Roger Corman: Interviews

Conversations with Filmmakers Series
Gerald Peary, General Editor

Roger Corman

INTERVIEWS

Edited by Constantine Nasr

University Press of Mississippi / Jackson

www.upress.state.ms.us

The University Press of Mississippi is a member of the Association of American University Presses.

Copyright © 2011 by University Press of Mississippi

First printing 2011
∞
Library of Congress Cataloging-in-Publication Data

Corman, Roger, 1926–
  Roger Corman : interviews / edited by Constantine Nasr.
    p. cm. — (Conversations with filmmakers series)
  Includes index.
  ISBN 978-1-61703-165-6 (cloth : alk. paper) — ISBN 978-1-61703-166-3 (pbk. : alk. paper) — ISBN 978-1-61703-167-0 (ebook) 1. Corman, Roger, 1926-—Interviews. 2. Motion picture producers and directors—United States—Interviews. I. Nasr, Constantine. II. Title.
  PN1998.3.C68A5 2011
  791.4302'32092—dc22
  [B]   2011013595

British Library Cataloging-in-Publication Data available

Contents

Introduction

Roger Corman once hired a first-time director and gave him this advice: "What you have to get is a very good first reel, because people want to know what's going on. Then you need to have a very good last reel because people want to hear how it all turns out. Everything else doesn't matter." Many years later, Martin Scorsese admitted that the guidance was "probably the best sense I have ever heard in the movies."[1]

After sixty-plus years of nonstop activity, Roger Corman has created a body of work that surpasses in quantity the output of workhorses John Ford, Alfred Hitchcock, and Michael Curtiz combined. As an independent producer and director, he was making more films per year than any other filmmaker in the 1950s and '60s. He became the first moviemaker to form a studio with its own distribution arm, both his most successful venture and a turning point for independent cinema. He launched the careers of most of the major players in the second half of twentieth-century Hollywood. His films still command retrospectives, and he recently won an Academy Award, two decades after he directed his last picture. Roger Corman may be in his eighties, but he foreshadows no hint at a closing act.

And yet the man Hollywood once christened its Wild Angel remains an enigma to his followers. He has notoriously remained typecast as a maker of exploitation flicks—those low-budget, non-studio productions aimed at secondary markets and suburban drive-ins. An overview of his most eclectic and creative period (1960–71) could place him among the most successful and promising young filmmakers of that era. He mastered the horror genre and explored its potential, more successfully and more inventively than any contemporary except Mario Bava. His movies spoke to that postwar teenage generation more than any other producer/director, essentially inventing the biker genre with *The Wild Angels* and the "drug film" craze with *The Trip*. Everyone has a Corman story to tell, building up a legend that has overtaken history, even in his own lifetime. For as it goes, "when the legend becomes fact, print the legend."

Since critics started paying attention in the sixties, many apologists have valiantly attempted to set right Corman's legacy, to pull him out of the ghetto of the "B" and help lift him into the stratosphere of the "A." He's never enjoyed the same praise that is lavished on acknowledged artists like Edgar G. Ulmer, a director who also defied his miniscule budgets, or Val Lewton, a producer who made art out of schlocky assignments. Toiling under similar conditions, Corman embraced his limited medium with gusto and ingenuity and delivered much more than his audiences had the right to expect.

"Some of my peers, making low-budget films, simply couldn't get up much enthusiasm for the work," Corman recalled in 1978. "Their typical reaction was, 'These quickies are ridiculous, and certainly not worth my serious effort. I'll just grind out something trashy, grab the money and run.' Well, anyone who feels his talent is greater than the crummy assignment in front of them is doomed to failure."[2]

Corman has always been a man about his work, pouring enthusiasm into the process and displaying little care for the accolades. He was, however, concerned that people didn't mix up "low-budget" with "B" pictures, a thing of Hollywood's block-booking past. He taught others to appreciate the freedom that comes with *free*, the resourcefulness bound by *lack of resource*. He might not have sought out the attention, but as he matured into an elder-statesman and grand-mentor of the indie movement, he certainly never turned it down.

Starting his Hollywood career as a runner for Fox in 1950, Corman quickly discovered he had very little tolerance for studio ways and its crumbling system. Unafraid to grab the bull by the horns, he produced movies before he directed them—a sure sign of things to come. Corman had an excellent grasp of story, and coupled with his business acumen, had a knack for turning out good product fast and cheap. In the realm that he worked, his movies stood out above the rest. His talent caught the attention of eager showmen Jim Nicholson and Sam Arkoff, and together they discovered the most important audience of the movie marketplace: teenage America. Forming American International Pictures (AIP), they specialized in fun, hip, sexy, and contemporary alternatives to Hollywood's stuffy spectacles and mundane melodramas. By satisfying this hungry portion of cinemagoers, AIP became the most successful independent film company in the world, of which no small part was due to Corman's entertaining and energetic pictures.

Note that word *pictures*. More often than not, Corman refers to his output as pictures, a subtle but telling distinction. Maybe this is because he was informed with an old Hollywood attitude that viewed films first and foremost as entertainment. He might also have been referring to cinema as the art of the moving picture, a form that he loves with passion, not pretense. But he was an artisan first, artist second, and he made pictures.

Throughout the fifties, he developed both his intuitive knack for staying ahead of the curve and his reputation for speed, key factors necessary to maintain his output. He produced nearly every film he directed and established a tight unit that allowed him both comfort and control; this period climaxed with his first real film of merit, *A Bucket of Blood*, in which Corman basically created the horror satire. The sixties gave us Corman at his peak, starting with the first of his classic Poe cycle, *House of Usher*, which re-established American horror as a viable and lucrative genre and properly launched Corman as a filmmaker with a vision; at the same time, he could still crank out an auspicious programmer like *The Little Shop of Horrors*, which to this day remains a remarkable black comedy whose celebrated reputation has lifted it well above its poverty-row roots. The seventies saw Corman turn from directing to producing and distributing through New World Pictures, a period crucial in his establishment of New Hollywood and his support of foreign artists; cinema after Corman, both at home and abroad, would never be the same. After selling New World in 1983, he remained exploitative, and usually profitable, but the critical value of his direct-to-video and television productions are far removed from the strength of his early work. Even his brief return behind the camera, aptly named *Roger Corman's Frankenstein*, was a throwback to an era that Hollywood had left behind.

His oeuvre is a mixed bag, but that comes with the territory he staked out. Remembered today as a "fearmaker," he worked in every known genre: comedy, western, musical, gangster, suspense / thriller, action, war, sci-fi, drama, period, swords-n-sandals, fantasy, and of course, horror. Even his singular big-studio picture, *The St. Valentine's Day Massacre* (1967), is remarkably at odds with Hollywood gangster fare, in structure and style, and yet it still nails down the consistent Corman anti-hero embodied by both Al Capone (Jason Robards) and Bugs Moran (Ralph Meeker).

Regardless of his milieu, Corman remains a thinking-man's filmmaker, passionate about the value of ideas. His deep fascination with human psychology boils below the surface of his stories and in the actions of his characters, who, like Corman, are rebels, distrustful and disdainful of conventional, even conservative, norms. They are social misfits, outsiders, strangers, intruders, all struggling to find their place in a senseless world, and there is no better example of the Corman complex than in his adaptations of Edgar Allan Poe.

Corman is fond of recalling his childhood fascination with Poe's stories. Certainly the decision to make these adaptations was driven by commerce, but never has an author been better matched with a filmmaker who consistently understood the essence of his stories. The unofficial series of eight films, all bizarrely compelling, wildly atmospheric (and all shot on fifteen-day schedules), contain several unquestionable masterpieces (*House of Usher, Pit and the Pendulum, The Masque of the Red Death, The Tomb of Ligeia*). Poe's deviant decadence is incarnated through the third partner in the pact, Vincent Price. Price, who once called Corman "dead serious, humorless . . . and full of a lot of psychological exploration for nose picking,"[3] revels in misanthropic madness, sometimes in blackest humor, other times in dispirited grief, but always deeply disturbed.

Corman never minces words. Writing for the *Hollywood Reporter* in 1957, he called out for intelligence in genre pictures. He sharply attacked Hollywood's misdirection of science fiction, a genre he helped popularize but that was already becoming stale. "Science-fiction today needs cerebral wings,"[4] he said, pointing to Ray Bradbury as an ideal to pursue. Through the years, he goes on record to state his personal yet unfulfilled desire to make movies of cerebral sci-fi, such as Frank Herbert's *Dune* and Robert Heinlein's *Stranger in a Strange Land*, movies that would have required budgets far greater than he would probably be willing to spend.

Corman appreciated competition, almost basked in it, and he wasn't afraid to copy a good thing, over and over, if need be. His detractors take jabs at his penchant for cheapness, but when it's your money on the line, the most important line *is* at the bottom. While his early features seem crude, they still hold audiences' attention for their out-of-the-ordinary plots and characterizations, as broad as Beverly Garland's feminist avenger in *Gunslinger* or Paul Birch's missionary alien in *Not of This Earth*. As AIP upped his budgets, his unique, often quirky leading heroes and heroines were matched by an equally stylized environment, to complement their Freudian histrionics.

Corman constantly acknowledges film as a collaborative medium, often giving credit to those key colleagues from whom he benefited: cinematographer Floyd Crosby, production designer Daniel Haller, composer

Ronald Stein, editor Ronald Sinclair, and key grip Chuck Hanawalt. Exceptional writing is difficult under any circumstance, but screenwriters Charles Griffith, Richard Matheson, Charles Beaumont, Mark Hanna, and R. Wright Campbell turned budget constraints into challenges to overcome, providing outrageous storylines populated by sardonic characters that elevated would-be claptrap like *The Wasp Woman*, *Attack of the Crab Monsters*, and *A Bucket of Blood*.

Part of Corman's appeal is that he remained in a field that he dominated; had he left the pond of exploitation for bigger studio waters, he'd have to compete against vets like Billy Wilder and Robert Wise or rising contemporaries like John Frankenheimer and Sidney Lumet. Studio budgets made room for excessive waste in time, talent, and overhead, financial flaws that baffled the business-minded Corman. Every studio experience reaffirmed his determination to remain where he was, because of the control he maintained, the constant pace of production, and the large amounts of money he stood to win or lose.

Which brings us to a pivotal film in the Corman canon: *The Intruder*. Made in 1961, when Corman was on the verge of commercial breakthrough, the picture was an acknowledged risk that would alter the course of his career. A controversy, financial failure, critical victory, and personal achievement all wrapped up in one, the topical anti-hate message movie was a venue for Corman to purge his convictions on-screen. "I believed so much in my subject matter," he said to Joseph Gelmis in 1970, "that I pushed my own personal thoughts a little bit too heavily into it and the film became slightly propagandistic." He learned his lesson never to make a movie that wouldn't entertain first. *The Intruder* is almost always brought up in conversation, as journalists and critics ponder the "what if" scenario of Corman's career, had it been a success.

"He does such marvelous spoofs, what does he want to go and turn serious for?" remarked critic Peter John Dyer, upon seeing the film. In his 1964 *Positif* article entitled "Z Films," Dyer tried to justify Corman's "degrading trash" (referencing *Red Death*) as the best of the bottom barrel—but it was still the bottom. It was only by the late sixties, mainly through efforts of European journalists, that opinions started to change. But by then it was too late; Corman was shifting his game, readying to quit directing in the same year that the Edinburgh Film Festival pronounced his Millenic Vision.

The Intruder did, however, reaffirm Corman's appreciation for those artists working amidst the human condition. And with that in mind, he established a secondary purpose for New World Pictures—the distribution of international filmmakers (Kurosawa, Fellini, Resnais, etc.) that might not otherwise find an American audience, usually in the same venues and with the same intense marketing strategies as his low-budget comedies and action films. Oftentimes he was also a silent financier, providing advance funding by way of theatrical pre-sales. Of this he was most proud: "We even showed a Bergman film in two or three drive-ins, against the advice of all the experts who foretold disaster," Corman recalled to *Positif* in 1990. "Surprisingly, the film finished a completely normal run, to the satisfaction of the theater owners, for whom the film didn't matter as long as it didn't fail at the box office. And I received a letter from Bergman, absolutely delighted that his film was shown in drive-ins."[5]

Although Roger Corman never attended film school, his self-established attitude didn't put him off from the students that they produced; rather, Corman was attracted to them in a practical way. Who better to put to work than a talented, knowledgeable, and *hungry* novice? He had a penchant for discovering talent and nurturing its potential, often handing over cast, crew, and cash to assistants like Francis Ford Coppola and Peter Bogdanovich with the expectation of a movie in return. He believed in giving almost anyone a chance to prove his worth, and more often than not, his gamble of faith paid off. Within these pages, Corman comments time and again on the reliability of these young filmmakers (most of which came from USC, UCLA, NYU, and his own alma mater, Stanford) when it came to making the most out of financial and creative resources.

"The obligatory first-director lunch before *Caged Heat* was the most extraordinary hour, just amazing," remembered Jonathan Demme, another Corman discovery. "The way he just machine-gunned the rules of directing to me. Like: 'Find legitimate, motivated excuses for moving the camera, but always look for ways to move it. The eyeball,' he said, 'was the organ most utilized in movie-going. If you don't keep the eyeball entertained, no way you'll get the brain involved. Use as many interesting angles as you can. Don't repeat composition in close-ups. Don't remind the eye it's already seen the same thing. Make your villain as fascinating as your hero. A one-dimensional villain won't be as scary as a complicated, interesting one.' It was amazing."[6]

His students, protégés, and disciples include Coppola, Scorsese, Bogdanovich, Demme, James Cameron, Ron Howard, Joe Dante, Sylvester Stallone, Monte Hellman, Jack Nicholson, Robert DeNiro, Dennis Hopper, Peter Fonda, Gale Anne Hurd, Irvin Kershner, Jonathan Kaplan,

Charles Bronson, Jon Davison, Curtis Harrington, Paul Bartel, John Sayles, Jack Hill, Curtis Hanson, and Robert Towne, just to name some of the more successful. Try and imagine modern cinema without *The Godfather, Easy Rider, Star Wars, Chinatown, Goodfellas, Rocky, The Terminator, The Silence of the Lambs, Raging Bull* . . . Thank you, Mr. Corman.

As to Hollywood's future, Corman's comments to an AFI audience in 1971 resonate with even greater import forty years later: "If you have a little picture, I now believe that maybe you're better off not to be with the majors, on the basis it costs them so much to distribute that they're not interested in the little picture." The gulf between the studio and the independent has never been wider.

And this brings us to the great mystery of Corman's unpredictable career. Why has one of the most promising talents of the sixties, one of the most successful, knowledgeable, capable, and inspiring of directors—who time and again maintains that he is most happy when on a film set—stopped directing? It's the $64,000 question that has been asked over and over again, only to receive the same direct answer: "there's still a possibility."

Part of the reason lies with whatever was left behind with *The Intruder*. If Corman had more to say, he'd now let others say it for him. As his interviews affirm, he was worn out. For a man to direct over fifty films in fifteen years, regardless of time, money, even success, there has to be a burning flame. After AIP's maltreatment of both *The Trip* and *Gas-s-s-s*, Corman had to protect that flame at all costs. He was too committed to making movies to just walk away, but too wary to deal with any devil except his own.

Corman needs to be in constant motion. He relishes the challenges of action, part and parcel with production. He celebrates film, which is why he is still making pictures: four hundred and counting. But he is now defined more by his offspring than his originality.

If these interviews offer any fresh perspective to the fashionable Cult of Corman, it is that his most significant legacy is not simply the dynamite films of his gifted youth, but the modern Hollywood motion picture industry that he has left in his wake. For better or worse, he paved the way for genre films to take over the mass marketplace. Nearly every tentpole film of the last decade has been, and will be for the foreseeable future, a genre picture in one form or another. They are no longer "B" fare, but the most expensive films ever made. Corman's impact may have been deeper, more complex than even his champions suspect. He motivated and influenced most of Hollywood's last fifty years of filmmaking, and, for all intents and purposes, he has earned his role as God-father of the A's.

"I think that to succeed in this world you have to take chances," Corman reflected upon receiving his honorary Oscar. "I believe the finest films being done today are done by the original, innovative filmmakers who have the courage to take a chance and to gamble. So I say to you: Keep gambling, keep taking chances." The abundant success in Roger Corman's story is the kind that has been both earned and shared.

First and foremost, I am grateful to Roger Corman, who took an interest in this book and allowed me the opportunity to interview him at length on multiple occasions. I would also like to thank all of the authors and publications who graciously allowed their work to be included in this volume. Corman has never shied away from the press, making the search and selection process a worthy challenge. I unearthed more articles than I could either clear or include. Qualifying musts were content and diversity, and many that have resurfaced in recent years had to make way for those most likely to fade from microfiche if not reprinted now.

With permission, I made room for selected writings by Corman himself, taken from actual articles and transcribed lectures. If the goal is to present the evolution of the filmmaker in his or her own words, these texts go a long way to reveal that gradual legend taking shape in print. They also remind us that these pieces were conversations Corman was having with students, enthusiasts, and peers. There is a dialogue at work, with Corman as teacher and Hollywood as his classroom.

While most of the interviews themselves are complete, some editing was necessary for the sake of space, particularly when it came to repetition. Film titles are presented in the same context in which Corman and his interviewers mention them. Historians can debate the value of adding or dropping the occasional article (*THE Day the World Ended, THE House of Usher*), but after fifty years, even Corman doesn't split hairs.

Film history has many friends, and this book couldn't have been assembled without the enduring aid, advice, and criticism of some very special friends: Steve Haberman, Tim Lucas, Lisa Majewski, Greg Mank, Joseph McBride, and Tom Weaver. I must also thank Rudy and Stacey Behlmer, Joe Dante, Jeffrey DeMunn, Scott Eyman, FX Feeney, John Gallagher, Mick Garris, Gale Anne Hurd, Stephen Jones, Richard Klemensen, Leonard Maltin, John McCarty, Patrick McGilligan, Kim Newman, and Ted Newsom; Lawreen Loeser at the Academy of Motion Picture Arts and Sciences; the exceptional staff at the Margaret Herrick Library; Mahn-

az Ghaznavi and Robert Diacopoulos at the American Film Institute's
Mayer Library; Ned Comstock, the USC Cinema-Television Library's
unsung hero and archaeologist; and my wife Mandy, who defines the
word *patient*. Special thanks go to Cynthia Brown at Concorde-New Horizons, whose encouragement gave my efforts a more personal meaning;
to Gregory Laufer for his excellent work in translating Corman back to
his original English. Finally, to my editor-in-chief, Leila Salisbury, who
saw that same value in Roger Corman's films and whose support never
failed; and her associate Valerie Jones, for lightening my load every step
of the way. Finally, I dedicate this book to Dr. Drew Casper, my longtime
mentor and dear friend.

CN

Notes

1. Roger Corman, with Jim Jerome, *How I Made a Hundred Movies in Hollywood and Never Lost a Dime* (New York: Random House, 1990), 185.

2. Marshall Berges, "Julie and Roger Corman," *Los Angeles Times Home Magazine*, October 22, 1978, 43.

3. Vincent Price, personal letter to author Tony Thomas.

4. Roger Corman, "Science-Fiction in Danger," *Hollywood Reporter*, November 18, 1957.

5. Robert Benayoun, Jean-Pierre Berthomé, and Michel Ciment, "An Interview with Roger Corman," *Positif* 348 (February 1990).

6. Corman, *How I Made a Hundred Movies in Hollywood and Never Lost a Dime*, 204.

Chronology

1926	Born on April 5, 1926, in Detroit, Michigan.
1940	Corman family moves to Beverly Hills, California.
1943	Graduates from Beverly Hills High School; co-edits high school newspaper *Highlights*. Attends Stanford University in Palo Alto.
1944-45	Signs up for the V-12 military service program as a Navy seaman; World War II ends before Corman is sent overseas.
1947	Graduates Stanford with a degree in Industrial Engineering.
1948-49	Hired as a messenger at Twentieth Century-Fox. Contributes an unattributed story which becomes *The Gunfighter* (1950), featuring Gregory Peck.
1950	Quits Fox. Studies English Literature at Oxford under the GI Bill.
1953	Develops the story for *Highway Dragnet* for Allied Artists.
1954	Produces his first film, *Monster from the Ocean Floor*. His second, *The Fast and the Furious*, is distributed through American Releasing Corporation (AIP).
1955	*Five Guns West*, his first feature as a director, is released. Followed by *Apache Woman*, *Swamp Women*, *Day the World Ended*, and *The Beast with a Million Eyes* (which he produces).
1956	Directs *Gunslinger* and *It Conquered the World*, both featuring Beverly Garland, as well as *The Oklahoma Woman*.
1957	His most productive year yet: releases include *Naked Paradise*, *Attack of the Crab Monsters*, *Rock All Night*, *The Undead*, *Teenage Doll*, *Carnival Rock*, *Sorority Girl*, *The Viking Women and the Sea Serpent*, and the cult hit *Not of This Earth* with Beverly Garland.
1958	Casts Charles Bronson in his first starring role as *Machine-Gun Kelly*. Releases include *War of the Satellites*, *She Gods of Shark Reef*, *Teenage Cave Man*, and *I, Mobster*, which he co-produces

with his brother Gene. Produces *The Cry Baby Killer*, Jack Nicholson's feature film debut.

1959   Launches Filmgroup with brother Gene, to produce as well as distribute their own films; their first films are *The Wasp Woman* and *Ski Troop Attack*. Also directs Dick Miller in the black comedy classic, *A Bucket of Blood*. Travels to Puerto Rico and makes three films back-to-back with the same cast and crew: *Creature from the Haunted Sea*, *Last Woman on Earth*, and *Battle of Blood Island* (directed by Joel Rapp). All released through Filmgroup. Legendarily directs *The Little Shop of Horrors* in two and a half days.

1960   Travels to Greece to direct the swords-and-sandals epic *Atlas* for Filmgroup. Directs Vincent Price in *House of Usher* for AIP. *Usher* will result in Corman's famous Edgar Allan Poe cycle, both creatively satisfying and financially rewarding for all involved. Price will star in nearly all of the films, ensuring his transition to horror icon.

1961   Directs William Shatner in the civil rights drama *The Intruder*, based on the book by Charles Beaumont and produced by his brother Gene. Directs his second Poe film, *Pit and the Pendulum*, with Price and Barbara Steele.

1962   Despite high praise at the Venice Film Festival, *The Intruder* is denied a Production Code Seal of Approval by the MPAA and fails at the box office. More Poe: Corman directs *The Premature Burial*, casting Ray Milland instead of Vincent Price in the lead role, and the anthology film *Tales of Terror*, this one with Price and Peter Lorre. Directs Price in the non-AIP period film *Tower of London*, produced by Gene.

1963   Directs *The Raven*, with Price, Lorre, and Boris Karloff; uses sets, crew, and star Karloff to shoot key scenes for *The Terror*. The remainder of the film is made over a period of many months whenever cast, crew, and funds are available. Directs *The Young Racers* in Ireland; gives his assistant, Francis Coppola, his cast, crew, and some funds to make *Dementia 13*. Directs the Lovecraft / Poe mash-up *The Haunted Palace* with Price and Lon Chaney Jr., and *X: The Man with the X-Ray Eyes*, starring Ray Milland, arguably his finest and most personal film.

1964   Goes to Yugoslavia to direct the war adventure *The Secret Invasion* with Gene producing. Shoots his two final Poe films in England: *The Masque of the Red Death* and *The Tomb of Ligeia*. Meets Julie Halloran.

1965	Signs a contract with Columbia; it is a period of creative frustration, in which Corman is unable to mount a single film. Takes on contemporary counter-culture with AIP's *The Wild Angels*.
1966	*The Wild Angels* opens the Venice Film Festival; the film is his biggest success to date and the genesis of the "biker film" genre. Columbia finally approves Corman to direct *The Long Ride Home*, from a script by Robert Towne; after shooting begins, he is replaced by Phil Karlson.
1967	Directs *The St. Valentine's Day Massacre* for Fox; it would be his only major studio film. *The Long Ride Home*, re-titled *A Time for Killing*, is released. Corman returns to AIP and directs *The Trip* from a script by Jack Nicholson. Produces (uncredited) Boris Karloff's swansong, *Targets*, written and directed by another former assistant, Peter Bogdanovich.
1968	Shoots an unsold pilot for ABC; it is released the following year as a TV movie under the name *Target: Harry*.
1969	Directs *Bloody Mama*, headlined by a strong cast led by Shelley Winters and featuring a young Robert DeNiro, and *Gas-s-s-s*, both for AIP.
1970	*Gas-s-s-s* is released in butchered form, which results in Corman's split with AIP. Directs *Von Richthofen and Brown* in Ireland for UA. Studio meddling pushes Corman into a nearly twenty-year "sabbatical" from directing. Founds New World Pictures, and quickly releases its first feature, *The Student Nurses*. The Edinburgh Film Festival promotes a career retrospective entitled "Roger Corman: The Millenic Vision." Marries Julie Halloran on December 26, 1970.
1970–83	Corman's New World order produces and distributes over 150 original, foreign, and independent films, becoming the most successful distributor of the decade. Among the careers he personally launches are Martin Scorsese, Jonathan Demme, Ron Howard, and Joe Dante. Fellini's *Amarcord* (1973), Kurosawa's *Dersu Uzala* (1975), and Volker Schlöndorff's *The Tin Drum* (1979) all receive the Oscar for Best Foreign Film.
1971	*Von Richthofen and Brown* is released.
1973	The Cormans move to a new home in Brentwood, close to his new office building on San Vicente Blvd., which will remain his base of operations for nearly forty years.
1975	*Death Race 2000*, Corman's biggest hit of the seventies, is released. Birth of daughter Catherine.

1976   Birth of son Roger Martin.

1977   The documentary *Roger Corman: Hollywood's Wild Angel*, is released, ironically through New World.

1978   Birth of son Brian.

1982   *Little Shop of Horrors*, a new musical based on the 1960 film, becomes a hit on Broadway.

1983   Sells New World Pictures and its library to a group of attorneys. Immediately launches what becomes a new independent company, New Horizons.

1984   Birth of daughter Mary Tessa.

1985   Establishes Concorde Pictures as a distribution company. Successfully sues the owners of New World for back earnings.

1986   *Little Shop of Horrors* becomes a major motion picture for Warner Bros., domestically grossing nearly $39 million. Corman proudly promotes the film.

1989   Merges companies to form Concorde-New Horizons, focusing on the direct-to-video market. Corman launches action star Don "The Dragon" Wilson with the highly successful *Bloodfist* series for home video. Agrees to direct an adaptation of Brian W. Aldiss' *Frankenstein Unbound* for Warner Bros. and Fox. Shooting takes place in Italy, with a budget of $11.5 million, his highest budget yet.

1990   Now titled *Roger Corman's Frankenstein Unbound*, the film opens to a disappointing $37,000 domestic gross. It will be the last feature film he writes and directs. Publishes autobiography entitled *How I Made a Hundred Movies in Hollywood and Never Lost a Dime*.

1991   Receives a Star on the Hollywood Walk of Fame.

1995   Launches *Roger Corman Presents* for the cable channel Showtime. Forms New Concorde, a production company based in Ireland, to produce more direct-to-video films.

1996–99   Receives the Career Achievement Award from the Los Angeles Film Critics Association, Lifetime Achievement Award from the CSA, and the Golden Eddie Filmmaker of the Year (1997).

1998   Launches the *Black Scorpion* TV series on Showtime.

1999   Stars as "Dr. Gorman" in the multi-part serial film *The Phantom Eye* for AMC.

2005   *House of Usher* is added to the National Film Registry.

2009   Produces and co-directs Joe Dante's web series *Splatter* for

Netflix. Also contributes commentaries for Dante's popular *Trailers from Hell*. Receives an Honorary Oscar from the Academy of Motion Picture Arts and Sciences on November 14. He is presented the award by protégé Jonathan Demme and is surrounded by his family, friends, and many of the Roger Corman Alumni Association.

Filmography

As Director

FIVE GUNS WEST (Palo Alto / American Releasing Corporation, 1955)
Producer: **Roger Corman**
Director: **Roger Corman**
Screenplay: R. Wright Campbell
Cinematography: Floyd Crosby
Editor: Ronald Sinclair
Music: Buddy Bregman
Cast: John Lund, Dorothy Malone, James Stone, Touch Connors, Paul Birch, Jonathan Haze
78 minutes

SWAMP WOMEN (Woolner Bros., 1955)
Producer: Bernard Woolner
Director: **Roger Corman**
Screenplay: David Stern
Cinematography: Frederick E. West
Editor: Ronald Sinclair
Music: Willis Holman
Cast: Beverly Garland, Carole Mathews, Touch Connors, Marie Windsor, Jil Jarmyn, Jonathan Haze, Ed Nelson, Lou Place
73 minutes

APACHE WOMAN (Golden State / American Releasing Corporation, 1955)
Producer: **Roger Corman**
Director: **Roger Corman**
Screenplay: Lou Rusoff
Cinematography: Floyd Crosby
Editor: Ronald Sinclair
Music: Ronald Stein

Cast: Lloyd Bridges, Joan Taylor, Lance Fuller, Morgan Jones, Paul Birch, Jonathan Haze, Dick Miller
83 minutes

DAY THE WORLD ENDED (Golden State / American Releasing Corp., 1955)
Producer: **Roger Corman**
Director: **Roger Corman**
Screenplay: Lou Rusoff
Cinematography: Jock Feindel
Editor: Ronald Sinclair
Music: Ronald Stein
Special Effects: Paul Blaisdell
Cast: Richard Denning, Lori Nelson, Paul Birch, Touch Connors, Adele Jergens, Paul Dubov, Jonathan Haze, **Roger Corman** (in photograph)
82 minutes

THE OKLAHOMA WOMAN (Sunset / American International, 1956)
Producer: **Roger Corman**
Director: **Roger Corman**
Screenplay: Lou Rusoff
Cinematography: Frederick E. West
Editor: Ronald Sinclair
Music: Ronald Stein
Cast: Richard Denning, Peggie Castle, Cathy Downs, Tudor Owen, Mike "Touch" Connors, Jonathan Haze, Dick Miller, Bruno Ve Sota
71 minutes

GUNSLINGER (Santa Clara / American Releasing Corporation, 1956)
Producer: **Roger Corman**
Director: **Roger Corman**
Screenplay: Charles B. Griffith, Mark Hanna
Cinematography: Frederick E. West
Editor: Charles Gross
Music: Ronald Stein
Cast: John Ireland, Beverly Garland, Allison Hayes, Martin Kingsley, Jonathan Haze, Dick Miller, Bruno Ve Sota, William Schallert
83 minutes

IT CONQUERED THE WORLD (Sunset / American International, 1956)
Producer: **Roger Corman**
Director: **Roger Corman**
Screenplay: Lou Rusoff, Charles B. Griffith (uncredited)
Cinematography: Fred West
Editor: Charles Gross
Music: Ronald Stein
Special Effects: Paul Blaisdell
Cast: Peter Graves, Beverly Garland, Lee Van Cleef, Sally Fraser, Russ
Bender, Jonathan Haze, Dick Miller, Charles B. Griffith
68 minutes

NAKED PARADISE (Sunset / American International, 1957)
Producer: **Roger Corman**
Director: **Roger Corman**
Screenplay: Charles B. Griffith, Mark Hanna, R. Wright Campbell (un-
credited)
Cinematography: Floyd Crosby
Editor: Charles Gross Jr.
Music: Ronald Stein
Cast: Richard Denning, Beverly Garland, Lisa Montell, Leslie Bradley,
Dick Miller, Jonathan Haze, **Roger Corman**
71 minutes

NOT OF THIS EARTH (Los Altos / Allied Artists, 1957)
Producer: **Roger Corman**
Director: **Roger Corman**
Screenplay: Charles B. Griffith, Mark Hanna
Cinematography: John Mescall
Editor: Charles Gross Jr.
Music: Ronald Stein
Special Effects: Paul Blaisdell
Cast: Paul Birch, Beverly Garland, Morgan Jones, William Roerick, Jona-
than Haze, Dick Miller, Ann Carroll, Tamar Cooper
67 minutes

ATTACK OF THE CRAB MONSTERS (Los Altos / Allied Artists, 1957)
Producer: **Roger Corman**
Director: **Roger Corman**
Screenplay: Charles B. Griffith

Cinematography: Floyd Crosby, Maitland Stuart (underwater sequences)
Editor: Charles Gross Jr.
Music: Ronald Stein
Cast: Richard Garland, Pamela Duncan, Russell Johnson, Leslie Bradley, Mel Welles, Beach Dickerson, Ed Nelson, Charles B. Griffith
62 minutes

THE UNDEAD (Balboa / American International, 1957)
Producer: **Roger Corman**
Director: **Roger Corman**
Screenplay: Charles B. Griffith, Mark Hanna
Cinematography: William Sickner
Editor: Frank Sullivan
Music: Ronald Stein
Cast: Pamela Duncan, Richard Garland, Allison Hayes, Val Dufour, Mel Welles, Dorothy Neumann, Billy Barty, Bruno Ve Sota, Dick Miller, Richard Devon
75 minutes

ROCK ALL NIGHT (Sunset / American International, 1957)
Producer: **Roger Corman**
Director: **Roger Corman**
Screenplay: Charles B. Griffith (based on the teleplay *The Little Guy* by David P. Harmon)
Cinematography: Floyd Crosby
Editor: Frank Sullivan
Music: Buck Ram
Cast: Dick Miller, Abby Dalton, The Blockbusters, The Platters, Robin Morse, Richard Cutting, Bruno Ve Sota, Mel Welles, Russell Johnson, Jonathan Haze, Beach Dickerson, Barboura Morris
62 minutes

CARNIVAL ROCK (Howco / Roger Corman Productions, 1957)
Producer: **Roger Corman**
Director: **Roger Corman**
Screenplay: Leo Lieberman
Cinematography: Floyd Crosby
Editor: Charles Gross Jr.
Music: Walter Green, Buck Ram

Cast: Susan Cabot, Brian Hutton, David J. Stewart, Dick Miller, Jonathan Haze, Bruno Ve Sota, The Platters, David Houston, The Shadows, The Blockbusters
75 minutes

TEENAGE DOLL (Woolner Bros. / Allied Artists, 1957)
Producer: **Roger Corman**
Director: **Roger Corman**
Screenplay: Charles B. Griffith
Cinematography: Floyd Crosby
Editor: Charles Gross Jr.
Music: Walter Greene
Cast: June Kenney, Fay Spain, John Brinkley, Colette Jackson, Barbara Wilson, Ziva Rodann, Barboura Morris, Sandy Smith, Dorothy Neumann
68 minutes

SORORITY GIRL (Sunset / American International, 1957)
Producer: **Roger Corman**
Director: **Roger Corman**
Screenplay: Ed Waters, Leo Lieberman
Cinematography: Monroe P. Askins
Editor: Charles Gross Jr.
Music: Ronald Stein
Cast: Susan Cabot, Dick Miller, Barboura O'Neill, June Kenney, Barbara Crane, Fay Baker, Jeanne Wood, Margaret Campbell
61 minutes

THE SAGA OF THE VIKING WOMEN AND THEIR VOYAGE TO THE WATERS OF THE GREAT SEA SERPENT (Malibu / American International, 1957)
Producer: **Roger Corman**
Director: **Roger Corman**
Screenplay: Lawrence L. Goldman, Irving Block (story)
Cinematography: Monroe P. Askins
Editor: Ronald Sinclair
Music: Albert Glasser
Cast: Abby Dalton, Susan Cabot, Brad Jackson, June Kenney, Richard Devon, Betsy Jones-Moreland, Jonathan Haze, Jay Sayer, Gary Conway
66 minutes

MACHINE-GUN KELLY (El Monte / American International, 1958)
Producer: **Roger Corman**
Director: **Roger Corman**
Screenplay: R. Wright Campbell
Cinematography: Floyd Crosby
Editor: Ronald Sinclair
Art Direction: Daniel Haller
Music: Gerald Fried
Cast: Charles Bronson, Susan Cabot, Morey Amsterdam, Jack Lambert,
Wally Campo, Bob Griffin, Richard Devon, Barboura Morris
80 minutes

WAR OF THE SATELLITES (Santa Cruz / Allied Artists, 1958)
Producer: **Roger Corman**
Director: **Roger Corman**
Screenplay: Lawrence L. Goldman, Irving Block, and Jack Rabin (story)
Cinematography: Floyd Crosby
Editor: Irene Morra
Art Direction: Daniel Haller
Music: Walter Greene
Cast: Susan Cabot, Dick Miller, Richard Devon, Robert Shayne, Jerry
Barclay, Eric Sinclair, Jay Sayer, Mitzi McCall, Beach Dickerson, Bruno
Ve Sota, **Roger Corman**
66 minutes

TEENAGE CAVE MAN (Malibu / American International, 1958)
Producer: **Roger Corman**
Director: **Roger Corman**
Screenplay: R. Wright Campbell
Cinematography: Floyd Crosby
Editor: Irene Morra
Music: Albert Glasser
Cast: Robert Vaughn, Leslie Bradley, Darrah Marshall, Frank De Kova,
Robert Shayne, Joseph Hamilton, Beach Dickerson, Jonathan Haze,
June Jocelyn, Ed Nelson
66 minutes

SHE-GODS OF SHARK REEF (L.H. Gerber / American International,
1958)
Producer: Ludwig H. Gerber

Director: **Roger Corman**
Screenplay: Robert Hill, Victor Stoloff
Cinematography: Floyd Crosby
Editor: Frank Sullivan
Music: Ronald Stein
Cast: Don Durant, Bill Cord, Lisa Montell, Jeanne Gerson, Carol Lindsay, Beverly Rivera
63 minutes

I, MOBSTER (Alco, 1959)
Producer: **Roger Corman**, Gene Corman
Director: **Roger Corman**
Screenplay: Steve Fisher, J. H. Smyth (novel)
Cinematography: Floyd Crosby
Editor: William B. Murphy
Art Direction: Daniel Haller
Music: Gerald Fried, Edward L. Alperson Jr.
Cast: Steve Cochran, Lita Milan, Robert Strauss, Celia Lovsky, John Brinkley, Lili St. Cyr, Wally Cassell, Frank Wolff, Dick Miller
80 minutes

A BUCKET OF BLOOD (Alta Vista / American International, 1959)
Producer: **Roger Corman**
Director: **Roger Corman**
Screenplay: Charles B. Griffith
Cinematography: Jack Marquette
Editor: Anthony Carras
Art Direction: Daniel Haller
Music: Fred Katz
Cast: Dick Miller, Barboura Morris, Antony Carbone, Julian Burton, Ed Nelson, John Brinkley, John Shaner, Judy Bamber, Myrtle Damerel
66 minutes

THE WASP WOMAN (Santa Clara / The Filmgroup, 1959)
Producer: **Roger Corman**
Director: **Roger Corman**, Jack Hill (uncredited)
Screenplay: Leo Gordon, Kinta Zertuche (story)
Cinematography: Harry Neumann
Editor: Carlo Lodato
Art Direction: Daniel Haller

Music: Fred Katz
Cast: Susan Cabot, Anthony Eisley, Barboura Morris, Michael Mark, William Roerick, Frank Wolff, Bruno Ve Sota, Dick Miller, **Roger Corman**
73 minutes

SKI TROOP ATTACK (The Filmgroup, 1960)
Producer: **Roger Corman**
Director: **Roger Corman**
Screenplay: Charles B. Griffith
Cinematography: Andy Costikyan
Editor: Anthony Carras
Art Direction: Daniel Haller
Music: Fred Katz
Cast: Michael Forest, Frank Wolff, Wally Campo, Sheila Carol, Richard Sinatra, **Roger Corman**
63 minutes

HOUSE OF USHER (Alta Vista / American International, 1960)
Producer: **Roger Corman**
Director: **Roger Corman**
Screenplay: Richard Matheson, Edgar Allan Poe (story)
Cinematography: Floyd Crosby
Editor: Anthony Carras
Art Direction: Daniel Haller
Music: Les Baxter
Cast: Vincent Price, Mark Damon, Myrna Fahey, Harry Ellerbe, Bill Borzage, Mike Jordan
80 minutes

THE LITTLE SHOP OF HORRORS (Santa Clara / The Filmgroup, 1960)
Producer: **Roger Corman**
Director: **Roger Corman**
Screenplay: Charles B. Griffith
Cinematography: Arch R. Dalzell
Editor: Marshall Neilan Jr.
Art Direction: Daniel Haller
Music: Fred Katz
Cast: Jonathan Haze, Jackie Joseph, Mel Welles, Dick Miller, Myrtle

Vail, John Shaner, Jack Nicholson, Charles B. Griffith, Wally Campo
70 minutes

THE LAST WOMAN ON EARTH (Santa Clara / The Filmgroup, 1960)
Producer: **Roger Corman**
Director: **Roger Corman**
Screenplay: Robert Towne
Cinematography: Jacques R. Marquette
Editor: Anthony Carras
Art Direction: Floyd Crosby (uncredited)
Music: Ronald Stein
Cast: Antony Carbone, Betsy Jones-Moreland, Edward Wain [Robert Towne]
71 minutes

ATLAS (Beacon Films / The Filmgroup, 1961)
Producer: **Roger Corman**
Director: **Roger Corman**
Screenplay: Charles B. Griffith
Cinematography: Basil Maros
Editor: Michael Luciano
Music: Ronald Stein
Cast: Michael Forest, Barboura Morris, Frank Wolff, Walter Maslow, Christos Exarchos, Andreas Filippides, Theodore Dimitriou, **Roger Corman**
79 minutes

CREATURE FROM THE HAUNTED SEA (Roger Corman Productions / The Filmgroup, 1961)
Producer: **Roger Corman**
Director: **Roger Corman**
Screenplay: Charles B. Griffith, **Roger Corman** (story)
Cinematography: Jacques R. Marquette
Editor: Angela Scellars
Music: Fred Katz
Cast: Antony Carbone, Betsy Jones-Moreland, Edward Wain [Robert Towne], Edmundo Rivera Alvarez, Beach Dickerson, Robert Bean
63 minutes

PIT AND THE PENDULUM (Alta Vista / American International, 1961)
Producer: **Roger Corman**
Director: **Roger Corman**
Screenplay: Richard Matheson, Edgar Allan Poe (story)
Cinematography: Floyd Crosby
Editor: Anthony Carras
Art Direction: Daniel Haller
Music: Les Baxter
Cast: Vincent Price, John Kerr, Barbara Steele, Luana Anders, Antony
Carbone, Patrick Westwood
85 minutes

THE PREMATURE BURIAL (Santa Clara Productions / American Inter-
national, 1962)
Producer: **Roger Corman**
Director: **Roger Corman**
Screenplay: Charles Beaumont, Ray Russell, Edgar Allan Poe (story)
Cinematography: Floyd Crosby
Editor: Ronald Sinclair
Art Direction: Daniel Haller
Music: Ronald Stein
Cast: Ray Milland, Hazel Court, Richard Ney, Heather Angel, Alan Na-
pier, John Dierkes, Dick Miller
81 minutes

THE INTRUDER (The Filmgroup, 1962)
Producer: **Roger Corman**
Director: **Roger Corman**
Screenplay: Charles Beaumont (from his novel)
Cinematography: Taylor Byars, Haskell Wexler
Editor: Ronald Sinclair
Music: Ronald Stein
Cast: William Shatner, Frank Maxwell, Beverly Lunsford, Robert Em-
hardt, Jeanne Cooper, Leo Gordon, Charles Barnes, Charles Beaumont,
George Clayton Johnson, William F. Nolan
84 minutes

TALES OF TERROR (Alta Vista / American International, 1962)
Producer: **Roger Corman**
Director: **Roger Corman**

Screenplay: Richard Matheson, Edgar Allan Poe (stories)
Cinematography: Floyd Crosby
Editor: Anthony Carras
Art Direction: Daniel Haller
Music: Les Baxter
Segment Casts: "Morella": Vincent Price, Maggie Price; "Black Cat":
Vincent Price, Peter Lorre, Joyce Jameson; "The Facts in the Case of M.
Valdemar": Vincent Price, Basil Rathbone, Debra Paget (Helene), David
Frankham
89 minutes

TOWER OF LONDON (Admiral Pictures / United Artists)
Producer: Gene Corman
Director: **Roger Corman**
Screenplay: Leo Gordon, F. Amos Powell, James B. Gordon
Cinematography: Arch R. Dalzell
Editor: Ronald Sinclair
Art Direction: Daniel Haller
Music: Michael Anderson
Cast: Vincent Price, Michael Pate, Joan Freeman, Robert Brown, Bruce
Gordon, Joan Camden, Richard Hale
79 minutes

THE YOUNG RACERS (Alta Vista / American International, 1963)
Producer: **Roger Corman**
Director: **Roger Corman**
Screenplay: R. Wright Campbell
Cinematography: Floyd Crosby
Editor: Ronald Sinclair
Second Unit Director / Sound: Francis Ford Coppola
Music: Les Baxter
Cast: Mark Damon, William Campbell, Luana Anders, Patrick Magee,
Roger Corman
84 minutes

THE RAVEN (Alta Vista / American International, 1963)
Producer: **Roger Corman**
Director: **Roger Corman**
Screenplay: Richard Matheson, Edgar Allan Poe (poem)
Cinematography: Floyd Crosby

Editor: Ronald Sinclair
Art Direction: Daniel Haller
Music: Les Baxter
Cast: Vincent Price, Peter Lorre, Boris Karloff, Hazel Court, Jack Nicholson, Olive Sturgess
86 minutes

THE TERROR (Alta Vista / The Filmgroup, 1963)
Producer: **Roger Corman**
Director: **Roger Corman**; uncredited: Francis Ford Coppola, Jack Hill, Monte Hellman, Dennis Jakob, Jack Nicholson
Screenplay: **Roger Corman**, Leo Gordon, Jack Hill
Cinematography: John M. Nickolaus Jr.
Editor: Stuart O'Brien
Art Direction: Daniel Haller
Music: Ronald Stein
Cast: Boris Karloff, Jack Nicholson, Sandra Knight, Dick Miller, Dorothy Neumann, Jonathan Haze, Leo Gordon
81 minutes

THE HAUNTED PALACE (Alta Vista / American International, 1963)
Producer: **Roger Corman**
Director: **Roger Corman**
Screenplay: Charles Beaumont, H. P. Lovecraft (novella)
Cinematography: Floyd Crosby
Editor: Ronald Sinclair
Art Direction: Daniel Haller
Music: Ronald Stein
Cast: Vincent Price, Debra Paget, Lon Chaney Jr., Frank Maxwell, Leo Gordon, Elisha Cook, John Dierkes
87 minutes

X: THE MAN WITH THE X-RAY EYES (Alta Vista / American International, 1963)
Producer: **Roger Corman**
Director: **Roger Corman**
Screenplay: Robert Dillon, Ray Russell (also story)
Cinematography: Floyd Crosby
Editor: Ronald Sinclair
Art Direction: Daniel Haller
Music: Les Baxter

Cast: Ray Milland, Diana van der Vlis, Harold Stone, John Hoyt, Don Rickles, Morris Ankrum, Dick Miller, John Dierkes
76 minutes

THE MASQUE OF THE RED DEATH (Alta Vista / American International / Anglo-Amalgamated, 1964)
Producer: **Roger Corman**
Director: **Roger Corman**
Screenplay: Charles Beaumont, R. Wright Campbell, Edgar Allan Poe (stories)
Cinematography: Nicolas Roeg
Editor: Ann Chegwidden
Art Direction: Daniel Haller
Music: David Lee
Cast: Vincent Price, Hazel Court, Jane Asher, David Weston, Nigel Green, Patrick Magee, Paul Whitsun-Jones, Skip Martin
89 minutes

THE SECRET INVASION (San Carlos Productions / The Corman Company, 1964)
Producer: Gene Corman
Director: **Roger Corman**
Screenplay: R. Wright Campbell
Cinematography: Arthur E. Arling
Editor: Ronald Sinclair
Art Direction: John Murray
Music: Hugo Friedhofer
Cast: Stewart Granger, Raf Vallone, Mickey Rooney, Edd Byrnes, Henry Silva, William Campbell, Mia Massin
95 minutes

THE TOMB OF LIGEIA (Alta Vista / American International / Anglo-Amalgamated, 1964)
Producer: **Roger Corman**, Samuel Z. Arkoff, James H. Nicholson, Pat Green
Director: **Roger Corman**
Screenplay: Robert Towne, Edgar Allan Poe (story)
Cinematography: Arthur Grant
Editor: Alfred Cox
Art Direction: Colin Southcott, Daniel Haller (uncredited)
Music: Kenneth V. Jones

Cast: Vincent Price, Elizabeth Shepherd, John Westbrook, Oliver Johnston, Derek Francis, Richard Vernon
81 minutes

THE WILD ANGELS (American International, 1966)
Producer: **Roger Corman**
Director: **Roger Corman**
Screenplay: Charles B. Griffith, Peter Bogdanovich (uncredited)
Cinematography: Richard Moore
Editor: Monte Hellman
Music: Mike Curb
Cast: Peter Fonda, Bruce Dern, Nancy Sinatra, Lou Procopio, Coby Denton, Marc Cavell, Buck Taylor, Diane Ladd, Michael J. Pollard, Dick Miller, Barboura Morris, Venice Hell's Angels
82 minutes

THE ST. VALENTINE'S DAY MASSACRE (Los Altos Productions / 20th Century-Fox, 1967)
Producer: **Roger Corman**
Director: **Roger Corman**
Screenplay: Howard Browne
Cinematography: Milton R. Krasner
Editor: William B. Murphy
Art Direction: Philip M. Jefferies, Jack Martin Smith
Music: Fred Steiner
Cast: Jason Robards, George Segal, Ralph Meeker, Jean Hale, Clint Ritchie, Bruce Dern, Leo Gordon, Dick Miller, Jack Nicholson, Paul Frees
100 minutes

THE TRIP (Roger Corman Productions / American International, 1967)
Producer: **Roger Corman**
Director: **Roger Corman**
Screenplay: Jack Nicholson
Cinematography: Arch Dalzell
Editor: Ronald Sinclair
Music: The Electric Flag, an American Music Band
Cast: Peter Fonda, Susan Strasberg, Bruce Dern, Dennis Hopper, Salli Sachse, Barboura Morris, Judy Lang, Luana Anders, Dick Miller, Peter Bogdanovich
85 minutes

TARGET: HARRY (The Corman Company, 1969)
Released January 1979
Producer: Gene Corman
Director: **Roger Corman** (as Henry Neill)
Screenplay: Bob Barbash
Cinematography: Patrice Pouget
Editor: Monte Hellman
Music: Les Baxter
Cast: Vic Morrow, Suzanne Pleshette, Victor Buono, Cesar Romero,
Stanley Holloway, Charlotte Rampling, Michael Ansara, **Roger Corman**
79 minutes

BLOODY MAMA (American International Pictures, 1970)
Producer: **Roger Corman**
Director: **Roger Corman**
Screenplay: Robert Thom, Donald A. Peters (story)
Cinematography: John A. Alonzo
Editor: Eve Newman
Music: Don Randi
Cast: Shelley Winters, Robert DeNiro, Bruce Dern, Scatman Crothers,
Don Stroud, Pat Hingle, Diane Varsi
90 minutes

GAS-S-S-S! . . . OR—IT BECAME NECESSARY TO DESTROY THE WORLD
IN ORDER TO SAVE IT (San Jacinto Productions / American International, 1970)
Producer: **Roger Corman**
Director: **Roger Corman**
Screenplay: George Armitage
Cinematography: Ron Dexter
Editor: George Van Noy
Music: Barry Melton, Country Joe and the Fish
Cast: Robert Corff, Elaine Giftos, Bud Cort, Talia Coppola [Shire], Ben
Vereen, Cindy Williams, Alex Wilson, Phil Borneo, Bruce Karcher
79 minutes

VON RICHTHOFEN AND BROWN (The Corman Company / United
Artists, 1971)
Producer: Gene Corman

Director: **Roger Corman**
Screenplay: John William Corrington, Joyce Hooper Corrington
Cinematography: Michael Reed
Editor: George Van Noy, Alan Collins
Music: Hugo Friedhofer
Cast: John Phillip Law, Don Stroud, Barry Primus, Corin Redgrave, Karen Huston, Hurd Hatfield, Stephen McHattie
97 minutes

FRANKENSTEIN UNBOUND (The Mount Company / 20th Century-Fox, 1990)
Producer: **Roger Corman**, Kobi Jaeger, Thom Mount
Director: **Roger Corman**
Screenplay: **Roger Corman**, F. X. Feeney, Edward Neumeier (uncredited), Brian W. Aldiss (novel), Mary Shelley (novel)
Cinematography: Armando Nannuzzi, Michael Scott
Editor: Mary Bauer, Jay Lash Cassidy
Music: Carl Davis
Cast: John Hurt, Raul Julia, Bridget Fonda, Catherine Rabett, Nick Brimble, Jason Patric, Michael Hutchence
82 minutes

As Uncredited Co-Director

THE BEAST WITH A MILLION EYES (1955)
A TIME FOR KILLING (1967)
THE WILD RACERS (1968)
DE SADE (1969)
DEATHSPORT (1978)
BATTLE BEYOND THE STARS (1980)

As Producer

Throughout his career, Roger Corman has produced close to four hundred films, and as of 2010, he is still making movies. Through his privately owned company, New World Pictures, he invested in and distributed many of the most celebrated foreign films of the seventies and eighties.

Below is a selection of key films for Corman the producer, credited and uncredited, and Corman the distributor (marked by an asterisk). For a more complete list, we recommend you consult the Internet Movie Database.

HIGHWAY DRAGNET (Dir: Nathan Juran, 1954)—also Story
MONSTER FROM THE OCEAN FLOOR (Dir: Wyott Ordung, 1954)
THE FAST AND THE FURIOUS (Dir: John Ireland, 1955)—also Story
STAKEOUT ON DOPE STREET (Dir: Irvin Kershner, 1958)
THE CRY BABY KILLER (Dir: Jus Addiss, 1958)
HOT CAR GIRL (Dir: Bernard L. Kowalski, 1958)
NIGHT OF THE BLOOD BEAST (Dir: Bernard L. Kowalski, 1958)
BEAST FROM HAUNTED CAVE (Dir: Monte Hellman, 1959)
T-BIRD GANG (Dir: Richard Harbinger, 1959)
ATTACK OF THE GIANT LEECHES (Dir: Bernard L. Kowalski, 1959)
NIGHT TIDE (Dir: Curtis Harrington, 1960)
BATTLE BEYOND THE SUN (Re-edit Dir: Francis Ford Coppola, 1962)
THE MAGIC VOYAGE OF SINBAD (Re-edit Dir: Francis Ford Coppola, 1962)
DEMENTIA 13 (Dir: Francis Ford Coppola, 1963)
RIDE THE WHIRLWIND (Dir: Monte Hellman, 1965)
QUEEN OF BLOOD (Dir: Curtis Harrington, 1966)
TARGETS (Dir: Peter Bogdanovich, 1967)
DEVIL'S ANGELS (Dir: Daniel Haller, 1967)
THE SHOOTING (Dir: Monte Hellman, 1967)
DE SADE (Dir: Cy Endfield, 1969)
THE DUNWICH HORROR (Dir: Daniel Haller, 1970)
THE STUDENT NURSES (Dir: Stephanie Rothman, 1970)
LADY FRANKENSTEIN (Dir: Mel Welles, 1971)*
THE BIG DOLL HOUSE (Dir: Jack Hill, 1971)
PRIVATE DUTY NURSES (Dir: George Armitage, 1971)
ANGELS HARD AS THEY COME (Dir: Joe Viola, 1971)
THE VELVET VAMPIRE (Dir: Stephanie Rothman, 1971)
NIGHT CALL NURSES (Dir: Jonathan Kaplan, 1972)
THE FINAL COMEDOWN (Dir: Oscar Williams, 1972)
BOXCAR BERTHA (Dir: Martin Scorsese, 1972)
THE BIG BIRD CAGE (Dir: Jack Hill, 1972)
SEVEN BLOWS OF THE DRAGON (Dir: Cheh Chang, Hseuh Li Pao, Ma Wu, 1972)*
CRIES AND WHISPERS (Dir: Ingmar Bergman, 1972)*
FELLINI'S AMARCORD (Dir: Federico Fellini, 1973)*
THE STUDENT TEACHERS (Dir: Jonathan Kaplan, 1973)
FANTASTIC PLANET (Dir: Rene Laloux, 1973)*
I ESCAPED FROM DEVIL'S ISLAND (Dir: William Witney, 1973)
THE ARENA (Dir: Steve Carver, 1974)
T.N.T. JACKSON (Dir: Cirio Santiago, 1974)

CAGED HEAT (Dir: Jonathan Demme, 1974)
COCKFIGHTER (Dir: Monte Hellman, 1974)
BIG BAD MAMA (Dir: Steve Carver, 1974)
LAST DAYS OF MAN ON EARTH (Dir: Robert Fuest, 1974)*
SWEET SWEETBACK'S BAADASSSS SONG (Dir: Melvin Van Peebles, 1974)*
CAPONE (Dir: Steve Carver, 1975)
DEATH RACE 2000 (Dir: Paul Bartel, 1975)
CRAZY MAMA (Dir: Jonathan Demme, 1975)
THE ROMANTIC ENGLISHWOMAN (Dir: Joseph Losey, 1975)*
THE STORY OF ADELE H. (Dir: Francois Truffaut, 1975)*
THE LOST HONOR OF KATHARINA BLUM (Dir: Volker Schlöndorff, 1975)*
DERSU UZALA (Dir: Akira Kurasawa, 1975)*
HOLLYWOOD BOULEVARD (Dir: Allan Arkush, Joe Dante, 1976)
JACKSON COUNTY JAIL (Dir: Michael Miller, 1976)
EAT MY DUST (Dir: Charles B. Griffith, 1976)
FIGHTING MAD (Dir: Jonathan Demme, 1976)
MOVING VIOLATION (Dir: Charles S. Dubin, 1976)
PIRANHA (Dir: Joe Dante, 1976)
SMALL CHANGE (Dir: Francois Truffaut, 1976)*
ANDY WARHOL'S BAD (Dir: Jed Johnson, 1977)*
GRAND THEFT AUTO (Dir: Ron Howard, 1977)
I NEVER PROMISED YOU A ROSE GARDEN (Dir: Anthony Page, 1977)
THUNDER AND LIGHTNING (Dir: Corey Allen, 1977)
A LITTLE NIGHT MUSIC (Dir: Harold Prince, 1977)*
DEATHSPORT (Dir: Henry Suso, Allan Arkush, 1978)
AVALANCHE (Dir: Corey Allen, 1978)
A HERO AIN'T NOTHIN' BUT A SANDWICH (Dir: Ralph Nelson, 1978)*
SAINT JACK (Dir: Peter Bogdanovich, 1979)
ROCK 'N' ROLL HIGH SCHOOL (Dir: Allan Arkush, 1979)
LADY IN RED (Dir: Lewis Teague, 1979)
THE TIN DRUM (Dir: Volker Schlöndorff, 1979)
THE BROOD (Dir: David Cronenberg, 1979)*
BREAKER MORANT (Dir: Bruce Beresford, 1980)*
HUMANOIDS OF THE DEEP (Dir: Barbara Peeters, 1980)
BATTLE BEYOND THE STARS (Dir: Jimmy Murakami, 1980)
CHRISTIANE F. (Dir: Uli Edel, 1981)*
SMOKEY BITES THE DUST (Dir: Charles B. Griffith, 1981)
GALAXY OF TERROR (Dir: Bruce Clark, 1981)

SATURDAY THE 14th (Dir: Howard Cohen, 1981)
ANDROID (Dir: Aaron Lipstadt, 1982)
FITZCARRALDO (Dir: Werner Herzog, 1982)*
LOVE LETTERS (Dir: Amy Jones, 1983)
SPACE RAIDERS (Dir: Howard S. Cohen, 1983)
SUBURBIA (Dir: Penelope Spheeris, 1983)
HOUSE (Dir: Steve Miner, 1986)
CHOPPING MALL (Dir: Jim Wynorski, 1986)
SORORITY HOUSE MASSACRE (Dir: Carol Frank, 1986)
STRIPPED TO KILL (Dir: Katt Shea, 1987)
BIG BAD MAMA II (Dir: Jim Wynorski, 1987)
DANCE OF THE DAMNED (Dir: Katt Shea, 1989)
MASQUE OF THE RED DEATH (Dir: Larry Brand, 1989)
TRANSYLVANIA TWIST (Dir: Jim Wynorski, 1989)
THE HAUNTING OF MORELLA (Dir: Jim Wynorski, 1990)
FULL FATHOM FIVE (Dir: Carl Franklin, 1990)
DRACULA RISING (Dir: Fred Gallo, 1993)
TO SLEEP WITH A VAMPIRE (Dir: Adam Friedman, 1993)
CARNOSAUR (Dir: Adam Simon, 1993)
THE FANTASTIC FOUR (Dir: Oley Sassone, 1994)
NOT OF THIS EARTH (Dir: Terence Winkless, 1995)
ATTACK OF THE 60 FOOT CENTERFOLDS (Dir: Fred Olen Ray, 1995)
THE WASP WOMAN (TV) (Dir: Jim Wynorski, 1995)
DILLINGER AND CAPONE (Dir: John Purdey, 1995)
BLACK SCORPION (TV) (Dir: Jonathan Winfrey, 1995)
A BUCKET OF BLOOD (TV) (Dir: Michael James McDonald, 1995)
PIRANHA (TV) (Dir: Scott Levy, 1995)
VAMPIRELLA (Dir: Jim Wynorski, 1996)
THE HAUNTING OF HELL HOUSE (Dir: Mitch Marcus, 1999)
THE PHANTOM EYE (TV series, 1999)
BLACK SCORPION (TV Series, 2001)
MARLENE DIETRICH: HER OWN SONG (Dir: David Riva, 2001)
THE ARENA (Dir: Timur Bekmambetov, 2001)
DINOCROC (Dir: Kevin O'Neill, 2004)
SEARCHERS 2.0 (Dir: Alex Cox, 2007)
DEATH RACE (Dir: Paul W.S. Anderson, 2008)
SPLATTER (Dir: Joe Dante, 2009)
DINOSHARK (Dir: Kevin O'Neill, 2010)

As Actor

THE CRY BABY KILLER (Dir: Jus Addiss, 1958)
THE GODFATHER PART II (Dir: Francis Ford Coppola, 1974)
CANNONBALL (Dir: Paul Bartel, 1976)
THE HOWLING (Dir: Joe Dante, 1980)
THE STATE OF THINGS (Dir: Wim Wenders, 1982)
SWING SHIFT (Dir: Jonathan Demme, 1984)
LORDS OF THE DEEP (Dir: Mary Ann Fisher, 1989)
THE SILENCE OF THE LAMBS (Dir: Jonathan Demme, 1990)
JOHN CARPENTER'S BODY BAGS (Dir: John Carpenter, 1993)
PHILADELPHIA (Dir: Jonathan Demme, 1993)
RUNAWAY DAUGHTERS (Dir: Joe Dante, 1994)
APOLLO 13 (Dir: Ron Howard, 1995)
THE SECOND CIVIL WAR (Dir: Joe Dante, 1997)
THE PHANTOM EYE (TV series, 1999)
SCREAM 3 (Dir: Wes Craven, 2000)
LOONEY TUNES: BACK IN ACTION (Dir: Joe Dante, 2003)
THE MANCHURIAN CANDIDATE (Dir: Jonathan Demme, 2004)
SEARCHERS 2.0 (Dir: Alex Cox, 2007)
RACHEL GETTING MARRIED (Dir: Jonathan Demme, 2008)

Roger Corman: Interviews

Science-Fiction in Danger

Roger Corman / 1957

From *The Hollywood Reporter*, November 18, 1957. Reprinted by permission of the author.

Science-fiction, which has become as staple a production category as westerns, is in danger.

The danger is not from outer space but inner man. The hazard was created by the very success of science-fiction, which predisposes to routine instead of imaginative plotting. That's a broad accusation to level against a form of film which depends for its success on imagination. But it is routine imagination that threatens the sci-fi feature. The paste-up of plots is clipping the wings of a kind of picture that can give wings to the audience mind.

There is a difference between the over-contrived science-fiction feature which recapitulates all the clichés of its category and the truly original, soaring feature. Logic is the missing ingredient from so many thrillers today. True, there is a false logic, a sophistry of science-fiction, but there is little of the grand imagination that captures a mind and transports it into the world of science on a realistic, here-and-now basis.

That world of science today, which formed a basis of science-fiction success on the screen, is the world's smartest activity. Science facts are beggaring, run-of-the-mill science-fiction. The producers in that category, therefore, had better start their imaginations going on a higher level if they don't want their product to wind up in the category of pulp publications.

The audience, which now takes fission, international Geophysical Year, twenty-mile-high flight, and other wonders in stride, is conditioned for the kind of film that reflects an imagination comparable to that of the great scientist. Science-fiction today needs cerebral wings, writers like H. G. Wells and Ray Bradbury. Until that kind of imaginative

3

brain is brought to the science-fiction feature film, we will have pleasantly routine, time-filling pictures in the category. With such minds
working in the field, there's no limit to the continuity and success of
science-fiction.

Corman Speaks

Bertrand Tavernier, Bernard Eisenschitz,
and Christopher Wicking / 1964

From *Positif* 59 (March 1964): 15–28. Reprinted by permission of Michel Ciment. Translated by Gregory Laufer.

Q: At the beginning of your career, did you have any connection to the movies?

A: No, just with thermodynamics and electronics, a whole world I no longer have anything to do with now.

Right in the middle of my studies at Stanford, I realized that I didn't really want to see them through. In fact, I got the highest grade on the physics exam in my first year at Stanford, and during my second year, I got the main part in a show. I remember the criticism from professors who thought I was ditching a good career to go lose myself in the theater. Then I enlisted in the navy, which made me pursue my studies. When I was discharged, I had only six months of coursework left to get my engineering degree. I also could have thrown myself into a totally different field and started over. But in the United States, a young man in school feels absolutely ashamed if he doesn't get his degree. It's a sure thing that his whole life will be a flop.

Since I had only six months left, I decided to keep going, and I got my degree.

I worked for four long days as an engineer and at the end of the fourth day, I went into the human resources office and said simply, "This is not going well. I'm leaving." I then thought that I wanted to go into filmmaking. The only problem was that I didn't know anything about it, but movies had always fascinated me. Because of the unions, all I could get was a job as a runner at Fox. From that point on, I got involved in the screenwriting department and I was assigned as a reader. I had written a few stories when I was in school, so I had a few ideas about how to go about it.

I was increasingly taken in by this work, which I had to give up to go to Oxford. I stayed there for only one trimester, and then I went to Paris. I lived on the left bank. I had my yellow sports car and we regularly hung out at the Deux Magots all afternoon. It was really nice. I went back to Paris two years later with a girl—an American I knew—and I told her, "I'm going to show you my Paris." I took her to lots of places and all of a sudden she said to me, "You didn't show me Paris at all. There were just Americans talking everywhere." I was struck by what she said. With the exception of one or two French girls I had met, I had only hung out with Americans, behaving like most students who go to Paris and spend their time talking.

Q: What were your real beginnings?
A: When I came back from Europe, I held various jobs—television stagehand, literary agent—and then I sold a screenplay that I had written at Allied Artists. I had called it *House in the Sea*, but they changed the title to *Highway Dragnet*, which they considered more commercial. I worked there as an associate producer, earned $2,000, and borrowed from several people. With a $12,000 budget, I made my first film as a producer and it was a hit. I threw myself into a second film . . .

Q: That was John Ireland's *The Fast and the Furious*?
A: Yes, and personally, I'm not very pleased with his work. It was after that film that I decided to become a director. That was the condition John Ireland laid down to act in that film: to direct it. He made another for that matter, a 3D western that went nowhere.
Q: The German credits said, "Based on an idea from Dorothy Malone . . ."
A: Actually, Dorothy gave us several ideas. Certain ones were follow-ups. She had left her agent and, having no work, accepted a part for next to nothing. At the time we had a tiny office, which was the waiting room of a literary agency. The production house was two girls and I, and the agency complained about losing clients because of us *(laughter)*.

But as for telling you which were Dorothy Malone's exact ideas . . .

Q: Have you continued producing films from time to time?
A: Yes. It was the beginning that was hard. Later on things moved along quite naturally. I was offered contracts and subjects. One year I directed

ten films and produced three or four others. The first one I produced was *Stakeout on Dope Street* by Irvin Kershner, which was an artistic and financial success. My brother told me that it was the greatest mistake of my career because on account of that success I reinvested my money in other productions that were all failures. I gave great freedom to the writers, since I myself do not like when people tell me what to do when I'm filming. I never said a word to Kershner. We would meet and have long talks in which everyone offered his point of view, and I would approve the cast and the distribution (Jack Hayes, Abby Dalton, and some of my actors would be there), but once the decision was made, I would say, "Go for it," and I would pull back. This was hugely successful. And I would set about looking around Hollywood for all the young people I knew: for a Dennis Sanders, a Francis Kobler, Irv Kershner, Bernie Kowalski, or Curtis Harrington. I bet on other names that I won't mention and whose films were horrible failures.

To be honest, *Crime and Punishment, USA* lost me a lot of money. *Night Tide*, which is a good film, has had difficulties at the box office. The *New York Times* and *Time* wrote very laudatory reviews and Curtis sent me a letter a few days ago saying that he hoped to reimburse me soon.

Q: You seem to operate cyclically in terms of the films you direct (rock 'n' roll, horror, detective). Is that because you have to? Is it a personal choice?

A: Everything springs from a network of factors that are both economic and artistic. In Hollywood, the cost of making a film is very high and there's no government assistance. I used to work on small budgets, very small budgets, but even then, I needed a hit. To survive, a director must have a long series of hits. That means that he depends more or less on what's in style, and has to bend to the flavor of the day. That said, I don't think that any genre is "inferior." Everything interests me: the adventures of a 120-pound monster, a gangster, or a student blown away by rock 'n' roll. I've agreed to handle such diverse topics because I thought I would learn my trade that way. Everything was useful to me; everything enriched me. But still, in every genre I've tried to innovate somewhat and to form original ideas. I've agreed to do any story at all provided I could make a true statement with it.

I don't think it's good for a director to become specialized. I am rather proud of having revitalized, in a certain respect, certain kinds of films, and especially of having been the first to cast them off once they've succeeded. I've also tried to vary my styles within a series. As a general rule, the basic idea for a film has come from me, but the subject has been written with a commercial eye.

Q: For example, your prehistoric film.
A: That was on contract. In reality, it wasn't a prehistoric film. The initial idea was really good. We showed cave men with a strange religion and weird rituals who worshipped difficult-to-recognize objects, and at the end it was understood that this was happening in the future, after an atomic disaster that had destroyed the world. In this religion, you saw certain elements from twentieth-century civilization, but totally distorted. The original title was *Prehistoric World* but, after the success of *I Was a Teenage Werewolf*, the distributors did away with that name and stuck it for a few weeks with the most horrific title in the entire history of filmmaking: *I Was a Teenage Caveman* (laughter). Despite that, the *Los Angeles Times* wrote that it was a very good film, which was a bit of a stretch.

Q: Have you learned a lot by filming in such conditions?
A: Yes, because, as I've told you, I feel that it's good for a director not to let himself be closed off in a single genre. I don't think, however, that this is the best method and I often vary genres and styles grudgingly. Legend has it that you learn in one year with Corman what you learn in four years at school. . . . But I would have preferred to have had another kind of training. Mine was sort of like a baseball player's: if he shows he's got talent, he'll start off on the Pocatello team, in the Idaho League. If he plays well, he'll be sent to Kansas City, and so on and so forth, until he's playing for the New York Yankees, but he'll have spent three or four years getting an education. It seemed to me that in France young people would burst out and were already brilliant. From their first films, they were already excellent directors. But their learning is different, more theoretical. It's all the same. You can learn as well by making films as by watching and understanding them.

Q: Do you think that your training is effective with respect to directing actors?
A: You know, there are plenty of things I would have done better if I had had more time. Starting now, I'm going to look after certain things more. I've made quite a few bad films.

Q: How do you introduce personal elements when filming so fast?
A: To begin with, every problem has to be settled in my head. It's on the

level of the script, in its preparation, that you have to introduce personal elements in order to be able to come onto the set with a whole scene in your head, even if it means tossing it aside in the event a better solution comes about. I don't believe in complete improvisation.

Q: But your speed is incredible. You filmed *Little Shop of Horrors* in a weekend?
A: Actually, the filming lasted two days and one night, a Thursday and a Friday. I hired my actors for a week. We rehearsed Monday, Tuesday, and Wednesday.

Q: It wasn't distributed in either France or England.
A: It wasn't shown anywhere in Europe, with the exception of a single time, at the Cannes Festival, where it was screened out of competition. I don't know how it got there. A friend called and told me that he could set up a screening. I had nothing to lose, so I sent him a copy. It seems it was well received, but no one knew how it had been made. It has overtones of pure comedy, of a horror film, and dark humor.

Q: Does it seem pretty close to *A Bucket of Blood*?
A: It came straight from that. If you strain your ear, you'll hear in the room next door the sound of a typewriter. It's Charles B. Griffith, the author of *Bucket* and *Little Shop*, writing the following film: *The Gold Bug*. We worked all night and destroyed our first version. We're starting over with a new idea.

Q: It seems that there's a good dose of comedy in your films. I'm thinking of *Swamp Women*, with that nymphomaniac's line, "Lemme cut my jeans shorter."
A: That made no sense, but it addressed a precise need. I had to make public and commercial films. So in these films there are certain things that apparently make them workable. They're often ridiculous things. But I had to put them in there, even when I was dealing seriously with history. For example, the girls cut their jeans just because the distributors wanted girls in shorts for publicity purposes. I couldn't find a valid justification for that gesture. It was completely illogical; the swamps were infested with mosquitoes. In fact, we had to cover up for protection and the best solution was to make the scene into a joke. If you have to get something illogical done for commercial reasons, do it in an even more illogical way. I remember making a small western in six days—sorry,

seven. (laughter) It rained for five days. It was a horrible experience. It was called *The Gunslinger.* My Texas distributor arrived in the city where I was filming and asked me how it was going. I told him that I thought that it was good but that there was too much violence and passion, and he answered, "Roger, I've been in this business for forty years, and you've been in it for just two. Let me tell you that no one has ever made a film with too much passion and violence." So I pressed on. Everyone was dying. At the end of the film half of the city was dead.

Q: That's the one where the heroine is a professional killer?
A: Yes, Beverly Garland, and it was a funny idea. I'm weary of prepackaged formulas, and when you try out a new idea, you necessarily think about shooting a hackneyed scene in a funny way without resorting to parody. This wasn't a parody, it was "Good God, how can I find a different sort of gunslinger?" Right away, I thought of a woman gunslinger, and the idea for the script came to me all of a sudden. It was the sheriff's wife. He's killed and she takes over for her husband. It was logical when it wasn't, but that was enough for a six- or seven-day western.

Q: *A Bucket of Blood* seems to be your first comedy?
A: Yes, it was the first of my films in which comedy had some importance, was part of the basic concept. In the others, there was sometimes a scene with a light tone, but here everything was comedic. It got huge laughs in America. I previewed the film at the same time as a Jerry Lewis film because I wanted to get the opinion of comedy lovers. However, the theater owner told me that I had gotten more laughs than the Lewis film and that it was the funniest film he had ever seen. I felt like I'd finally taken a big step forward. The very next day, Chuck and I started on *Little Shop. Bucket* wasn't a huge success, but I think we were ahead of our time, because *The Raven*, which is a triumph, is far less funny. Maybe the film was too modest, filmed in five days on sets that came from a film about youth. The distributors didn't know what to make of a movie that didn't belong to any particular genre. They were always scared of comedy, so they never mentioned in ads that *The Raven* was a comedy. Few people went into horror comedy, and we wanted to warn moviegoers that they were going to laugh without broadcasting the effect. Furthermore, in all three films I tried to imagine a beginning that would put the audience in the mood. But I was perhaps too subtle or not clear enough. No one got it. Still, in *The Raven*, when Vincent Price gets up and gets into a telescope in two stages, the film you're going to see is by all appearances

a comedy. *A Bucket of Blood* was a satire for beatniks. Since the beatnik movement was well known at the time, the very subject and the way in which we addressed it made audiences burst into laughter within the first few minutes. They knew what we were doing and there was no issue.

Watching it again a short time ago, I realized that the distribution crew was made up of all the guys and gals who came to our "parties." There was Dick Miller, Tony Carbone, and Barboura Morris, whom I was seeing at the time, and plenty of friends of mine.

Q: In *War of the Satellites*, you have a small role?
A: Yes, I was an engineer who shot off satellites. I thought that my scientific training authorized me to sit down and speak that dialogue. I act occasionally, but never as often as Alfred Hitchcock.

Q: What do you think of *She Gods*, which seems, at least in terms of its filming, to be linked to New Wave cinema?
A: That was partly on contract. I had to make certain kinds of films and, since I like to travel, I thought it would be great to get a few guys (I always work with a small crew) and take them to Hawaii, to one of the remotest islands. We settled in there for a while and made two films. And then we went home (laughter).

Q: We haven't seen *Naked Paradise*.
A: That was one of the films.

Q: But there seems to be a trilogy of these exotic and erotic films?
A: *Naked* was actually linked to gangster films. We took quite a long time. It was fun, and it's always fun to make money at the same time. A good number of my films were made like that. *Little Shop* was filmed in two days because I wanted to know if I could make a film that fast.

Q: The adaptations of Edgar Poe make a series. Were you annoyed by the fact that you filmed them one after the other?
A: Of course. It's part of that carefully honed formula that is always applied in the same way. I don't want to do that anymore now. You feel like you're repeating yourself too much. For a long time I had wanted to change but my producers didn't want me to. I asked to direct *Usher* in order not to make small-budget monster stories. The market was so glutted and it didn't interest me anymore. I suggested *Usher* to them, showing them that it could be a good film in the terror genre, that we could

make something classic. They took time making up their minds because it was their most expensive production and they were losing money at the time. They invested what they had left and gave me free reign. But later, each time I brought a new idea to them, they begged me to make another little *Edgar Poe* for them.

Q: We are bothered by the artificial similarity that exists among all these films: the fog, among other things, that you see on the outside of buildings, the color scheme . . .
A: Yes, of course (laughing). It was hard for me to change anything at all in a genre that was very successful. I thought on the other hand that it would give me the chance to use color as a precision tool. Through color, I could home in on the meaning of certain details, highlight such and such a notion. I didn't want it to be perfunctory.

I used fog at first to cover up the lack of set designs. In the majority of cases there was nothing but the studio wall. And also because Poe requires stylization and rejects realism. Fog is the easiest means of creating a romantic atmosphere even if it means demystifying it.

Q: Do you feel a kinship with Poe?
A: Yes, I read Poe when I was very young, when I used to read a lot. When I was six, seven, eight years old, I devoured book after book. My father had given me Poe's complete works and I loved them. In fact, there are undertones of comedy in Poe that people do not notice because he's not as good when he writes comedy. But a great number of things have commonalities with satire and even with farce, and I liked all of that.

On the other hand, and this hasn't been spoken about enough, Poe wrote in the first person. He was one of the first subjective writers, and also one of the first writers to have pierced human consciousness. The nineteenth century saw several artists, several men like Dostoyevsky, attack the unconscious. What Freud did consciously, Poe had done unconsciously. He literally penetrated the interior of the human spirit. I think I've stayed faithful to his spirit, even though over the course of the series I've gotten further and further away from him, notably in *The Masque of the Red Death*. *Usher* is very faithful. In *The Pit and the Pendulum*, we wrote the first and second acts and ended with Poe. In his exploration of the consciousness, Poe uses a symbolism that is very close to modern psychoanalysis. I remember writing when I was nineteen years old a gangster story that was never published. I recently found it and realized that it was in fact the story of Oedipus blow by blow. I had found one of the essential complexes without realizing it.

Q: In *Bucket*, there is a walled-in cat. Was that already a tribute to Poe?
A: It was one of those things that you put in there unconsciously. I don't remember intending to make an exact reference to Poe, but I thought perhaps unconsciously of *The Black Cat*, which is one of my favorite short stories.

Q: Which of your adaptations of Poe is your favorite?
A: I think that the series makes up a whole. There's a progression from one film to the next, especially in the directing. These films are full of dialogue, and to create movement, I made my actors move constantly, and the camera as well. I tried to locate with my camera the motivation behind each movement, for each gesture, for each shift. Maybe in the beginning, there was something gratuitous about it. In the final films in the series, there's less movement in terms of the equipment. Maybe I was wrong. My favorites are *The Pit and the Pendulum*, then *Usher* and *The Raven*.

Q: Was the choice of Vincent Price yours?
A: Yes, because Vincent fulfills several requirements. Poe's heroes are all highly cultured and intelligent. A horror film hero *must not* be a benighted brute. I think that people identify horror with something that is above them, a superior force, an intelligence, a culture that they may make fun of but that they in fact fear.

Price offers a very interesting and very personal interpretation of fear. He recreates the basic feeling of horror: that felt by a child alone in the night whose parents have left home alone. There's a storm, a vast and terrifying world around him. There is a bit of child in every character that I've had Price take on. At the same time, he plays characters who are very refined, but whose culture does not dispel fear. Quite the contrary. The more things they learn, the more their fear in the face of the unknown increases, and the closer they get to the child. Price is the last descendant of a civilization of refinement, that has been driven to the brink of decadence by an excess of culture, another element of concern. It's the end of a civilization, or the beginning of its decadence. Same with Ray Milland, who has an English accent, which, for American audiences, means culture. In *Premature Burial*, I wanted a younger and more romantic hero than Price. Milland isn't a lot younger, but in the public mind, he is associated with the notion of a romantic lead.

Q: Do you look for authenticity in your sets, in terms of Boston civilization?
A: Yes, we tried to build sets that were faithful with respect to the time in which Poe lived. I was greatly helped by my set designer Daniel Haller and I don't think (unless you pay great attention) that you would notice the degree to which the sets are almost identical from one film to the next. The audience doesn't see it.

But this faithfulness is more a question of the story than the sets, details or design. It's the whole that counts, that stylization that is faithful to Poe.

Q: Why was it Charles Beaumont who wrote *Premature Burial*?
A: It was a more romantic story. I had had an argument with A.I. [American International Pictures] and I started *Premature Burial* all by myself.

I convinced Pathé to front me some money and, all of a sudden, in the middle of filming, the president and vice-president of A.I. came onto the set, shook my hand, and said, "Dear partner." We had stayed good friends despite our argument, but I asked them, "What does that mean, dear partner?" And they answered, "We just bought Pathé, so we own half the rights to the film." And I found myself with A.I. unexpectedly.

Q: There are several moments of comedy in this film . . .
A: Yes. I wanted to make it a bit tongue in cheek. When you play with terror, it seems a bit simplistic to bank only on that feeling. But sometimes people will make fun of some idea that seems important to you, and sometimes joking will make it even more important, more frightening.

Q: Is it a sort of defense?
A: Exactly. For example, I just got a script from Columbia, with an offer to direct it when I get back. I read the beginning and, on the second page, the heroine cries out, "I'm going back home to discover who I am." You have to have that said with a smile. If I directed it (I don't know if I'll do it, probably not), the girl would have to smile while saying that. I understand what she means, but it sounds so clichéd that, unless you're presenting the girl as a total idiot, she must realize that that line counts for her, but that at the same time it's a bit overused.

Q: Was your approach to Lovecraft different from your approach to Poe?
A: My approach to Lovecraft came about in unfortunate circumstances. We had to make Poe's *The Haunted Palace*, but the script wasn't ready in time. In our drawers there was a script for *The Case of Charles Dexter Ward* that had some similarities to Poe. But the distributors only wanted films from the Poe series (given the success of the earlier ones). We used Lovecraft's short story, mixed in elements of Poe, and introduced *The Haunted Palace of Edgar Poe*. It was actually cheating. It was only partly Lovecraft, and I didn't really try to penetrate the inside of his universe.

However, I prefer Poe. His symbols are subtler. Lovecraft is direct. He consciously applied what Poe had found unconsciously. For example, we see pits in Lovecraft, but they're presented as an obvious sexual symbol, whereas in Poe, there is something more. The symbolism in *The Pit and the Pendulum* with the author of *The Raven* is obvious after reading Freud, but while Poe didn't present it as such, Lovecraft did.

Q: Lovecraft is more realistic, more outward.
A: Yes. He ascribes importance to landscapes, which are more tortured with Poe, where everything, in my opinion, is artificial. That's why I filmed all my outside shots in the studio. A real-life landscape would introduce a realism that I reject. In *The Pit*, you see the ocean twice but it's only because of the strange effect of the flood tide and the ebb tide, an almost hypnotic effect. At the beginning of *Usher*, we see a forest. There had just been a big fire in the area and I wanted to film that sequence in a burned-down forest. But I can't compare for the reasons I've told you: Poe's and Lovecraft's styles. I could set them against the style in *The Intruder*, where each scene is filmed in a natural setting, where there are fewer complicated movements, less searching with the camera. It's a more direct way of looking at life. But the audience accepts Poe's stories more easily because they occur in the past. You're forced to rely on plastic effects. You couldn't show one of those characters. You couldn't show a monster walking down a modern street. Though yes, that would be interesting. . . . Or else that would be the hero in *The Intruder*.

Q: What we find remarkable in this film is the way in which you present William Shatner. For a few moments, he looks like a hero.
A: Yes, that's what I wanted. And in fact there were plenty of other things, other ideas that trended that way and that I had to do away with. When he arrives in that little town, he's presented like a very nice guy. As soon as he gets off the bus he helps a little girl. He then goes down

the street and I had a panoramic that showed the town as seen from his eyes. It's the approach, the positioning of a battlefield that we didn't yet know was such.

Q: We see that already in the bus.
A: Yes, but I forced the idea. The panoramic ended on a nice scene of a crossroads, and we homed in on a small dog at Shatner's feet. Shatner bent down and petted the dog, which wagged its tail in a very friendly way. I had to cut this scene because the camera was quivering slightly during the panoramic. In fact, there was a break in the editing, because it eliminated a transition scene. That panoramic would have shown the town, and that in that very town, dogs like Adam Cramer (laughter).

Q: Wasn't the playground a symbol?
A: No, not at all. Or else it was unintentional. I've started to think that even the choice of an exterior has a symbolic meaning you're not immediately aware of. What I tried to say at the end of the film was that Shatner wasn't completely defeated. He was defeated in that town and remained alone, which meant that he was free to go to another town, where he very likely would use different tactics. What had started him off would make him continue on that same path until his death. People thought that ending was vague. I didn't want to show his career as having ended. His defeat wasn't irrevocable. In the South, men of his kind aren't easily defeated. He's a modern Lenin who may have lost the battle, but who hopes to come back to rule the whole country.

Q: What can you say about *The Dubious Patriots*[1]?
A: Well, I signed with my brother, a year and half ago, a contract for several films with Associated Artists. We were supposed to make serious films but everything we proposed was rejected. In the end, *The Dubious Patriots* became a compromise.

We thought we could do good work and, at the same time, meet Associated Artists' demands by giving them the kind of films they were asking for, despite long speeches about "Art" that they had made to us while pens were hanging over the contracts. We decided to do a sort of grand war story, in which there would be interesting subjects and characters.

---

1. The working title for *The Secret Invasion*, which Corman was working on at the time of this interview.

That's what I mean by compromise. It may be that this is not the best way to conceive a film, or that it might turn against the film itself. But, from another perspective, I think that we came through with a rather good war film and that we took one more step, in an entirely different direction, even though *The Dubious Patriots* may only be a modern translation of my first film, *Five Guns West*.

Among all the films I've made, many (God knows how many) were bad films. But each time, I did my best. There are some I never should have done, but even with those, I learned something, so I have nothing to regret. I don't have the right to say that it's horrible to have made those films because I don't think it was.

Q: Are you often your own producer?

A: Yes, and when I was only the director I had problems. For example, I had a contract for three films with Eddie Small. The first, *The Tower of London*, was the most foolish thing I've ever filmed. Every night he would come to see me or call me. The script was changed, reworked without my consent. Lots of strange things were happening all the time, and finally I asked him to tear up our contract. He realized he wouldn't get anything worthwhile out of me and tore it up. I have nothing against Eddie Small. He's an old man who had lots of success during the thirties, and who doesn't know that times have changed. In several cases, people tried to force my hand, so I preferred to go my own way. In general, I agree on the type of film, on its budget, and then I feel totally free. That's why I'm both a producer and a director. That doesn't prevent you from being owned by the distributors, like in the case of *The Dubious Patriots*. Associated Artists wanted "new and bold" films. How many times have I heard those words! Columbia has offered me a very tempting contract, but I sought to clarify right away what my projects would be. I would like to remake *Lost Horizon*, among others things.

Q: But Capra has the same idea . . .

A: If that's true, it's out the window.

Q: How would you have shot *The Rhinoceros*?

A: Oh, I would really like to make that film. It would contain a real message and at the time would be very fun, entertaining. It must be fantastic to direct a film that has an exact meaning and at the same time offers a satirical approach to certain things. I think that in *Intruder* I pushed too hard. It's my best film but I think I was too academic. I believed so much in the ideas espoused by the film that I handled them too heavily. That kind of subject calls for a simpler, subtler touch.

For example, in *The Gold Bug*, which I wrote with Chuck Griffith, and which will be very different from the other Poes, the action will occur in the South immediately after the Civil War. It will be a real horror comedy where we'll sprinkle lots of satirical features that we won't make much of in the least. It will be in the same vein as *The Intruder* but in a less direct way. Someone will make a comment about the "Old South" and that'll be all—a sort of joke—and the audience will laugh. Then they'll think, "Hey, wait a minute," but we'll have gone on to something else. It will be a lightning bolt.

Q: We see that in certain detective films, *Machine Gun Kelly*, for example.
A: Yes, I tried to show in that film that Machine Gun Kelly was a poor guy at bottom. The majority of gangster films show gangsters as heroes in the mold of Robin Hood. . . . But they weren't like that. Maybe some of them tried to rebel against certain social pressures, but not many. Most were just illiterate poor guys and I wanted to show that Kelly was just a coward and a giver, without giving social or psychoanalytical reasons for his cowardice. He was a rotten guy, a sort of Hitler.

Q: It's the only gangster film with *Legs Diamond*[2] that adopts this bias.
A: I didn't see *Legs Diamond*. In my case, it was very conscious. Even though most elements of a film (especially the directing, and by directing I also mean the positioning of the equipment, set choices, and directing actors) are unconscious. The basic idea must be premeditated. I could have filmed such and such a scene in twenty different ways. The fact that I chose one of them comes from a sort of unconscious determination. I personally couldn't give you a worthy explication, but if I did it one way or another it's because there must be a reason, in keeping or not with the basic idea.

To get back to Kelly, I threw myself into historical research and I found that he was neither a hero nor a totally cowardly guy. So I built the film entirely around his final lines, which are historical. Kelly was shut off in his mountain hideout and when he was told to lay down his arms and turn himself in, he did. And the FBI agent told him, "Kelly, you come off as being the toughest man in the country and we thought that were go-

---

2. *The Rise and Fall of Legs Diamond* (1960), directed by Budd Boetticher.

ing to put up a fight. Why didn't you?" And Kelly responded, "Because you would have killed me." We put the film together based on this dialogue. He didn't want to fight for nothing. His wife kept on fighting, which was true. That gives us the concept for the film.

Q: What do you think of Charles Bronson?
A: He's a great actor. Actually, one of the best actors I've worked with. You know he's a former boxer. He has tremendous physical strength. He has to control his movements, because he could easily knock out his partners.

Q: In that film, there was an admirable first reel, almost silent . . .
A: At that time I didn't know much of anything. Today I'd like to direct a similar sequence, *consciously*. That one was made instinctively. You see the holdup in the shadows on the floor because I didn't have enough money to build a set for a bank. At the same time, I had an initial idea and I got rid of a purely practical problem. It's the best solution. The film began with silent characters. Then I wondered, "Am I going to have them say anything?" The further along I got, the more I realized that they *could not* speak. They had nothing to say. Everything was rehearsed and went down as planned. Without intending to, I recovered the silent film style and that sequence earned me very good reviews.

Q: Don't you think science fiction and thrillers have to be approached in the same way? The two genres are almost identical.
A: I had never thought about that, but now that you've pointed it out to me, I think that there do indeed exist several similarities between these genres. Yes, you're totally right. Their approach is almost similar. In both cases, there is a mystery to solve and we're dealing with an investigation. The departure point may be improbable, but the unfolding of the story must be totally logical. The directing has to be spontaneous and without elaborate effects. You have to show rational beings in a rational setting, unlike in horror films.

This resemblance explains the failures suffered by certain good directors who have tried to treat science fiction like its own genre with its own rules. I'm thinking of Michael Anderson's *1984*, which a more modest director would have made more interesting.

Q: *Not of This Earth* was almost a thriller.
A: Yes, that's true. The basic idea for the film would have suited a de-

tective film and certain sequences could have appeared in a biography about gangsters.

Q: Where did you film it, since in Switzerland it's called *The Vampire of San Francisco* and in Belgium *The Vampire of New York*?
A: In Los Angeles (laughter).

Q: Why haven't you ever adapted any famous science fiction novels?
A: I don't know. Probably for economic reasons. In the first sequence you have rockets, in the second an unknown civilization, in the third Martians attack a spaceship.

Q: Matheson's novels, for example, are different.
A: You're right. But I don't know science fiction novelists very well. As a general rule, I prefer short stories because the basic scenarios are what's most interesting and you find them more readily in short stories. I wanted to do *I Am Legend* three years ago when I was just starting to be known, but the project was rejected. Salkow did it with Vincent Price. I have nothing against Salkow, I'm just sorry that the producers whom I made a lot of money for took my idea. I had gone to England to get a silly project ready—*I Flew U-2 Over Russia*—a spy film that would have looked like the James Bonds that are being filmed nowadays. It was the story of an American pilot who flies over Russia (there are those who do that for money and whose job it is). This pilot gets caught by the Russians. He finds himself involved in fights that pit two sides against each other, one of peace and one of war. It's really crazy and the English producers rejected it, panic-stricken. I then proposed *I Am Legend* to them, but I wasn't well known enough. I think that Price will be very good, but I wouldn't have gotten him. I saw an actor in the mold of a U-2 pilot, not at all cultured, young and athletic.

I have a science fiction project with Ray Bradbury. We have taken it on with my brother, and it's very possible that we'll do it. Under the ice of the pole, an atomic submarine discovers *Nautilus* in a state of hibernation. Inside is Captain Nemo, who's been asleep for five hundred years, fed up with his contemporaries. He is woken up. He's furious and we witness Nemo's wrangling with the modern world.

In this very specialized world, Nemo's science sets him back in every domain, but his intelligence stays more synthetic, more general. He can be used to connect, to coordinate the thoughts of men. The first thing he tackles is cancer, and we had a sequence in which the *Nautilus*, shrunk down to microscopic size, goes up blood vessels and does battle with the cancer virus.

Science fiction interests me when it allows you to show the interaction between man and science. For that matter, I think I'll soon come back to that genre.

Q: What do you think of the films made by Hammer?
A: I find them good, but frankly I prefer my own. They seem rather superficial and foreign to me. They don't make enough effort to get to the heart of things. They stay surface-level. So Hitchcock, for example, is interested in the unconscious. He builds all his films around that idea. The best scene in *The Birds* is a scene that makes audiences scream, but you don't see any birds, just a girl in the street. I used a similar scene at least five times. It's essential in my view. I've taken nothing from Hitchcock and he's taken nothing from me. We're interested in the same type of biases.

Q: What do you think of other directors at American International: Ray Milland, Edward L. Cahn, William Whitney?
A: I didn't see Ray Milland's film. The subject was exciting, but the technicians who worked on the film, who were *my* technicians, told me that Ray had been somewhat overwhelmed. He wasn't organized enough to act and direct at the same time. He lost time on a three-week scene and forgot his scenes . . .

Edward L. Cahn was a really good guy. As soon as he was given a good script he got along magnificently. Billy Whitney is an excellent director but one who had no luck. My brother produced two of his films and they had lots of problems.

Q: To get back to *Tales of Terror*, it seemed to us that a whole part of the dialogue was made up of song titles?
A: That's correct. It's funny because the actress who was supposed to speak that dialogue, Joyce Jamison, was a singer. In addition, that enhanced the grotesque side of the story. You see, I run the risk (like everyone) of becoming a bit pretentious, of getting too far from the audience. I don't believe in great films that no one liked.

In the copy of *Tales of Terror* that you saw, there were two gaps made by the English censors: the fight between Morella's ghost and her daughter, then at the end of the final panoramic, which showed Price's corpse, totally decomposed.

Q: As for *The Young Racers*, was that the working copy?

A: The fact remains that you've seen scenes that I had cut: the Belgian ambulance in England, the arrival of the brother who became a racecar driver in Monte Carlo. Maybe the company added back those scenes in the European version without my consent? It's not a good film. In fact, you can leave after the credits, but this is an unpleasant surprise for me. Would those people who always ask me for longer films have put back those scenes (that I had eliminated) for Europe in the belief that no one would notice? I mean, what happened to my seventy other films?

Roger Corman: A Double Life

Digby Diehl / 1969

From *Action!*, June 1969. © 1969 by Digby Diehl. Reprinted by permission of the author.

At forty-three, Roger Corman is getting used to living a double life. In the United States he has earned a vivid renown as "King of the Grade B's" from a series of inexpensive horror and sci-fi films. Abroad, however, he has been praised for cinematic brilliance and is the youngest director to have a retrospective showing at the French Film Institute.

Corman was born in Detroit but went to high school in Beverly Hills. From 1944 to 1946, he served in the Navy, after which he earned a B.S. from Stanford and later studied at Oxford on the G.I. Bill. He produced his first film, *Monster on the Ocean Floor*, in 1953 and two years later debuted as a director with *Five Guns West*.

Although influenced by the "classics" of the genre (*Caligari*, the original *Dracula*, etc.) Corman's own horror films became a unique blend of gasps and guffaws, as self-consciously campy dialogue and ever-so-solemn performances were mixed with the usual horror elements. Labeling him "the titillater," *Newsweek* praised Corman's "stylish cleverness" in his Edgar Allan Poe films and found that he "shows a flair for Gothic weirdness that is the dark side of America's sunny optimism."

This "dark side" was explored more directly in *The Wild Angels* (1966), a sordid story of motorcycle gang violence directed in a semi-documentary style with an innovative use of rock 'n' roll music. The *Independent Film Journal* predicted violent controversy about the film and noted that Corman "gives the characters no backgrounds, no particular motivations and his film makes no judgments . . . at no point does Corman say this is right or wrong, merely *this is how it is*." Since *The Wild Angels*, Corman has directed the equally controversial *The Trip*.

Diehl: You're known as one of the few professionals in the motion picture industry who takes particular interest in young filmmakers. Why is that true?

Corman: Well, I've helped some in their first pictures, because I think it's worthwhile. When I got out of Stanford, it took me seven years of doing everything in the world to get going in films. I came out with all the honors and I got a job as a stage hand. Actually, first I was a messenger at 20th Century-Fox and then I was a stagehand at KLAC. So, anyway, I think it's a worthwhile thing to help a young person of some talent get his start in films. It's enjoyable and stimulating and I generally have made money at it although recently the margin of profit has dropped. The ones at UCLA have gone far over budget and so I've decided to stop backing any new filmmakers until I can re-assess the situation.

Diehl: Although abroad your films have achieved critical acclaim, your reputation in the U.S. is not as great. How do you explain this difference?

Corman: In general, I believe the standard of criticism in Europe is higher than in the United States. Film has been respected there as the twentieth-century art form for a much longer period of time than it has here. In Europe, the critics are brought up in a different tradition and are taught to look for different elements. At the same time, however, there are American critics who are more perceptive, intelligent, and informed, but they are the minority. Ordinarily, there is a great deal of snobbery from American film critics. They will accept a film directed by Stanley Kramer as a work of art before they see it. Or a film from a European director. Or even a low- budget from New York. But they unloose their ire against a low- or medium-budget Hollywood production. Now generally, I've gotten fairly good reviews in the U.S., most often better in New York than in Hollywood: as a matter of fact, only in my last couple of times out have my receptions fallen off. When I was making the Poe pictures, I would hardly ever see an unfavorable review either in Europe or America. The only time I really began to be knocked was after doing *The Wild Angels* for American International. And, again, I can't say I was knocked *everywhere*: The *Los Angeles Times* listed it as one of the top ten films of the year! It seems, however, that when I turn to what I consider a truthful rendering of the American scene is the point where I run afoul of American critics.

Diehl: In your years of making horror and science fiction films, you must have developed some theories about the genre. You've been quoted as saying that your aesthetics is essentially Freudian.

Corman: Yes, specifically with horror films. To me, the horror film is essentially the recreation of childhood fear. The small child, alone in the world: he's worried, he's frightened, he depends upon the love and protection of his parents. But for some reason sometimes they are not with him. And at such times he can become very frightened. Now, as he grows older, these events are forgotten by his conscious mind or he learns to cope with them, but he will usually carry some residual fears about some aspects of the world as an adult. I think it's the function of the horror film, and it's a useful function, to expose those fears and show they are baseless. The unconscious minds of most people have common underpinnings. After all, we've all been raised in Western civilization in basically the same ways so there are similarities between us. I try to reach what I consider the uniform elements of the unconscious by building up a sense of suspense and then cracking through it quickly, moment by moment, and it reacts. Very often, if it's done correctly, you'll get a scream from the audience, for you've affected their unconscious, followed by a little ripple of laughter, which is when the conscious mind takes over again and says to the unconscious, "Okay, you didn't need to scream." And this why in my later films I added humor and made essentially comedy-horror films. These are a lot of fun to make but are also challenging, like a complex piece of music.

Diehl: Can you give me some specific examples of this theory in your films?

Corman: Okay. Say *The Pit and the Pendulum.* In that, Vincent Price is awakened in the castle by what seems to be the voice of his dead wife. Before this happened, we've set up several elements—that his wife may have been buried alive, that her ghost may still walk the castle, etc.— so that we've, as it were, sowed the ground. He wakes up and instantly he's frightened. And the audience begins to sense a little fear with him. He walks down the hill, trying to find the source of the voice; in other words, trying to investigate. At the same time, the audience is saying with him: "Find out what the secret is," but they're also warning "Don't go any farther down the hall." There are other elements working as well. I think the actual movement down the hall is another kind of fear-attraction combination. It's like a young boy dying to find out—"dying" is the right word I think—about sex. He's drawn irresistibly to it, yet at the same time he's frightened because he knows it's going to change his life. He doesn't know yet if he's going to meet the test adequately, yet he must meet the test. Now the movement down the hall, I'd say, is to a certain extent the symbolism of the vagina. It's generally dimly lit in our films, which may add to it as well.

Diehl: So the secret he's trying to discover is the primal secret . . .

Corman: Right. There's a theory that mystery stories are always an attempt to solve that primal secret. Very often what's going on down the hall, behind the door, has with it the question "What is father doing to mother?" It could be murder because it sounds pretty violent: the bedsprings are bouncing around, he hears cries and that's pretty frightening to him because his parents represent the only security he has in the world . . . Anyway, back in *this* hallway, Vincent Price is proceeding further and further. Soon, the audience begins to be caught up with him. We have point-of-view dolly shots moving backwards on his face. Once we get into it, I try to keep all the shots moving, so the audience is with him at all times. He goes down the stairway, into the underground crypt, it appears that the voice has been calling to him from his wife's tomb. He breaks through the bricks and pulls the coffin open and his wife sits up quickly and looks him straight in the face.

I've seen the film a number of times and at that point, the audience has never failed to scream—and *really* scream! And then they laugh a little bit and it's all right because they know you did something to them. And the laughter is always appreciative laughter because that's what they came for. When they bought their ticket, that's what they paid for—they didn't know what that moment would be, or exactly what was going to happen, but they came for the moment when they were going to scream, and, whether they knew it or not, they came for the moment when some part of a childhood fear was going to be exposed after which they were going to be told "It's okay."

Diehl: When you were at Stanford, did you study psychology?

Corman: I took a number of psychology courses but my degree was in engineering. But, of course, I've also read a great deal on psychology.

Diehl: When you talk about a Freudian aesthetic, how is this translated into filmic terms?

Corman: Well, film is the best medium in the world for a Freudian aesthetic because the unconscious predates language; it seems to deal with predominantly visual images. We dream primarily in images and therefore using the motion picture enables you to create an experience closely related to the unconscious, particularly as we know it in dreams. In a movie theater, you sit back, passively, in a darkened room. A passage of light appears before you and you concentrate your attention on it as you would on a hypnotist. You are in a near dreamlike state and your conscious mind relaxes because of your surroundings, breaking down some of the barriers to the unconscious. But the beauty of the form is that your conscious mind can still function on a critical level just as you react to it on an emotional level.

Diehl: When you take a Poe story, how extensively do you work it out?
Corman: Most of Poe's works were extremely short so I would utilize them as a third act of a structure which I create to lead up to it. In *The Pit and the Pendulum*, everything in the original story took place in that room containing the pit, the pendulum, and the prisoner. We utilized that scene by taking a young man and bringing him to the caste of Vincent Price and in the first and second acts, we prepared for it. In the third, he was in that room. With the art director, I would work out, say, 80 to 90 percent of the picture's shots in advance, sketching them in the script on the blank pages opposite the text. I would then follow that—70 or 80 percent of the time. If there was any particular style or technique of working, it was of having as much time as possible, as much preparation, but then never be wedded to it. If I came to the set and saw a better way of working, I would always throw out the work that had been done before. If you become too rigid, you may get a very technically excellent result but it may also lack life.

Diehl: Obviously, it is easy to produce emotion on the screen by violence. But this can be done glibly, and I would be interested in knowing how you feel about resorting to such practices?
Corman: Actually, there is very little violence in the horror films. Matter of fact, sometimes there's none at all. The essence of the horror is fear of the unseen—the image behind that door. Some of the most frightening sequences I've shot are simply a dolly coming up to a strange door and hearing some strange noise—not necessarily a violent noise. In *The Masque of the Red Death*, there was no violence whatsoever. We were dealing with the plague, a perfectly natural phenomenon and it was fear of Death, *per se*, not fear of any violence.

Diehl: In *The Masque*, Death was personified, much like it was in Ingmar Bergman's *Seventh Seal*. Did you get inspired from his work?

Corman: Somebody once said I had, but all I can say is that I took my concept from Poe's story which was written one hundred years before Bergman made *The Seventh Seal*, and I believe that both Bergman and I took our inspiration from that story. I never started to do a series on Poe. I just wanted to do a version of "Fall of the House of Usher." It was a success, and AIP asked me to do another one. Poe's next two most famous stories were "The Pit and the Pendulum" and "Masque of the Red Death." I couldn't decide between them, but finally chose the latter because "Masque of the Red Death" was very close to *The Seventh Seal*. And as the series grew, I always came back to *The Masque* as the logical film to do next, and I always rejected it in favor of a lesser Poe work because of the similarity to Bergman's film. Finally, I had used up all suitable Poe material and had no choice. Of course, both *The Masque* and *The Seventh Seal* deal with the Middle Ages and in each the leading character confronts Death as an individual. But in making my film, I tried as much as possible to avoid the similarities.

Diehl: Harold Pinter's plays and films emphasize the "something sinister lurking in the background" you mentioned earlier. Are you an admirer of his?

Corman: Very much so. In *The Birthday Party*, there's always the feeling of a sinister quality out there—which is our modern world as I interpret it. And there *is* horror in the modern world, believe me. One time, AIP asked me to do a prehistoric picture. The beauty of it was that they would let me alone to do pretty much what I wanted as long as I stayed within the scope of the type of film they wanted and their budget limitations. I came up with a very strange film with Bob Vaughn called *Prehistoric World*, and as you began to follow the story and learn about the tribe the young man belonged to, you could hopefully see the growth of religions built around strange belief, superstitions, and fears. And at the end, you found that it all took place in the *future*; that the world had been destroyed by an atomic bomb; that the man was *re-building*. And just as his original beliefs came from attempts to cope with a world he didn't understand, he was now doing the same thing in a different world. Part of it was contaminated and his religion told him, it was an "evil" area— that devils were lurking there. I think that we were dealing in that film with the same kind of sinister element you mentioned—but in a different way.

Diehl: Does science fiction fit into your theoretical framework for horror films?

Corman: I think that they represent different aspects of the same basic drive: to know the unknown. If you say that there is a superior civilization on another planet you are answering the same basic question as if you say the spirits of the dead can come back and haunt us. In each case you are seeking to discover what is out there, either in the stars or in the world around us. The finest example of science fiction I've seen in my life is Stanley Kubrick's *2001*. Kubrick was saying that in moving beyond what we already know, we eventually enter a mystical religious experience. Just as in my film *Man with the X-Ray Eyes*, what started out as a simple experiment in vision ended up as a kind of quasi-religious parable. The man had to pluck out his eyes at the end because he had seen too deeply and too much. And could not stand it.

Diehl: Many of the New Wave filmmakers cite you and Hitchcock as being heavily influential. Why should you be coupled that way?

Corman: Of course, as mentioned, both Hitchcock's and my films are heavily psychoanalytical in their use of symbols. In *Psycho*, for example, Hitchcock uses a great sexual symbol with that old house on the hill. A house is accepted traditionally as a female symbol. And at the same time, he had a long, low motel that pointed straight at the house. Guess what that is? And the whole interaction was built around Tony Perkins, playing a man and a woman, moving back and forth between the phallic symbol of the motel and the feminine symbol of the house. In many of Hitchcock's films, he used the male symbol of the train. Now on a train, you are able to put people in a contained environment but with an ever-shifting background—which are good enough cinematic reasons for setting his film on one. But Hitchcock continued putting his people on trains after the time when everyone travelled by plane. An airplane is not as clear-cut a symbol as a train—you can't have it go through a tunnel, for instance—and so he had to resort to wild excuses explaining why someone in a film took a train when nobody takes trains anymore. In *Psycho*, he came up with the magnificent substitute symbol of the motel—which, if you look at it clearly, has no relationship to reality. I mean the whole thing is a soundstage affair, which is in keeping with a fantasy film. If you want to keep the fantasy, you don't want to show the real world.

Diehl: What do you call the type of film you're doing now?

Corman: AIP likes to call them "protest films," and so many have involved motorcycle gangs, people just call them "motorcycle films." But I only made one motorcycle film—the first one—*The Wild Angels*. I never intended to initiate a cycle. (No pun intended.) I've done nothing more or less than taken a hard objective look at life in the United States today. The Hells Angels represent the dark forces in society that people ignore but which are always with us. They're part of a movement of people who have no part in a technical society—who are frozen out. Formerly, these people might have been field workers or janitors. But such jobs are being automated now, and I think we have to anticipate a future when a large part of our society will be unemployable. It is beginning to be that right now.

Plus there's something else. The Angels have their own society, their own mystique, and they talk about how they don't want to be part of our society. It's partially because they can't be part of it because they are not capable of functioning within it on any reasonable level. It's therefore natural to drop out and say the former society is no good. But if you come from a society, you will take most of its values with you. And, one more thing, if some advertising executive can say, "I want out of this rat race; it's not good enough," how much easier is it for some guy who can only hope for a job as a garage mechanic to drop out. And to a certain extent, he's right. Why should he spend his life doing that? So I think the Angels are symptomatic of something in society today—and a growing something, too.

The Trip was the same way, only it dealt with the taking of LSD. I think that discoveries come about in the world when they're needed—not through any divine operation but simply the mind of man turns to the problem at hand. I think one of the problems "at hand" will someday be the growing leisure, and it's very possible that LSD or later chemical discoveries will be there so that people who work two or three days a week can spend most of their time tripping out. After all, how many pro football games can a guy who's free from his job watch until he says "I just don't want to see another pro football game"?

Diehl: Thematically, do you connect *The Trip* with trying to know the unknown?

Corman: Yes. Both *The Trip* and *The Wild Angels* show us possible projections of the dark side of society and possible ways society may go in the future. People don't like to talk about these elements—except to put them down in an unsavory way—and both those films were highly criti-cized. Yet they both were shown at film festivals, so, I believe, there must be something there.

Diehl: What are your plans now in terms of future filmmaking?
Corman: Well, I haven't directed a film in a year—which is the first year since I started when I haven't directed at least three. It's partially a re-lief—that reassessment I mentioned. I got tired and simply said "Enough! I'm tired." I financed a couple of films in this time and have a deal with United Artists on some projects. But I haven't anything definite at this moment. I would like to work along the lines of *The Wild Angels* and *The Trip*, possibly not with such sensational subjects but simply on some-thing which has relevance to human beings today in our world.

Diehl: Would you like to do one of those multi-million-dollar epics?
Corman: I would have no objection. I'm not snobbish and I have noth-ing against that kind of film. Should a particular picture call for that kind of budget, I'd be happy to work within it.

Diehl: What is the total count of your films to date?
Corman: I'm not certain. I've lost track somewhere along the line. But as a producer, I've done over one hundred. As a director, I must have done over fifty.

Diehl: Where would you say that the greatest improvement is needed or the greatest advance could come in the Hollywood film?
Corman: The greatest opportunities for the director will come as the studios and the financiers learn more and more to leave him alone and let him make the film he wants. A lot of the executives would be making films if they could—for it's a lot more fun and profitable to be making films than to be an executive. But the executive must not tell the film-maker what to do. Now, this then puts a burden on the filmmaker who can no longer say "the front office wrecked my film." The responsibility is squarely on his shoulders. He makes the film and he stands or falls by it. And the front office sticks by this decision: if he makes a good film, hire him back. If he makes a bad film, fire him. I think operating under those conditions, the filmmaker will understand where he stands—he will live or die on the quality of his work—and the quality of his work will, at last, be his.

Roger Corman

Joseph Gelmis / 1969

From *The Film Director as Superstar* (New York: Doubleday, 1970). © 1970 by Joseph Gelmis. Reprinted with permission of the author.

Joseph Gelmis: How many films have you directed?
Roger Corman: I don't know exactly. I've directed somewhere between fifty-five and sixty. And I've produced somewhere between 100 and 110, including some of the ones I've directed.

JG: What time period does this span?
RC: I think from about 1954 or '55. I produced my first film in '54 and directed in '55. I produced a film called *Monster from the Ocean Floor*. And the first film I directed was a western called *Five Guns West*.

JG: What's the highest budget you've worked with?
RC: *The St. Valentine's Day Massacre*. It was budgeted at $2.5 million, but it only went to $2.1 million. We came in $400,000 under budget. Now that's misleading, however, because that was shot at a major studio carrying 20 per cent overhead charge. You can really figure that if I made that picture at Fox, at $2.1 million, I could have made the picture myself for about $1.1 million or $1.2 million independently.

JG: A million dollars' difference? That's more than 20 per cent. Where are the other hidden costs?
RC: It isn't so much hidden. It's the fact that they work through department heads. When they do a set, for instance, the head of the art department gets added to our payroll. They have a set designer, they have two or three draftsmen, they have a couple of sketch artists. In other words, our film helps pay the studio overhead by having its permanent staff charged to our budget. And then, on top of that, there will be 20 per cent

32

added to all of their salaries. When I do a set, Dan Haller is my normal art director—has been until recently; he's become a director. Dan would just take a pad and paper and sketch out the set. One man can do it.

JG: What about the exploitation end of it, and the distribution?
RC: There's studio publicity included with it, not distribution publicity.

JG: Where would you have made a film like that if you were going to do it outside the studio, in order to cut the 20 per cent overhead?
RC: I would have rented a small rental studio. There are a number of rental studios around town. For the exteriors, I probably would have shot them on location in Chicago. We had considered doing it for Fox but to make such a move for a major studio is prohibitive. They would take probably 100 to 150 men on location. I would have taken maybe two or three men from Hollywood and picked up a skeleton crew in Chicago. Now, I'm making it sound overly easy, because it isn't quite that simple. There's an additional problem in that this was Chicago of 1929 and it's a little bit difficult to get the right atmosphere in cars and so on. Yet I think in the long run I'd rather take my chances in the streets of Chicago than the back lot of Metro, which is where I shot.

JG: Where would you have picked up the skeleton crew you are talking about?
RC: Just out of the Chicago local of the union. There are three basic divisions of the international union, and that's New York, Chicago, and Los Angeles.

JG: Is that the way you would usually work on your earlier films—pick up a skeleton crew somewhere, and just go with two or three guys?
RC: Right.

JG: How does the union feel about that?
RC: It all depends on who you pick up. In other words, when I say "pick up," I'll be picking up union people. So there's no problem there. But I'll be going with the absolute minimum. I'll go with a three-man camera crew and that's it. I'll go with a three-man sound crew. Currently I'm trying to get a two-man sound crew because of the newer, lighter sound equipment. You don't need three men anymore.

JG: What kind of sound equipment is that you're talking about?

RC: The Nagra is probably the standard of today. The Perfection was also a good unit a few years ago.

JG: And what kind of camera do you use in situations like that?
RC: I still prefer a Mitchell. It really, in my opinion, is the best camera in the world. It's a heavier camera, however. I have shot on location with Arriflex or with Camoflex, which is a version of the French Eclair. They're much lighter. They're more portable. They're not as good a camera, however. If I'm shooting inside a studio, I'll always go with a Mitchell. If I'm shooting on location, I'll probably trade a little bit of the quality of the Mitchell for the ease of handling of the Arriflex or the Camoflex.

JG: How do you feel about hand-held work versus a Mitchell? I take it you prefer a more stable platform?
RC: For certain scenes. I use a lot of hand-held work. But I use hand-held work primarily when there is movement within the shot itself. I feel that when there's violent movement the hand-held camera leads you into the movement. So if I'm photographing a fight or a chase or something like that, as I did in *The Wild Angels*, possibly a fast group of people dancing, something like that, I'll go among them with the hand-held camera.

Whereas if I have a close-up of somebody sitting in a chair and he's more or less stationary, I want my camera to be stationary also. There's no point in having a hand-held camera bobbing up and down if the man is sitting in his chair.

JG: Do exhibitors object to too much hand-held camera work?
RC: The exhibitors like it as rock steady as possible, but what seems right for the film is what I do.

JG: In *The Wild Angels*, for example, I imagine you must have used a lot of hand-held camera work.
RC: Yes. The scenes on the road were all hand held.

JG: Did you use special lenses for those scenes on the road?
RC: It's very fashionable today to use long lenses, 500 mm, or 1000 mm, and I use them at times. Yet at other times, I like to use the wide lens. I'll use an 18 mm or a 25. In the first shot on the road in *The Wild Angels*, I used either an 18 or a 25, deliberately, to give the sense of the Angels coming out of tremendous depth. There is a 9 but that causes such distortion, I don't like to use it.

JG: In *The Wild Angels*, did you use more than one camera?

RC: I didn't, much, on *The Wild Angels*, as a matter of fact.

JG: How was that possible? You had a lot of people involved in any given scene.

RC: Generally I just moved through the scene with a hand-held camera. I would be more likely to use multiple cameras in something like *The St. Valentine's Day Massacre,* when Hymie Weiss sent his parade of cars down the streets of Cicero and blasted Al Capone's headquarters. I had laid something like a thousand squib (simulated bullet explosions) on the front of the building when the cars came through so it was a one-take shot. I think I had three cameras mounted around in different areas, photographing that, because once they shot up the front of the building, that was it. On something like that, I'll use multiple cameras.

Other than that, though, I prefer to use one, on the basis, hopefully, that there's one best way to photograph a scene.

JG: Why is there one best way to photograph a scene? Because of the lighting, because you're lit for a particular camera, or is there some other reason?

RC: It's a combination. First, simply, my vision of the scene. I say, "I want the camera to be here to photograph this. This is what the scene is about." At the same time, particularly on the interiors, lighting becomes crucial because you light basically for one camera. You can light for multiple cameras, but you tend to flatten your lighting out. Exteriors, you're better with multiple cameras because basically you're using the light of the sun.

JG: How much lighting do you think is necessary with either fast lenses or fast film? A filmmaker told me that there's some sort of formula that lighting cameramen have always used.

RC: I think that's probably true. Most cameramen have modified not so much their lighting style but the way in which they get the light. In other words, at one time it was necessary to go out there with large heavy equipment, to get the necessary light into a scene. Now you can go out with much lighter, much more portable equipment, and you can light the scene much better. It's very possible the cameraman is still getting roughly the same effect on film. But he's doing it faster and easier.

JG: Is it more difficult to shoot in color, in terms of lighting or preparing sets?

RC: I think it's easier with color. With black and white it was necessary to cast a certain amount of shadow to give an impression of depth into a scene. You saw probably a more dramatic, sometimes an overly dramatic style of lighting in black and white, whereas color gives its own depth to a scene and it becomes easier.

For instance, you see, the cameramen on European films like *A Man and a Woman* are using a kind of diffused area lighting now in color which is quite fast to work with and is quite pleasing to look at. That same type of area lighting in black and white would just wash everything out. It would be very flat.

JG: When and where did you learn film technique? Such things as how to use a camera, the correct exposures, and how to deal with actors?
RC: I learned it simply by doing it. I've a degree in engineering. At any rate, I started in the motion picture business as a writer and then became a producer and then became a director. And what I learned I learned as I went along. I think had I had the chance to go to a film school I could have saved myself a lot of time and a lot of bother, learning to do things on feature films that were then exposed to the public. I think it's much better to do these things on 8 or 16 mm in a film school. I think the film schools, particularly the ones I know here on the west coast, at USC and UCLA, are invaluable.

JG: Could you elaborate on that?
RC: They are taught to handle technical things. They're taught to handle cameras and sound and light. They know how to cut a film. Before a man is, say, out of his sophomore year in UCLA or USC he is at least reasonably familiar with all the technical workings of making a film. He's not an expert, as I found out, unfortunately, on a few student films I financed. I slightly overrated their expertise.

And they're able to experiment. They know there is no rule that says you have to do any such thing at a particular time. They are simply getting the grounding in making a film. I'm not positive, though, that they are taught by people who *know*. That may be one of the weaknesses of the film schools. I think there are a few veteran directors, or cameramen, older men, semi-retired, who lecture occasionally in the film schools. And I think probably the students will get more out of them than from their instructors. Although I'm not knocking the instructors as such.

JG: You worked within the system as an apprentice, to learn your craft.
RC: That's true.

JG: What did you learn from writing that you were able to use later on?
How to mold and shape a script?
RC: Yes, to a great extent. Also, to be able to control the type of film I
wanted from the inception. Very often the producer or director is somewhat at the mercy of the writer. The writer has one idea, the producer
has another idea, the director has another idea, and they do not always
mesh.

JG: As a writer, have you written most of your own films?
RC: I haven't written screenplays recently. Generally, I'll write the original idea. And then I'll work very closely with the writer on the screenplay.

JG: How did you learn to work with actors?
RC: I learned through the painful process of simply working with them
on the set. And then I did do some studying. I went to Jeff Corey's acting school here in Hollywood for a year or two, as a student actor. I was
directing at the time and I felt I just did not know enough about acting
and I'd better learn.

JG: At what point in your career were you finally satisfied you were getting the kind of performances you thought you wanted?
RC: I've never been satisfied, or gotten the performances I wanted. I've
gotten good performances. I can remember individually good sequences
in a film, a good job by a specific actor. But I've never been able to look
back and say, "I really did it that time."

JG: What's involved in getting a good performance out of an actor? Is it
just picking the right person or is it motivating them or is it luck or is it
the editing process that makes them look good?
RC: It's everything. How do you become a great football coach? You get
a bunch of really good football players. You start, hopefully, with a good
script. You then find good actors, and then you work with them the best
you can to get the best performances out of them. And then you work in
the cutting room to cut to what you hope are the best of moments.

JG: Is it slower shooting in a studio?

RC: Yes. On the other hand, let me say this. The Hollywood technicians are extremely good. They're the best in the world, in my opinion. So although you're working at a slower pace in a major studio, and spending a great deal more money, you're getting technically the best work you can get.

JG: When you work within the system, does one do it fairly traditionally—the master shot, for example, and then the various setups?

RC: No, it isn't that rigid. They will let you have a fair amount of freedom.

JG: What's the difference between the way you shot *The Wild Angels* and the way you shot *The St. Valentine's Day Massacre*?

RC: I probably shot a little more traditionally in *St. Valentine's Day*, due to the fact that I was in a studio and had a certain amount of lighting and control and so forth. I was probably a little freer in *The Wild Angels*. That was not necessarily dictated by a studio hierarchy.

The differences are more in what happens in getting the camera and the actors into position. Once the camera is there and the actors are there I can say, "Action," just as easily on the streets of Mecca in *The Wild Angels* or on Stage 17 at 20th Century-Fox. At that point it's all the same. It's how you get to that point that makes the difference—whether you're there with a 12-man crew in the desert or whether you're in a studio with a 120-man crew. But it still ends up with actors in front of a lens.

JG: How long did it take to make *The St. Valentine's Day Massacre*?

RC: It was about forty-five days. It was the longest schedule I've ever had.

JG: How long did it take to make *The Wild Angels*?

RC: Three weeks. The budget was about $320,000.

JG: The film has supposedly grossed several million.

RC: That's right.

JG: How much of *The Wild Angels* did you make with a rigid script and how much of it did you shoot on the basis of the locations and the day-to-day conditions?

RC: I was very loose with *The Wild Angels*. The script was in a constant state of flux. I was rewriting as I was shooting. I never had a really finished script on *The Wild Angels*.

JG: Why was that? Was it because your own feeling about what the film was about changed from day to day?

RC: It was partially that my feeling changed from day to day, and partially that I was never really satisfied with the script. I had a definite start date. I was actually under contract to Columbia at the time and I had a leave of absence to do this picture for AIP. I had to shoot it at a specific time, though the script I had I felt was not right. So I said, "I have no choice. I will shoot at this particular time, but I will continue to work on the script, hopefully trying to improve it as I go along."

JG: Looking back on it, was there something specific that you know now that you would have liked to have done differently?

RC: I probably would have gone a little deeper into the characters of some of the Angels. I had previously done a film that I had believed in very much, *The Intruder*, which I shot in the South on natural locations. It was about white and black relationships. The film was a magnificent critical success but did not make money. Thinking back on it, I decided that one of the reasons the film was not a commercial success was the fact that I believed so much in my subject matter that I pushed my own personal thoughts a little bit too heavily into it and the film became slightly propagandistic. So on *The Wild Angels* I determined to withdraw and to shoot in an objective and documentary style as much as possible. Now of course I was dealing with fiction, so it was impossible to do so. But I did pull back a little bit.

JG: What film are you working on now?

RC: I'm working on a couple of films. I'm working on one film called *The Labyrinth*, which is a modern suspense or horror story. It's my own original idea. I'm working on another one called, tentatively, *Millennium*, which is a science fiction fantasy story based on another one of my own ideas. I used to do quite a bit of science fiction and fantasy and I haven't done it for a number of years. I've always liked it, and I think I'm going to move back into the field again.

I've got one other film at work at the moment and that's the story of the German ace in World War I, von Richthofen, and Roy Brown, the Canadian who shot him down. A dual story that cuts back and forth between the lives of both men.

JG: How far in the future are any of these projects?

RC: I'm working on the first-draft screenplays of all of them. As yet I don't even have a first draft.

JG: Are you working for a studio at this point, or are you working on your own?

RC: I'm independent, but I'm working through United Artists. This is a setup I like, since they give me a great deal more freedom of operation. I am preparing one picture for AIP I might mention, called *The Great Peace Scare*.

JG: Is that an original script too?

RC: Yes, more or less. A friend of mine and I developed the idea jointly. It startled a few people, and they must understand that we're doing a satire. We will attempt to prove that war is the natural and normal condition for humanity and that peace is a perversion. I got some nasty letters when I said that at one time.

JG: You've been quoted as saying about modest-budget pictures: "This is an art business, but the majority of people who run the business do not know how pictures are made. Thus a man who brings in better pictures cheaper becomes not only a threat to other directors but also to the committees that give pictures to him." Do you still feel that way about the business?

RC: It seems like a rather harsh statement that I made. I don't remember phrasing it exactly that way. But I think it is a threat. For instance, if *The St. Valentine's Day Massacre* could have been made at a major studio for $2.1 million and it can be made independently for $1.1 million, there must be some cause for thought somewhere as to why an extra million dollars is spent on a film.

JG: Where, for example, did you shoot the studio stuff, the interiors, for *The Wild Angels?*

RC: Everything was natural. There were no studios.

JG: You mean that church where the orgy was held was a real church?

RC: That was a church. We almost got thrown out for a variety of reasons. I explained that we were going to have a funeral in the church and that there probably would be a moment or two of violence. The preacher would then call the police. Which is a fairly accurate statement.

JG: Yes, but he didn't know the minister was going to end up in the coffin or that there was going to be an orgy. Was anybody there witnessing this thing?

RC: Yes, there was some unhappiness.

JG: How much of that was improvised?

RC: A great deal was improvised. As a matter of fact, the business of the preacher and the coffin. It's very funny you mention that, because the writer saw the rushes with me and he said, "Why did you put the preacher in the coffin?" And I said, "I just shot the script." And he said, "I never wrote that." And I said, "Sure you did. It's in the script." We looked up the script and it was not in the script. I started thinking it was in the script but it wasn't. But I did not believe that I was making up any ideas.

JG: Directors keep talking about instinct all the time.

RC: I'm a believer in both instinct and preparation. I think you have to go in prepared and then you have to be able to throw away your preparation, if something better occurs. But if you go in just with the vague hope that something brilliant will happen on the spot you could be in a lot of trouble.

JG: Is there a Corman technique for making films so quickly, when other people seem to have to take twice as long?

RC: If there is, it would be just what I've said. The idea of preparation. Trying to go in with an efficient, small crew, very well organized and very well prepared. And then be able to throw all of the preparation out if you want to change.

JG: What about the independent filmmakers who are coming up right now? It seems to me that the film students who are learning how to make documentaries or how to make low-budget features don't have any place to go right now. Unless they start a whole new industry of their own.

RC: Well, they do have a place to go. For instance, some of the fellows I've backed on their first films—going back a few years to Irv Kershner, and Bernie Kowalsky, and Monte Hellman, and Peter Bogdanovich, and Francis Coppola, and a few others—they've all found their way into the industry. You can come into the industry a variety of ways. Maybe by shooting an interesting short subject that gets somebody's attention. Maybe by writing a screenplay that somebody wants and saying, "Look,

I've shot some documentaries and if you want the screenplay you must take me as the director." Maybe starting away from Hollywood and working in the style of the New York underground.

JG: You mentioned before that you had backed some student films. In what sense?
RC: I just put up the money.

JG: Students come to you and say: "We want to make a film. Here is our project, our script"?
RC: Yes.

JG: You seem to think the best young directors are going to find their way into the system. You don't think it's necessary to form a third force someplace between the underground and Hollywood?
RC: It would help. But the best men do work their way up. I think it would help to make it a little easier for them, and let them work up a little bit faster so that they can get recognition at an earlier age. On the other hand there may be something to be said for suffering a few years before you get that recognition.

JG: What about distribution and exhibition? Isn't that a tremendous problem for the independent? You probably solved it for yourself with an outfit like AIP, by which you both serve each other. But what's the alternative for the independent filmmaker who presumably has some talent but hasn't had a chance to get much financing and has a very low-budget film? He doesn't really have a place to distribute it.
RC: There are a number of independent distributors who can handle a low-budget film. And he can place his film with them. The real problem, I think, is that most low-budget filmmakers and most new filmmakers fall into a trap where they're unwilling to make a straight commercial film and they're afraid to invest their or their backer's money in a full art film. And they've come up with a film that's not really quite commercially successful, not really artistically satisfying, and they can be in some trouble on that basis.

JG: What do you think about television within the next couple of years, either Pay-TV or some other form of TV, as an outlet for independent films so you don't even have to go through the exhibition stage?
RC: I have no faith whatsoever in Pay-TV. I just can't believe for one min-

ute that anybody is going to pay money to see something he can see free. So I don't think there's any chance at all that that will happen. I think, however, there will be an increasing outlet on television on the UHF stations, on educational stations, and so forth for serious works of young filmmakers which will probably never be shown in theaters or maybe only one or two theaters in either big cities or university towns and then straight on to television. Television is today what the second-feature market used to be for films I wouldn't push that analogy too far, but it's true in a general kind of a way.

JG: The last film you made was *The Trip*, and it was released two years ago back in 1967. "Why haven't you worked for two years? Is it true that your encounter with big budgets has somehow slowed you down?
RC: Possibly just disenchantment. With the industry, and with my own work within the industry.

JG: The multimillion-dollar Robert E. Lee script, for example, never came to fruition, did it?
RC: I have the script. I may yet do it. But I was never really satisfied with it.

JG: So are you back to thinking in terms of more manageable budgets?
RC: Probably, yes.

JG: For realistic reasons?
RC: Right.

The American Film Institute Seminar with Roger Corman

American Film Institute / 1970

This is a selected except from the AFI Harold Lloyd Master Seminar with Roger Corman, held on March 11, 1970, and moderated by James R. Silke. © 1970 by the American Film Institute. Reprinted by permission of the Louis B. Mayer Library, American Film Institute, Los Angeles, CA.

Q: Do you presently use IA crews?
A: It divides up in various ways. In the films that I've personally directed, I've always used an IA crew until the very last picture I did in which I used a Nabet crew. On the films I've financed because I backed some low-budget films, we will sometimes go IA, sometimes Nabet—most generally, we have not gone for a seal of any kind.

The way the seal, the IA-bug, works is the major studios—that is the old line majors—have contracts with the IA that states that every film they make must have an IA bug on it and the film that they release, that they make in the United States, almost must have it. We've done such things, frankly, as buying the seal. A few thousand dollars into the IA pension fund and if it's a new filmmaker, somebody with his first picture, they will generally put the seal on. However, if you're not distributing through the established majors, that is through Metro, Fox, Paramount, whatever, you do not need the IA seal. For instance, I've sent a number of pictures through American International, through Walter Reade, through a number of other of the newer distribution companies and as far as I know, with none of them do you need any seal at all. You do not need the area seal and you do not need the Nabet seal either.

Q: Are those screened in theaters?
A: Yes, they are. And it really is nothing more than a myth that the pro-

jectionist in the theaters will not screen a picture that doesn't have the IA bug on it. As you know, the projectionists don't even look at the films; they're out of focus, they're misframed; they have no way of knowing if there's an IA bug on it or not.

Q: I was going to ask, this term "low-budget film" is kind of a relative term, at least it should be. With most of us sitting around here, it certainly means something different than what you're engaged in. What is a low-budget film, now, cost-wise? What kind of general averages?
A: Well, it varies from year to year and each year, when inflation moves in it costs a little more. I wouldn't want to pick any hard and fast area and say this is a low-budget figure. In general, anything under, say, $200,000 or $300,000 would probably be a low-budget film. I've made films for as little as—well, the first one, as I say, came somewhere in the $20,000 area and after that we did a few films in the $30,000 to $40,000 range. I would say those were extremely low-budget feature films, but we've been doing some low-budget films—for instance, the film Bruce Clark out of the UCLA film school did for me—a year and a half ago, the forty-second consecutive motorcycle film, *Naked Angels*, cost about $120,000. I would say that is a representative figure for a low-budget film in 35 color and without any names in it.

Q: In what areas do you feel you cut the cost of your films most consecutively?
A: Well, I went over that with Norman Herman, the AIP production manager, a couple of days ago because I had just done a film for them which cost about $600,000 and then I turned around and did another film on my own, which I then am giving to AIP for a lease, which cost about $250,000. Both films shot in about four weeks and Clint was in the first one, *Bloody Mama*, the one we did with Shelley Winters in Arkansas, and as Clint will testify we didn't throw the money around needlessly on that. Nevertheless, it cost considerably more than the second one, and we tried to figure it out and what it was there was no specific one area. It was that everything was down a little bit. The fact that the second one was Nabet and the first one was the IA was probably the biggest contributing factor, but the Nabet rates these days are very close to the IA rates. The only real difference as far as budget is concerned, is you can go with a slightly smaller crew, Nabet, but since the IA has come up with their current concessions, the differential isn't even that great. We did not work with Teamsters with Nabet, which was one advantage. The

IA generally is tied in with the Teamsters and it just means that many more men and as far as I'm concerned, that's really money down the drain because all they do is drive your equipment to the set and the location in the morning and they play cards, or one thing or another all day and drive you home at night. Whereas, with Nabet, the grips will drive the truck, anybody can drive. The grips drive the trucks, the equipment, to the location and then work during the day and at the end, you drive back. So, there's a fairly substantial saving there, but other than that, it's just a general watching of the money from start to finish. Little things, like for instance, shooting in color—I will always print either in black and white off the colored negatives or the one light colored print. I've never had in my lifetime color prints on the dailies. It's a true luxury.

Q: What kind of ratios do you shoot with?
A: I used to shoot on a very low ratio. I used to shoot—as against the finished film; if I'd have a finished film, of let us say, 6,000, 7,000, 8,000 feet, I would shoot maybe 30,000 feet, but now I'm shooting maybe 100,000, 150,000 feet to get just the same thing. It's one of the luxuries as you move up a little bit. Once you get beyond your immediate coverage of your cost, I believe that you should shoot a lot of film on the basis that everything is there. You're paying for lunches, you're paying for dressing rooms, you're paying for all this. You're paying for all these things that don't show on the film and when it's done, all you have is the film itself. So I now believe in shooting a great deal more film.

Q: What sort of controls do you have over, let's say, when you finance a student filmmaker?
A: Generally, not a great deal of control during the shooting on the basis I don't think anybody can have a great deal of control in the shooting unless they just come in and take over. Most of my controls are before the shooting and afterwards; for instance I'll check out the script very carefully, the production staff, the casting, and so forth, and then I'll probably have some sort of control over the cutting. During the actual shooting itself, on most of the films that I've backed, I never even go to the set. I really feel it's best on the basis that I say, "O.K., I'll back this man as a director. He should have the opportunity to simply go and direct his film." The only time I'll generally step in is when I'm looking at the rushes, when I see something that really causes me to jump out of my chair looking at the rushes, I may have words with him about that. Or if he falls a great deal behind schedule. But if the work looks even

somewhere near what I would consider to be commercial, acceptable standards and he's near his schedule and his budget, I prefer, frankly, not even to talk to him; just let him make the film. After completion, I'll generally go in and look at his second or third cut and just tell him my thoughts on it. That would be on a film that will go very smoothly. On others, I'll go into the actual cutting room with him when I think we're in some problems. The majority of the films that I've backed, I had never been on the set and I've never been into the cutting room; I simply will look at the film in the projection room and talk with the director. On many of these low-budget films, I think this is very good, the director is his own editor.

Q: Would you say something about the cast and crew comforts on location?
A: Cast and crew comforts are very nice for morale, but when you're really strapped for money, you have to con a little bit and dolly people along as much as you can. Again, if you're trying to make a good picture for $100,000 or less, it's very, very difficult—you want to put your money where it shows on the screen.

Q: Where do you cut costs first?
A: In the basic deal, right in the beginning with the director. For instance, with Bruce Clark, on the last film of this type I've done—and with Frances Scofield on one a few years ago and with Irv Kershner, I'm thinking of three directors that I've backed and the first picture that I thought did a very good job. On each one of them, their deal was to write, direct, and cut. So I had, as it were, three elements in there right at the beginning and, frankly, they did not get a great deal of money for doing this. The reason was this: I was giving them an opportunity to make their first film on the basis, hopefully, that I would make a profit and, hopefully, their career would take off from this. In each of these director's cases, it did. Monte Hellman had roughly a similar thing and Monte's career took off. It took Monte a little bit longer that some of the others. On that basis, a couple of people have said to me I should take options on the directors I back. I've never done that for this reason: On the basis that it's an even trade on the first film. He gets a small amount of money and makes his film; I get the profit off the film and he gets the opportunity to start his career. If I were to take options on him for his second film, at that point I would think it would become unfair and I'd be starting to exploit him, I feel, to a certain extent. And from there on in, getting back to the origi-

nal question, it's just a matter of cutting out the frills. There's no magic statement that you cut this specific thing out. Generally, shooting on natural locations, you're cheaper than shooting in a studio. On the other hand, you can balance that back. Peter Bogdanovich on *Targets* shot a good part of this picture in the studio—a little rental studio on Santa Monica Boulevard, and did not spend more particularly than some of the people shooting on natural locations.

Q: Is a four-week shooting schedule the norm?
A: No. A four-week shooting schedule is a little bit long for this type of picture. There is an answer. Now, it has varied. For instance, Monte Hellman shot in two weeks. He did two westerns and a science fiction picture. Monte Hellman was generally working with two-week schedules.

Frances Scofield was with a picture in Ireland and had three weeks. Bruce Clark, on *Naked Angels*, went a little bit beyond that and we did have some small words on that—and he finished the picture fairly quickly thereafter. Generally, I would say three to four weeks. We haven't done one in two weeks for some time now. When we were doing the two-week pictures, there was more of a market for second features and I felt at that time you could make an adequate second feature on a two-week schedule, but with the second-feature market gone, we feel we'd move up to three- and four-week schedules and aim for the top of the bill.

Q: Do you still feel you can shoot 100,000 feet of film in four weeks?
A: No. I probably didn't make myself clear. On the films I'll direct myself, I'll shoot maybe 100,000 feet. On these lower-budget films, around $100,000, I don't remember, honestly, exactly what they shot, but I think it was less than that; probably in the neighborhood of 60,000 or 70,000 feet.

Q: How about the problems of mixing your crew? Do you want an IA cameraman or a cameraman who's Nabet and a production manager who's IA or a couple of other people who you can get very cheaply, or none of the unions at all? What kind of problems do you have?
A: Well, first, from the standpoint of the first one that you mentioned, the production manager, there's no problem at all because the production managers are generally not in either the IA or Nabet; they're members of the Directors Guild. Directors Guild handles directors, assistant directors, and production managers or they're working independent.

There's no problem there. For the crew itself, that can sometimes become difficult, mostly with the IA. You will sometimes find IA men who will not work with other workers who are not members of the IA, the IA not only being the most established union, but having fought its way up during the kind of terrible days for unions in the thirties when there was a real feeling as against the scab worker and the union worker.

Times have changed a little bit. The Nabet men will be more likely to work with men who are not in a union. I generally have not tried too much to mix unions. If I'm going IA, I'll go straight IA. If I'm going independent, it's straight independent and occasionally I will mix some Nabet and independent. Overseas there's no problem. When I've shot overseas, I've generally taken an IA cameraman and one or two key people out of the IA and the rest either from the local country or from here.

Q: Do you ever use the IA for first unit shooting and then do a lot of second unit work?
A: Yes. They frown on that very heavily, but we've not done it for a long time, however. As a matter of fact, Don was with us on one picture on the trip which we did a few years ago which we shot in three weeks, with an IA crew and then we had a few days to pick up shooting after that.

Q: Why did you use IA when you had the option of using Nabet in these past years?
A: Well, I had signed with my company at the beginning, standard IA agreements, so I had contracts that only expired a short while ago. So each time I made the pictures specifically myself, I moved up to the IA contract and when I invested in a picture, I treated that simply as an investment and so I didn't have to live up to the IA contract. Now that my IA contract has run out, as I say, my last picture I did with Nabet and from here on in I'll probably stay flexible. For instance, if I were to do a picture for major release, the chances are they would require the IA and I would work with the IA on the basis I had nothing against the technicians in the IA. As a matter of fact, I think they're the best in the world. The men who retain their enthusiasm, most of them are veterans and some of them get tired and they figure they're there for the job but many of them are sincerely—As a matter of fact, the majority of them and the IA are sincerely interested in working in films and you find guys who have got more energy and more enthusiasm than anybody I've ever seen.

Q: How did you come about signing an IA contract originally? That presumes that they give you something and then you give them something.

A: As I say, when I first started, fourteen years ago, the strength of the IA was dominant. In other words, there were essentially no feature films being made in Hollywood that were not IA. As during the last fourteen years, the power of the major studios has weakened so you can go to other distribution companies and Nabet has come up and independent workers have come up. The fact of the matter is at that time just about anybody who was any good was in the IA in the crews and when you moved away from the IA, you moved way downhill in quality of work. Whereas now, you can move elsewhere. In my last picture from the IA, I had Johnny Alonzo, a cameraman who is very good, but when I moved to Nabet I had Ron Dexter who is equally as good—they're both good cameramen. Whereas, at one time you wouldn't have found a Ron Dexter who was not in the IA.

Q: Well, back in those days, if you wanted to mount a feature film, couldn't you simply go to IA and say I have a film I want to do without signing a contract that would extend over a number of productions?
A: No, you could not do that. In other words, they had the control, they had the monopoly. Today, they're talking a different story because they don't have the control anymore.

Q: What's the smallest IA crew you've worked with?
A: Oh, probably twelve, thirteen, or something like that.

Q: Could you say what that consisted of?
A: It consisted of three men on camera, three men on sound, a couple of grips, possibly an electrician, and a prop man. Now, this is varied because at one time, they required four men on sound. At the time they required four men on sound there was a minimum of one man on props. But when the bulky sound equipment became condensed, the number of sound men dropped down to three, but just about that time the prop local decided you had to have a minimum of two prop men. So you gained on one end and you lost on the other. The IA has just come up with what appeared, on paper, to be very, very good concessions. They've cut the number of men on their crew for pictures costing $1 million or under, which I assume anybody who's going to make a picture under $3 million, is going to cut say, $900,000 and you're going to go with that minimum crew. If they really live up to what they are saying, the reasons for moving to Nabet, and the reasons to move independently, have been diminished greatly because the Nabet scale is roughly now equal to IA and

if the IA will really live up to their statement about the small crew, I think they will be back as a stronger force in low-budget filmmaking than they had been for the last year or two.

Q: How long do you spend in pre-production?
A: A lot of time. I believe the only way to make a film efficiently on a low budget is with a tremendous amount of preparation.

Q: What is a lot of time?
A: Generally, a couple of months. That is, for me, a lot of time. Possibly somebody else might require more than that.

Q: What does that consist of, scouting locations? Do you do storyboards for your pictures?
A: No, I don't do storyboards, but I scout the locations very thoroughly. I have every location picked in advance. I know pretty much how I'm going to shoot. I'll have a picture which I'll design and I'll design the shots myself. It's always the myth that I will design all my shots before I start the picture and it has never happened, but I'll sometimes get up to 50, 60, 70 percent of my shots worked out in advance. That is one of the greatest advantages to shooting well on a low-budget film, knowing exactly what you're going to do in advance. On the other hand, after having planned that much in preproduction, you must stay flexible enough so that if it doesn't work, you throw it out, even if you've spent weeks working on something. You're there on the set and you're working with the actors and it doesn't work, you've got to say, "O.K., I'm going to throw out the couple of weeks' work and I'll do it another way." Or you may get a better idea at that time. So, there are big differences between, say, an Alfred Hitchcock who will design every shot and stay very, very closely. I read an interview with him and he said very logically, he thought better in his office than he did on the set. So he figured his pictures in advance—or somebody like Francis Coppola who, on *The Rain People*, actually didn't know where his locations were going to be. It was part of his method of shooting. He started off from New York with a crew and some of the cast who were friends of his on the basis it was going to be a tour of the United States shooting as they went in, hoping that this would give him a certain amount of spontaneity. I think Francis will not be quite that spontaneous in the future. On the other hand, you don't have to lock yourself in quite as much as Hitchcock does and that's why I feel there is middle ground there.

Q: How about rehearsals? Do you have rehearsals?

A: I have a small amount of rehearsals. I don't have a great deal and the reason is you have problems with SAG on rehearsal time. So, again, it's a matter of knowing that a little bit of rehearsal helps you and a great deal of rehearsal—with Screen Actors Guild, you end up paying your actors so much money, you might as well be shooting with them on a bigger budget—I would go for rehearsal. In other words, on a low-budget film, if you're going Screen Actors Guild, which you almost always have to do, even when we've gone independently. We've never gone away from the Screen Actors Guild with the exception of one or two brilliant young actors just about to make it. Everybody who is really good, or 99 percent of them are really members of SAG.

Q: When you say you have your shots worked out in the beginning before you begin to shoot, do you mean that you have it in your mind?

A: No, on paper. I don't work with a sketch, I work—I have an engineering degree so that probably comes back to the way I was trained. I'll have a kind of a plan with certain symbols that I've invented for myself, arrows and dots and moving things so it's looking down that way and I'll see actors moving this way and the camera moving over here, and so forth. Dan Haller, who is a good friend of mine, who was trained as an art director, as an artist actually, works totally differently. He sketches what he will see. And I think the difference between what he does and what I do is simply a matter of our early training, the way we were organized at one time.

Q: Do you always have an assistant director? And a production manager?

A: Yes. Well, not a production manager. Since I'm a member of the Directors Guild—when I came out of college I tried to get in the Directors Guild and they kept me out for seven years and when I said I was going to become a director, within twenty-four hours, I got a call from them and said "You must join the Directors Guild." So, as a member of the Directors Guild, I must, whenever I work in the United States, use a first assistant director and a second assistant director. I will sometimes carry a first and a second and also a production manager, but that's very seldom and when I back a film myself I've never carried all three. I have certain first assistants who are production managers as well—specifically, Jack Boyer and Paul Raft who have worked with me for a number of years and they will combine the two jobs.

Q: At what point do you put them on?
A: As late as possible. I try to do as much of the advance planning myself. I'll put on the production manager—assistant director combination job probably about three weeks before I shoot. I used to put them on a week before I shot, when I was making very low-budget films. The second assistant I'll bring in at the last minute. I'll bring him in at whatever the Directors Guild minimum was, which is generally just a couple of days preparation.

Q: What does Boyer do for you at the point where he comes on?
A: He would break down the script. I never really believe that the picture is going to be done right until I see it on the board, until I see the script broken down, I see a shooting schedule, I see a list of locations, I see where the actors work and can visualize the whole thing from that. Now, I'll break it down roughly myself in advance, but I'll do a very short-hand thing; I'll go through a script in two hours and just get a general idea of what I'm going to do so that I can plan from that. But his first job is to break it down to put it on the board and to get a shooting schedule and to lock in specific things such as the crew, the locations, rental of equipment, and so forth. But the first step to me is always the breakdown of the script.

Q: And the cost estimates?
A: The cost estimate I'll generally do myself. I'm not a believer in accurate budgets on the basis we work in such an intangible medium. A couple of pictures that I've done for the majors, they will have the picture broken down to the penny, which is ridiculous. They'll have a picture broken down—$2,176,000.42 is going to be the cost of the picture to it. So I go, again, possibly from my engineering training and knowing in statistics, that no set of figures is accurate beyond the loosest item in it. There's no point in figuring out to the penny how much a film is going to cost you if you're estimating to the nearest $1,000 on location rentals. So if you're estimating to the nearest thousand dollars on location rentals, and this is accurate, nothing else should be estimated closer to the nearest $1,000, which is the way I do it. Normally, I will have some problems with studio production managers so we generally then start faking in little figures after the 1,000. But left to myself, I'll never break down a picture closer than $1,000. And even then, I know statistically I'm not even right in getting a picture to $1,000. You're better to go to the nearest $10,000—it's just simply working in decimal points.

Q: Could you go into the problem of deferments that you mentioned before? I can see how you can defer salaries and certain things, but how do you defer lab costs and then how do you then relate that to what you just said about dividing up percentages?

A: Well, the biggest individual deferment is the last one you mentioned, which is generally the lab. Most labs, if you have any track record at all, will give you credit and do your entire lab work for nothing providing you have a contract with them that states they get the first money returned on the basis that any film, if it's at least reasonable, has got to get back $15,000 to $20,000, $25,000 that it costs to do lab work in color today, on the basis it's worth that on television, if nothing else. And sometimes they will back you with no track record. On the first picture I ever did, the lab came to me and we talked for awhile and they said, "Yes, we will give you the lab work on credit" and I'd never done a film in my life.

Q: Which lab was that?

A: That was Consolidated, at that time. And that's not that unusual; most labs will give you credit on this basis. Lab work doesn't really cost them a great deal because of the fact they've got the machines turning at night anyway and whether they throw an extra amount of film through is not important to them. As a matter of fact, the money they make off the lab work on your film is not even important. They will ask that they do the release printing because that's where they make their money. They're not going to make a great deal of money off just printing and developing and giving you an answer print on a film. They will get their money when and if you have a successful film, when they make one hundred or two hundred or three hundred release prints for you and that's what they're gambling for. So that kind of deferment is fairly standard.

The other deferments are whatever you can negotiate at the time. I used to give percentages of profits and I don't anymore. I now like to give a flat amount of money. The reason is that the first film I ever made, which is fourteen years old, I'm still sending out percentages of profits every six months and it's just a tremendous headache because now—it was a picture that cost, say $20,000 or so fourteen years ago and we're sending out checks to some guys for eleven dollars and it's ridiculous. There's another way to do it, which I thought of recently and I don't know why I was so dumb that I didn't think of it earlier, which is to give a percentage of the profits, but limit it to a certain number of years. On the basis, you have a percentage of the profits of all the money we make over the first seven years. On the basis after seven years the profits are going to be so small, we're not going to bother—that would be one way to work with it. I do remember now why at the beginning I gave a percentage of the profits rather than fixed amounts of money. Most people were more willing to gamble for percentages of the profits on the basis that if you have a real winner, the percentage of the profit can become astronomical where if they have a flat amount of money, they're just working for that flat amount of money. So you're not putting a limit on their potential earning ability with a percentage of the profit.

Q: What percentage went into the crew?
A: I always paid the crew. I never gave percentage to the crew except sometimes the head cameraman. Once or twice, some people who did more than just work on the crew, brought some equipment, I would sometimes give a little percentage.

Q: You say "better off." What do you mean by "better off"?
A: I don't remember what I was talking about when I said "better off."

Q: You said better off to pay the crew.
A: Yes, it's just a feeling of my own. Say you're doing a picture in a couple of weeks, let's say, and a crew member gets a couple of hundred dollars a week. If you're starting to divide up your profits down there on the basis of a couple of hundred dollars, you're in real financial trouble at that stage. I would prefer to save the percentage of the profits for people who are contributing more than, say, $400 or $500 worth of their wages, on the basis, it's simply better to pay them their wages.

Q: We're considering establishing a basic wage that everybody would be entitled to and defer a major part of that specific amount all the way down the line, actors and crew. Do you think that's feasible?
A: Yes, it's perfectly feasible. It's just that I chose not to do it. There are a million ways to go. You might have a slight problem with SAG. However, they now have made some concessions, but I read their concessions and it didn't seem to be a big concession to me. I didn't even see where anybody was gaining by taking what their concessions were. The problem there is with the actors. Most of the good actors are in the Guild so you're forced to give them Guild minimum anyway and when you're making a very low-budget film and you're working with beginning actors, all they're really going to be asking is Guild minimum, so there's no particular reason to give them . . . unless guys, you know, young men

playing lead or something. Again, you're better off just to pay him his Guild minimum.

Q: What if his minimum was like $420 a week and you want to pay him $200 a week?
A: All I can say is there, it's a good idea except you're breaking your Guild contract and that's very tricky.

Q: What percentage of independently made pictures, crew-wise, are finished not Nabet, not IA?
A: Again, even when we've gone with an independent crew, we've just paid them generally.

Q: How many such films are made that way today?
A: There's an increasing number; I couldn't give you an actual answer to that, but you can look at the production columns in the *Reporter* and *Variety* whenever it comes out, and you will see under independent production, a tremendous number of companies that nobody ever heard of and you start to look at some of the names connected, and I know some of the guys working independently and I'd say in that bracket, 75 percent of those films are being made, not Nabet and not IA. You look in the other area where it says Metro's production, that would be all IA.

Q: If they don't get released through AIP, where would they get released? You mentioned Walter Reade, but he has a relatively small thing.
A: There are a number. There's a growing number of distribution companies and I'm getting involved in one myself as a matter of fact because I think the business is changing very rapidly right now and it's moving faster away from the majors than the majors themselves are really aware. Of course, the biggest company handling independent product is AIP. Allied Artists, which was in financial difficulties for a number of years, is making a comeback and they are a functioning distribution company once more and quite a good one. Walter Reade.

Q: They don't require any kind of union seal?
A: If you make the picture for Allied Artists, they do require it, but if you just make it, they don't require it if you distribute through them. Crown International does not require a union seal and this is one of the better small distribution companies.

Q: Where do these pictures play?

A: They play everywhere. They'll play in art theaters, or they'll play in drive-ins, depending upon the picture. This is what has been happening to the business, that I think is extremely healthy. The power of the major distributors is fading very, very rapidly. For instance, in the distribution company I'm involved in starting, our sales manager is the head booker for the biggest drive-in chain in the South and he's leaving that job to come join this company because, as he says, "A few years ago, a salesman would come in from Metro and a salesman would come in from a small company. We'd kick this guy's ass out the door from the small company. Now we welcome him in and say, what do you have, because we lose too much money with the major films." And it's really going that way. Little distribution companies nobody ever heard of are cleaning up right now.

Q: Where, for instance, would one of these films play in New York soon?

A: It would play—I would say the majority of films in the art houses in New York City are probably not handled by the majors. So right there, you know, in the art house circuits, the art house method of distribution, you don't need the majors at all. I'm not now that familiar and I can't give you names of houses in New York. I don't know that much about individual houses, but I know the showcases in New York consist of, say, a couple of houses in Manhattan and then neighborhood theaters all around, as much as the saturation bookings in L.A., you play a straight showcase booking just like anybody else. There still is a slight preference for the major, but not much.

Q: Well, I guess *Targets* is a good example. I mean, I tried for six months to see that picture. Why was that?

A: *Targets* was not a small company, as a matter of fact. *Targets* went through Paramount. As a matter of fact, if you have a little picture, I now believe that maybe you're better off not to be with the major, on the basis it costs them so much to distribute that they're not interested in the little picture. I was a little shaky on the picture myself. I was not convinced that we had a potential commercial success. So Paramount gave me a part advance and part guarantee that was slightly in excess of the negative cost. So I said, O.K., I got my costs back, let's see what Paramount can do. They did nothing. They opened it up in New York and got, as you may know, sensational reviews. It just got magnificent reviews and didn't do any business. They opened it in an art house in Los Angeles and the same thing happened again. Brilliant reviews and no business and they just pulled it out on the basis they didn't want to spend the money on the prints. A company like AIP would have pushed that picture on the basis that if they could have even picked up $10,000, $20,000, $30,000, it was worth their while. To Paramount it was not worth the while of the company to screw around with this stuff and so they just passed the picture totally and said, "We'll sell it to television and get our money back later on." So in that case, we were worse off with the major, but on the other hand, the major had given me my money back, which generally the small companies will not do. They will not give you such an advance unless you really have a great picture that they're very confident of.

Q: Now, you make the distribution deal after the film is finished?
A: Generally. That's very risky, however. There are certain rules of thumb and one of them is get your distribution before you make the picture because if you make a bad picture and you don't have distribution, you're in real trouble.

Q: How do you specify how ambitious a distribution effort they will make on the film?
A: It's very, very difficult. For instance, when I was negotiating with Paramount, and I said I wanted a guarantee and they were saying, "You're not with AIP now." And I said, "That's why I want the guarantee from you guys." And it's exactly that, a small company will probably try harder. You would be more advised to get a minimum allocation from a major than from a small company. With a major you're better to get it written into the contract, that they will open it in a certain number of houses, they will spend a minimum amount of money on the advertising campaign because they will slough it off if you don't have that in. We had that in *Targets* and Paramount lived up exactly to their minimums and they never spent a penny more. We had it written in that they had to open once in New York and once in Los Angeles. That's all they ever opened. One house in New York, one house in Los Angeles and then they did strike a few prints and sold it off as a second feature with one of their bigger pictures, but they know that there's no money in the second-feature market anymore because the cost of your color prints is roughly equal to what your rent was going to be. So they were just playing games at that point.

Q: How much money was to be spent on advertising?

A: We had specified a minimum amount of advertising because there are certain areas you can't control. For instance, you have to go to a certain extent on the good faith or the intelligence of the people you're working with. If you and they specify that they're going to spend a certain amount of money to open the picture, you all know it's to their interest and to your interest to have the thing run as well as you can.

Q: If you had a distribution deal up front, with someone like Allied Artists or AIP, would you then have to go IA crew?
A: No. Only with the majors. With Allied it's a different thing. If Allied finances you, then you'd get into a grey area that I'm not positive of, but it's my understanding Allied, at the moment, is not requiring an IA seal.

Q: But if you had private financing and they just distribute it . . .
A: You'd be completely clear—no problems.

Q: Then these distribution contracts involve no front money at all. In other words, when you deliver the picture, they don't pay you anything.
A: Generally. Sometimes they do. Again, as I say, these things are subject to a wide amount of negotiation. It depends upon how much you want them and how much they want you.

Q: Is there a chance that you can renegotiate, have a contract that didn't specify some front money and then when you delivered the picture, that you said, let's have a little money for it?
A: If it's so great, you don't need the front money because you know they're going to earn it back right away. I've never heard of a contract being renegotiated at that point. But it could happen.

Q: Has your experience with distributors been that they are generally fairly reputable and polite?
A: Not particularly. Some of them are. Surprisingly, the smaller ones have been more honest. I have had a tremendous thing with a major studio once where I protested bitterly and we signed a contract finally in which they gave me several hundred thousand dollars more than their distribution agreement said I was due, and I, in turn, signed the paper saying that I accepted the distribution report as true and accurate on the basis they could not go on record as stating that there was anything wrong with their distribution request. I remember, a veteran producer that I worked with a number of years ago, told me that he made all these

Randolph Scott pictures in the forties and fifties that were very successful at the time and then made a fortune on television in the early days
of television. He had something like fifteen color Randolph Scott westerns and they just made money hand over fist, and he didn't know how
much money there was and he was getting no reports that anything had
been sold to television; this was with Columbia. So he went into the Columbia offices in New York just bluffing and he had no idea what was
happening and he said, "I know you guys are making a fortune off my
westerns, where's the money?" They said, "There's a little bookkeeping
problem, you'll have it." He said he got a check for $700,000. So that's
the way the business goes.

Q: When you spoke about a three-week shooting schedule, could you
give me some idea what that means in terms of the number of set-ups
you do in a day?
A: It varies. It varies according to whether you're shooting interior or exterior on location. On location, exterior, you should be able to get thirty
to forty set-ups a day. You can get many more.

Q: How about location interior?
A: Location interior, you'll slow down heavily because lighting anywhere is slower than shooting with the sun and lighting on natural locations is slower than lighting in a studio. So if you're getting, say, forty
set-ups a day, day exterior, that might drop to twenty-five a day interior.
It can vary tremendously. One of the things I found on this last picture
I backed with these guys from UCLA is that they were working much
slower than I had ever been accustomed to or known anybody to work
and yet they were conscientious, they were trying. I attributed it to the
fact, really, and I don't know if it means anything for the Institute here,
the fact that working in school, they didn't have any particular incentive
or concept that they had to really stay in there all day long. It was on a
much looser basis and so the idea of really getting a certain number of
set-ups a day had not particularly been told to them by their instructors
and they were not accustomed to doing it. Whereas, the same guy out
working on one picture will learn that very quickly, and I did not quite
realize that because when I had backed people like Francis Coppola . . .
Francis had been my assistant for something like eight to ten months
and had worked on two pictures before I backed him in a picture and
he'd already learned the difference as to what was necessary. So, I would

say right there is one of the biggest things you yourselves can learn when you start to work in an area that is more commercially oriented than you are now.

Q: How long does it usually take from the time you get the script until you get a release print?

A: Well, I'd rather put it another way. From the time you get the script to the time you start shooting; break it down into sections, because you might very well be still rewriting your script the day before. Or on *Wild Angels* and *The Trip* we were rewriting while we were shooting, or on the last picture, *Gas-s-s*, we're rewriting now and the picture was shot sometime ago. So start from the time you shoot, figure that your script might be ready two months before you shoot. Ideally, the longer the period you have between the time your script is finished and the time you start shooting, the better it is because you can plan more carefully. So that's really up to you. But from the time you start shooting, to the time you get an answer print something like *War of the Satellites*, where we were trying to grab the headlines, we did it in something like five weeks there, but that's extreme and is, needless to say, not particularly good. On most of our low-budget films, I would say we ran anywhere from ten to fourteen weeks. We're running longer now and spending a little more money.

Q: When you're doing thirty set-ups a day, would you say how much time for each set-up is devoted to physically setting the equipment up and how much time is to go to rehearsals and how much time is devoted to filming. Can you give any sort of a rough idea?

A: That would be just a guess . . . I don't know . . . I would say the physical aspect would take 50 percent of your time, maybe even a little more.

The Making of *The Wild Angels*:
An Interview with Roger Corman

John Mason / 1972

From *The Journal of Popular Film and Television* 5, no. 3-4 (1976): 263-72. Reprinted by permission of Taylor & Francis Group, LLC, http://www.taylorandfrancis.com.

In the following interview, producer/director-now-distributor Roger Corman talks about the making and broader social significance of *The Wild Angels* (American International, 1966). The preface to the film reads, "The picture you are about to see will shock you and perhaps anger you. Although the events and characters are fictitious, the story is a reflection of our times." The film is about a lawless, Nazi-oriented group of motorcyclists in rebellion against conformity whose constant partying ends in one member's accidental death, followed by his funeral during which the gang ties up and assaults the minister, destroys the church, defiles the dead youth by taking him out of his coffin, and rapes his girlfriend.

The film generated a storm of controversy. Bosley Crowther called it "a brutal little picture . . . a vicious account of the boozing, fighting, pot smoking, vandalizing, and raping done by a gang of 'sickle riders . . . ," and *Newsweek* labeled it "an ugly piece of trash." Yet in spite of adverse criticism in some quarters, the film opened the 27th Venice Film Festival and achieved impressive box-office success in both the United States and abroad. In addition, *The Wild Angels* spawned a number of imitations which, according to film sociologists Louis Savary and J. P. Carrico, "formed a kind of underground folk literature for a certain segment of American youth. The films fabricated a myth to express what this group resented (order and establishment) and what was yearned for (excitement, perhaps death)."

Corman was the king of the B-picture in the 1950s and 1960s. He made films of all types—"youth," horror, sci-fi, western—and he made them quickly and cheaply. In one five year span of the fifties, he made twenty-five films. *Bucket of Blood* (1959), a typical Corman action quickie, was shot in five days. He began to attract the attention of serious critics and *cineastes* as an important director with the release of *The Fall of the House of Usher* in 1960, the first of a series of intensely atmospheric adaptations of Edgar Allan Poe's works. Corman is presently head of New World Films, a film distribution company located in Los Angeles.

JM: Would you describe the circumstances which led you to produce *The Wild Angels*? How did the idea come to you? What influenced you to make the cycle picture? Were there any unusual persons or occurrences connected with the origination of the project?

RC: The circumstances which led to it were primarily within the motion-picture industry. That is, I had made a number of pictures successful with American International, for whom I made *The Wild Angels*, and I had left American International about a year earlier, and had signed a contract with Columbia Pictures on the basis that I was going to have an opportunity for bigger pictures. Columbia, immediately after getting me under contract, offered me a series of low-budget pictures, and I turned them all down. I was getting somewhat frustrated at Columbia when Sam Arkoff and Jim Nicholson, the men who run AIP, called me, suggested we have lunch and stated that they thought they could get me a leave of absence from Columbia if I would like to come back and make a picture for them—this was in the winter and they wanted a picture shot in the spring to come out for the summer drive-in season. I had lunch with them and it was one of those ideas that we all more or less came up with. I say yes, I'd like to come back and do a picture. They first asked if I'd like to do a horror film and certain other types I'd done before and I said no, I wanted to do a contemporary film about young people today and I wanted to shoot it all on natural locations. We discussed various aspects of what was going on in the country at the time and I mentioned that the Hell's Angels were very much in the headlines—that was when they first came into national prominence—and we jointly decided that I would do a picture on the Hell's Angels.[1]

Now, as to how I actually did it, I contacted the San Bernadino Hell's Angels from an article I'd read in the *L.A. Times* saying that they hung out at the Blue Blaze Café in Fontana. I called the Blue Blaze Café and there were no Hell's Angels there, but I spoke to the manager and I told him what I was going to do and said I'd like to talk with them, not only about doing a picture about them, but about having them in the picture.

I got a call back a couple of days later, saying that they could meet us either at the Blue Blaze or at a place called the Gunk Shop in Hawthorne, where they also hung out, and Hawthorne was closer than Fontana, so Chuck Griffith, a good friend of mine whom I hired to write the picture, and I went down to the Gunk Shop and met with them. They agreed they wanted to be in the picture and I said I wanted it to be as close as possible to their actual experiences. So they got started telling us stories of things they had done, and we sat around drinking beer and smoking a little pot and talking about the whole concept of being Hell's Angels and we based the script to a large extent on what they had told us. Almost every event that took place in the picture actually happened to Hell's Angels, and what we did was to put them together in one unit. The breakout of the Loser from the hospital had actually taken place south of the border. One of their men had been arrested and was put in a hospital in Tijuana, and they sprung him out and brought him back across the border, and it was a big thing for them that they had done this. I didn't want to get involved in a Mexican shooting and I felt that made my storyline a little bit too loose, so I put it in the desert in Mecca, and constructed a story line, as I say, based on what they had actually told us.

I had a theme in mind that came to me based upon what they told me and upon what I'd read in the *Economist*, an English economic and political science magazine, in which they had pointed out some of the destructiveness of lower-class American youth and said that similar things had taken place on the docks in Hamburg and in some of the industrial cities in the Soviet Union, and it was the same theme of the *Economist* that showed this unrest among young people, particularly among unemployed, underemployed, or employed with great dissatisfaction. It went beyond capitalism and socialism and was a factor of modern civilization as we go into more of a technologically oriented society. Those people who formerly held jobs at the bottom of society no longer have a job or existence available to them which gives them even a modicum of pride in what they do, and they become essentially dispossessed. And I felt that this was a good analysis of the Hell's Angels—these guys were at the bottom. Having talked with them, they were not highly intelligent, they came, to a large extent, from broken homes, and in general they had very little schooling. And I was involved in my own thinking at the time in various aspects of dropping out of society. I thought about the $50,000-a-year advertising executive who says, "I give up. I drop out. I don't like this." How much easier is it for a $150-a-week garage mechanic? They say this isn't for me, and they drop out. So I thought of the Hell's

Angels as essentially people who were dropping out of the lowest level of American society and attempting to form a society of their own, which, although it was different in many respects from American society, inevitably mirrored the society which they had dropped out, because they were born in that society.

JM: I would like to ask you two things then to follow up on that—one deals with the opening sequence of the movie, and the second, the end of the movie. To me, the opening sequence—where a little kid rides out of his yard and bumps into Blues's bike, and his mother spanks him or scolds him and takes him back in the yard—seemed to be a frame for the entire movie. From that point on, the gang encountered—well, the movie was about breaking away from various maternal figures and authority figures just like this young kid.
RC: Right.

JM: . . . which is what I wanted to ask you: if that was a key to the viewing.
RC: Yes, that was one of the keys. The picture, I would hope, has some complexity to it, but that at least is one approach to the picture. As a matter of fact, you know I shot the picture five years ago, so I can't remember exactly, but as I recall I shot the opening of the picture through some vertical wooden fence stakes which I wanted to give a slight prison effect—like, you reached for this, if nobody picks up that it's a prison, okay—but in the back of my mind was the fact that at the end of the movie we also shot through bars of the cemetery to see Blues at the grave of the Loser—so that was a framework, and it *was* part of the theme.

JM: I saw a basis for interpreting the ending of the picture two ways: one, pessimistically. The gang leaves Blues, the police close in on him—and the cycle of crime and punishment seems likely to continue. About the last thing he says is, "There is no place." Mike wants him to go and he says, "Go where?" There simply is no place where they can avoid this kind of encounter with police and parents and ministers—the people they want to get away from. Yet, on the other hand, he stays to face the music. Does this mean he has grown, that there is a way, any way, out, or it is just a statement of complete abandonment . . .
RC: He has grown, but it's not optimistically. He has grown enough to see the futility of the existence he's been leading. But he has not grown to the point where he can see any truly constructive answer. The only

thing he knows is there's no particular point in continuing to run. By standing, he may learn something; he may change. I myself would not be particularly optimistic about his chances. I would simply say that he has progressed one step up a very long ladder.

JM: Why is Loser's death such a calamity for him? I know it ultimately leads to his estrangement from the gang and its destruction. Is it that his loyalties have been tested, does he feel responsible for Loser's death, or is it just a growing sense of futility at their way of life?

RC: It's a combination of all three; and let me say now that, as I said before, I shot the picture five years ago and I've done a number of pictures since, and a lot of these pictures fade somewhat in my mind. But the points I was working with there were pretty much what you said. One, as leader of the gang he is responsible for what happens to everybody within the gang. At the same time the member of the gang that he is closest to is the Loser, so he not only feels a sense of responsibility, but he has a great sense of loyalty to the Loser. It's also involved with the growing sense of futility of what they're doing, and I think there's an additional point. That is, the Loser, probably being the freest spirit in the gang, represents something special. If they're moving from this society and they're various steps on the road of moving away, the Loser has probably progressed the furthest.

JM: May I ask you a couple of related questions about your role as producer? One is—how did you envision the picture when you began it? What was your original thinking as far as budget, and what kind of audience were you shooting after? Where did you plan to distribute and exhibit the picture?

RC: Alright—first, budget. Budget was about $350,000, and it was shot on a three-week schedule, which makes it a low-budget film.[2] And the fact that I shot it with a full union crew—the same $350,000 non-union could have bought me a seven-week schedule—so I prefer to think in terms of schedule, rather than budget, because the most important thing is time. So as a three-week picture, it was a very fast, low-budget film. It was an attempt to do an action film that would appeal to drive-in audiences, yet at the same time, I was hoping to make a statement beyond just that of an action film. I was trying to ride two horses, attract two types of audience, that it would play at art houses and it could play at drive-ins. I think the best American films move in that direction, that they are successful in both the commercial and artistic levels. I was trying to get to both, and I partially succeeded. By no means a perfect film, but as you know, it won a few awards. It was on a couple of ten best of the world lists of that year, it was the opening night film, which is something of an honor, at the Venice Film Festival. It was beaten, and beaten deservedly, by *The Battle of Algiers*, which, when I saw *The Battle of Algiers*, I said I'm not hanging around for the awards of this festival, that's obviously a better picture than *The Wild Angels*. But still, it did get quite a bit of critical acclaim, and until *Easy Rider*, it was the highest-grossing low-budget picture ever made in the United States.[3]

JM: As director, how much creative freedom did you have? You mentioned Griffith who wrote the script—did you follow it pretty much as he wrote it, did you compromise during the shooting of it, did you add things to it?

RC: I did all of those. I worked with Chuck on the script, so the script is something of a collaboration. And then I did make changes during the shooting. Peter Bogdanovich, who has recently done *The Last Picture Show*, which is a very good picture, was working as my assistant at that time.[4] Peter and I rewrote several sections as we went along, and then as the director, I worked, as I always do, which is to use the script simply as the starting point. And I did add in changes, although the basic line followed the original script.

JM: How about working with the Hell's Angels . . . did that present any particular problems for you as a director as opposed to working with trained actors?

RC: Surprisingly few. I determined in advance what my approach to the Angels would be and then followed it and it worked. I felt that I was in no position to give them orders and try to push them around, yet at the same time if I appeared weak and tried to ask them too much to come and work in the picture they would push me around. So I adopted a somewhat objective stance to the Angels, which is not a stance I would take with trained professional actors, but it worked with them. Which is simply to treat them as equals and say, all right, fellows, this is the shot, you are on the bikes here, you will go around that corner, you do this, and just tell them specifically what the problem was and then have them solve the problem.

JM: As you mentioned, this film kind of reached the status of a cult film. Did you expect that this might happen, did you anticipate that making a cycle picture would start a new direction, even though in the fifties there was one . . .

RC: There was one. Marlon Brando in the fifties, about fifteen years earlier, had done *The Wild One.*[5] We saw *The Wild One,* because we didn't want to copy it, and I remembered having seen it when it came out, and I do remember it very well. I remember being very impressed by it. And so Chuck Griffith and I screened *The Wild One* just to make sure that we didn't inadvertently copy something because that's been known to happen. You have a completely original idea and it's based on something you saw so long ago you've forgotten it. And *The Wild One* is a strange picture. I didn't like *The Wild One* the second time I saw it. But I was tremendously impressed with the acting. Looking at *The Wild One* again, it's got nothing to do with this, but if you want a quick criticism, I thought it was not a particularly good picture. But it was redeemed by two brilliant performances, Marlon Brando and Lee Marvin, who were both outstanding; they were what made the picture go the first time out. I would say our picture was much, much closer to the truthful way of looking at the Hell's Angels. But also, we did not have any performances that were really as good as Brando or Marvin.

JM: The content of the picture, in terms of the middle 1960s, was rather original. The style of the picture, too, seems rather unique, at least in relation to many of the other films I've studied.[6] Did the style emerge from the form of the picture itself, the content of the picture, or did you want to do some experimental things technically . . . stylistically?

RC: Again, many things went into it. One is the way in which I work on any picture. Any director brings something of himself in. Most of my pictures have had a certain energy and generally a fairly fast pace to them, no matter what subject. I just work that way. Secondly, I was looking for a picture of excitement. I thought, if I'm doing a picture about the Hell's Angels, it must have something to do with the image and the truths of the Angels, which is one of the powerful, almost sexual—I shouldn't even say almost—obviously sexual sublimation through the concept of the motorcycle. The subject matter itself, just a photograph of a motorcycle, a chopper, roaring down a road, brings a certain feeling of mind. Plus I used a rock music score, which is one of the first pictures to use contemporary music against the natural background. As a matter of fact, the blues theme from it became for a little while the number-one record in the country, and they took the actual mixed track out of the picture, so that you heard the music and you heard the roaring of the motorcycle behind it.

JOHN MASON / 1972   **69**

JM: A couple of last questions about the concept of the Angels as you saw it, and the kind of truth you were after. Can you elaborate a little bit about that, particularly to what extent you feel your concept matched what you understood about the Angels themselves, and how it came across in your film?

RC: Well, I thought we went into it in a variety of ways. One, as dropouts who did not fit into society, because frankly, the society had gone beyond what they were capable of—what job they might perform within the society. And two, having dropped out, I saw them as the modern equivalent of the cowboy; that is, the cowboy on his horse drifting through the West with no roots. The Hell's Angel is almost the same thing: he drifts through the West on his horse, with no roots. I think there's something within the American mystique that created the cowboy in the nineteenth century, and the mystique of the cowboy and the biker is composed partially of the truth of their lives and partially of the wishful thinking of other people who imposed their fantasies on the life of the cowboy, so that the image that's presented of both the Hell's Angel and the cowboy is partially true and partially fantasy. I would say with the Hell's Angel it's closer to the truth than the cowboy because the Hell's Angel may be acting out the fantasy he himself has created of the cowboy.

JM: It seems to me the film tends to glamorize the Angel way of life, his violence and his decadence. As frenzied as it is, both to himself and to other people, there's still a glamour and a romance to it. Were you aware of this—or do you think that it's a valid criticism?

RC: I think it's a valid criticism, and I was not working for that. I was trying to be very accurate and very truthful, and I think you're right, there is a feeling of glamour about their way of life, and it was unintended. I didn't mean to look at it that way. I think what may have happened, I may have been swept up in their stories, and gotten, as I shot the picture, a little involved and a little excited about their way of life, because I know I look at them a little bit differently now than I did at that time, and I look at them with . . . a little bit less . . . of an admiring eye.

JM: About society itself—it seems also that in spite of all the senseless violence inflicted on society, that in a curious way much of the violence seems justified, that the gang is never really doing anything, but is always under some kind of surveillance, especially by police, and that this kind of assumed guilt does indeed precipitate some tragedy or trouble of some sort. But it is not until they are judged guilty beforehand that something happens. I was just wondering if perhaps this is part of the element of sympathy that enters into it.

RC: It may be, because as we were shooting the picture we had the San Bernardino Sheriff's Department, the California State Highway Patrol, and I think several local cities sent their policemen out to keep us under guard at all times, and I felt this was a little out of hand, and I explained it to one of the guys from San Bernardino Sheriff's Department—he wanted to arrest some of them on some charges they had—I said, hey look, these guys are just doing a job. As a matter of fact, for some of them, for the first time in their lives, they are getting paid to do a job and do what they want to do. They're riding their bikes, having fun, being out in the desert and getting paid—what do you guys want to bust them for? And at that time my sympathies did start to go a little bit to them for that reason. They were, in many respects, being unjustly hassled by the law.

Notes

1. California-based Hell's Angels were indeed very much in the news in 1965 stemming from widespread public outrage and media coverage of the infamous Monterey Labor Day rape case of 1964 in which a number of frenzied Angels allegedly dragged two girls off into the sand dunes and repeatedly raped them. That scandal led then California Attorney General T. C. Lynch to launch an official investigation into Angel activities, a report whose lurid but largely unsubstantiated details were made public in March 1965. Newspapers and magazines across the country gave considerable attention to the findings of the Lynch report and related stories about the Angels. See, for example, William Murray's "Hell's Angels" in the *Saturday Evening Post*, 238L 32–9, Nov. 2, 1965: Hunter Thompson's *The Hell's Angels: A Strange and Terrible Saga*, New York: Random House, 1967, a freelance journalist's account of a year riding with the Angels, and the autobiographical account of the Angels by Freewheelin' Frank in Frank Reynolds *Freewheelin' Frank, Secretary of the Angels*, as told to Michael McClure, New York: Grove Press, 1967.

2. Low-budget, youth-oriented films made for the summer drive-in circuits like *The Wild Angels* are known in Hollywood as "product pictures."

3. In 1966, *The Wild Angels* was listed as one of the top-grossing films in the United States by the *Motion Picture Herald* and *Motion Picture Daily News*. The *Los Angeles Times* also selected it as one of that year's ten best films.

4. At the time of this interview with Corman, in the winter of 1972, Bogdanovich's *Last Picture Show* had just been released.

5. The motorcycle films of the 1960s, beginning with *The Wild Angels* (1966), are the direct descendents of *The Wild One* (Columbia, 1953), the first of the entire genre. The

latter film, which deals with the takeover of a small town by a motorcycle gang, began the film myth about terrorist, outlaw motorcycle gangs, and Marlon Brando's characterization of Johnny, the leader of the gang, established the prototype of the motorcycle rebel.

The film script for *The Wild One* was based on a short story, "The Cyclists Raid" by Frank Rooney, which in turn was based on an actual event in 1948, when a large number of riotous motorcyclists allegedly "took over" the town of Hollister, California. Unlike the short story, the movie presumed to be an honest effort to portray underlying social conditions responsible for producing gang violence. However, the film gained its reputation more on the basis of its portrayal of violence than because of its sociological revelations. Brando, for one, was quoted as expressing his displeasure at the film's ultimate impact: "We started out to explain the hipster psychology, but somewhere along the way we went off the track. The result was that instead of finding out why young people tend to bunch into groups that seek expression in violence, all we did was show the violence" (Louis Savory, and J. Paul Carrico, eds. *Contemporary Film and the New Generation*, New York: Association Press, 1971).

6. *The Wild Angels* was one of twenty-two films studied as part of the author's dissertation on "The Identity Crisis Theme in American Feature Films, 1960–1969." Stylistically, this film is significant for its quasi–cinéma vérité quality and, as Corman points out, for its integral use of rock music scoring.

Roger Corman Interview

Todd McCarthy and Charles Flynn / 1973

This interview was conducted on September 6, 1973. From *The Kings of the Bs: Working within the Hollywood System* (New York: E. P. Dutton, 1975). © 1975 by Todd McCarthy and Charles Flynn. Reprinted by permission of Todd McCarthy.

Roger Corman, businesslike as always, suggested we interview him at his New World Pictures office. The office itself, decorated with posters for Rohmer's *L'Amour, l'après-midi* (1972) and the British Film Institute's Corman retrospective, is on the top floor of a Sunset Strip building. One reaches New World by ascending in a glass-enclosed elevator.

After speaking to an associate who was setting up the East African distribution of *The Student Teachers* (1973), Corman turned to the interview.

Roger Corman rode the crest of just about every major film trend of the last twenty years: teenpix, sci-fi movies, the Poe cycle, motorcycle movies, and finally, the soft-core, R-rated, sexploitation genre.

After several disappointing experiences with major studios, Corman realized his longstanding dream in 1970 when he formed his own company, New World Pictures. He started by speaking about the firm.

Roger Corman: It's growing a little more than we counted on . . . the company is growing a little faster than we had originally planned. . . .

Anyway, in regard to the B movie, just as Al Zugsmith may say he doesn't make formula movies, I'd say I don't make B movies and nobody makes B movies anymore. The B movie was really the second feature movie in the great days of the major studios when they turned out vast numbers of motion pictures. A certain number were specifically earmarked as A and a certain number were specifically earmarked as B. And the B's were always the second feature, the supporting picture. Occasionally, of course, one well-made B would come up and become an A, but that was an exception. The changing patterns of distribution, and

72

the cost of color film specifically, has just about eliminated the B movie. The amount of money paid for a second feature is so small that if you're paying for color-release prints, you can't get it back. You can't get your negative costs back distributing your film as a B or supporting feature.

I don't know how this affects your book, but if you stay with the concept of the B movie as such, you're writing about past history.

Charles Flynn & Todd McCarthy: Would you call television films today's B movies?
RC: Yes. I think you can now start to expand upon the meaning of the word B. And I would say to a large extent they take the place of the B movies, because they're slotted into a certain area the way the B movie was. They know roughly how much money they're going to get for them before they make them, which was one of the hallmarks of the B movie.

For motion pictures, everything is made to try for the top half of the bill. The picture that fails then goes to the bottom half. Or, very often, a picture that had previously been top half will be brought back on the bottom half the second time around, as a second feature. A lot of our films do that. We'll play *The Student Nurses* as a first feature, then we'll come up with our sequel, *Private Duty Nurses*, and we'll bring back *The Student Nurses* as a second feature with *Private Duty Nurses*.

CF & TM: To go way back into history, would you call the films you did in the fifties, your first few films, B movies?
RC: The first one or two. The first picture I made was a science-fiction picture called *Monster from the Ocean Floor*, and that was probably somewhere in between a B movie and what is today considered top half. Because it played in some areas as a second feature, and in some areas, because of the subject matter, science fiction, it did play top half. Although the picture cost, as I recall, something like $12,000, cash, and was shot on a six-day schedule. But it did play top half.

My next picture, *The Fast and the Furious*, which was a road-racing picture, was probably a little bit closer to the traditional B movie. Because, again, of the subject matter, it fit more into the second feature category. Although it occasionally played top feature.

By the time I did the third one, *Five Guns West*, the first picture I directed, I did that picture in color. And the very fact that it was in color put it top half through most of the country, although in some major-city situations, such as the New York circuit break, it became a second feature. So at that time, we were bridging the two.

CF & TM: We wanted to ask about some of the people you've worked with over the years, like Daniel Haller and Floyd Crosby, who worked on all your Poe movies, and, of course, the actors you've used many times. How did you happen to come across these people? And then, why did you keep them from film to film?

RC: I kept them because they were good. It's as easy as that. When I started off, I found that a large percentage of the crew and cast were not particularly competent at their jobs, but a small percentage were. So when I did my second feature, I simply hired back the ones I thought were good, dropped the ones I thought were bad. I repeated that process on the third and fourth pictures. So by the time I had made four or five pictures, I had assembled a crew who were the best men I could find. And I worked with that crew for many years. It got to the point where they worked together much like an athletic team. One man knew in advance how another man would function, and they knew how I would function. They were so good they began to be hired by other producers as a unit. When I wasn't working, many other producers would simply pick up Floyd Crosby, Dick Rubin, the whole crew.

With actors, it worked roughly the same way, but of course that had many more intangibles because it was dependent on the picture. Someone might be a very good actor I had worked with, but there might be nothing specifically for him in one picture.

CF & TM: Could you describe some of the releasing companies you went through in those days, like Woolner Brothers, Howco, and Filmgroup?

RC: These were primarily small, independent companies. On my first picture, I just raised $12,000 and made the picture. Then I made a deal with Lippert Releasing to release the picture. I took the money from that and made a second picture, and realized that producing independently was a very slow process. You had to wait for the money to come back from one picture to put it in the other. That means that you might do one picture a year. So I made a deal with Jim Nicholson and Sam Arkoff, who were starting a company called American Releasing. On my second picture, *The Fast and the Furious*, I had offers from Republic and Columbia, but they were just straight deals.

I made a proposition to Nicholson and Arkoff: that if they would take my picture and give me an advance, I would make a three-picture deal with them, getting money from the franchise holders (that's kind of a states' rights operation throughout the country) in advance of each picture so that I would have financing. So Jim Nicholson and I flew around the country together, carrying the print of *The Fast and the Furious* with us. He talked about his distribution company and I talked about the three pictures I was going to make. And we signed up all the major franchise holders. I actively started making a series of pictures at that time and American Releasing, which later became American International, started on the basis of that plan.

The pictures were successful, and I was immediately offered other pictures—but by other little independents. For instance, there would be other independent companies like American Releasing operating through the same franchise holders. My picture, *The Fast and the Furious*, went out and was successful. Other people, such as Howco, which was George Houck's company, or the Woolner Brothers, who were both theatre owners and had connections with the franchise holders, became aware that these little pictures were doing business. So they would come to me with an idea.

CF & TM: Does that states' rights system still exist today?
RC: Yes, it still exists. Now that I have my own distribution company, I am basing it somewhat on my original formula with AIP. I have modified it because we're making bigger pictures, and I'm putting much more of my own money in, with the states' rights operators. Now that we're in our third year of operation, we are starting to open our own New World branch offices. We have our own offices in New York and part of the East Coast and the entire West Coast, but we go states' rights in the rest of the country.

CF & TM: We wanted to ask when you plan to go public. . . .
RC: We have no plans to go public! I think Sam Arkoff regrets AIP went public. It's given him additional sources of capital, but has given him additional problems as well.

CF & TM: Was the Filmgroup your own company?
RC: Yes. And it did well. In fact, Filmgroup never had a losing year. One year we made $3,000, another year we made about $1,500! It was too small a company. I was making pictures for $30,000 to $40,000, and getting my money back and making a little, tiny profit. I wasn't much interested in it. It was a sideline, and I was making pictures for other companies that were more expensive, so I finally made an arrangement with American International to take over the distribution of the Filmgroup pictures. In return, I made some pictures for AIP.

But I've always remembered it as an idea that, had I been more interested or had more capital, could have gone, and that's why I started New World.

CF & TM: What was the average budget for your fifties' sci-fi films?
RC: On the ones I was making for American International and Allied Artists, I would say anywhere from $70,000 to $100,000.

CF & TM: Didn't you once say that *War of the Satellites* was released within a few weeks after the first Sputnik in 1957?
RC: Yes.

CF & TM: Would you call that the essence of the exploitation film?
RC: Yes . . . it really was! Actually, it was released within a month or two. What happened was this: The Sputnik went up [October 4, 1957], and the day after it went up I told Steve Broidy, the president of Allied Artists, that I could deliver the picture in eight weeks, I think it was, and that if they would start the ads right away, based upon what I told them the picture was about, and if they would give me the money, I would deliver the picture. He said yes, because I had had a couple of pictures that had been successful with Allied.

We did it exactly on that schedule, and it was one of those rare times when everything meshed. I delivered the picture on the exact date I promised, and they had the advertising campaign ready at the same time. We booked it directly into the theatres, and the picture did very well.

CF & TM: Why did you go to Fox to do *I, Mobster*?
RC: They came to me; I really didn't go to them. I had done *Machine Gun Kelly* for American International, which, again, had done nicely, so Eddie Alperson, who was actually an independent releasing through Fox, came to me with the script of *I, Mobster*, and asked if I and my brother [Gene Corman] would do this picture for him, and we said yes.

CF & TM: But that was your last film for a major as big as Fox for a while?
RC: Yes.

CF & TM: Do you consider yourself a black humorist?
RC: Probably . . . right. If you talk about *The Little Shop of Horrors*, *A Bucket of Blood*, *Creature from the Haunted Sea*, and, more recently, *Gas-s-s-s*, I

would say they're somewhere in that vein. We did the first one before the term black humor was used. But they're probably somewhere within that genre.

CF & TM: What happened to *Gas-s-s-s*?
RC: AIP became very, very frightened of the picture, and when I was in Europe working on another film, they completely re-cut it, taking out "God," one of the major characters, and eliminating the entire end of the picture. They took every questionable or controversial point out of the picture; and that was what the picture was all about. So it became an extremely innocuous and slightly meaningless picture. And that's what went out. No one ever saw the picture as it was made—and the picture did not do well.

CF & TM: Would you say that's the most disappointing experience you have had?
RC: Probably that and *The Intruder*. *Gas-s-s-s* I believe was wrecked by AIP; on *The Intruder*, I can't blame anybody. I made the picture; I got extremely good reviews on it. It was a picture about integration in the South in the mid-1950s, and the public just didn't want to see that picture, at that time.

CF & TM: Does *Gas-s-s-s* more or less sum up your attitude toward the whole Poe thing, or is there a film in the Poe series that you consider your ultimate statement?
RC: No, no one in particular. I'd say each one was an attempt to deal with the individual short story of Poe. At no time did I try to put it all together in one unit. I let each one speak for itself. And *Gas-s-s-s* wasn't that closely related to the Poes. It was actually a second thought when we put Poe in it. We just started putting things in. In the original concept, he wasn't in it. And we just decided to put him in on a motorcycle—it seemed appropriate.

CF & TM: Of course, you also poke fun at the Poe films in *The Trip*.
RC: Yes . . .

CF & TM: In fact, most of the Poe films seem to be somewhat tongue in cheek themselves.
RC: Toward the end, yes; not at the beginning. *The Fall of the House of Usher, The Pit and the Pendulum, The Masque of the Red Death*—although

that was later—were serious films. It was starting with *Tales of Terror*, which was a trilogy, one of the three I played for humor. And then *The Raven* we played for humor.

CF & TM: About visual style: going back over your career the Poe films seem visually much more elaborate, if you will, than the films that came both before and after . . .

RC: I think that's true, and there are two reasons. One, on the Poe films I had a three-week schedule, which was the longest schedule I had ever had, so I had more time to shoot in an elaborate style. On the earlier pictures, *Little Shop of Horrors* was shot in two days, *Bucket of Blood* in five, and most of the others were shot in five to ten days. So there was simply no time to get into an elaborate camera style. I had to shoot very quickly, and relatively simply, although I tried to get as much interest into them as I could, within the schedule.

With a three-week schedule on the Poe pictures, I had a little more time to work with the camera. And also, I felt the subject matter lent itself to that. On the pictures that came after that, say, *The Wild Angels*, that was also a three-week picture. But I was looking for more of a realistic style, so I deliberately came back to a slightly simpler camera movement.

CF & TM: Why did you shoot the last two Poe films, *The Masque of the Red Death* and *The Tomb of Ligeia*, in England?

RC: Simply economics. We had offers from England, the Eady Plan, which was a heavy subsidy from the English government, and we went there for that reason.

CF & TM: Is it true that you used the leftover sets from *Becket*?

RC: Yes, for *Masque of the Red Death*. And *Ligeia* as well . . . I've forgotten which was which. I don't remember, but I know that in both pictures we used units from major English pictures, and one of them was *Becket*.

CF & TM: *The Secret Invasion* was shot in Yugoslavia, wasn't it?

RC: *The Secret Invasion* was shot in Dubrovnik . . .

CF & TM: And some of your New World productions have been shot in the Philippines . . .

RC: Yes, we've shot in the Philippines a great deal.

CF & TM: Do you feel, then, that economics forces you to seek out new locations?

RC: Right. Two things: the look for an interesting, unusual location, and the economics as well. With New World, I'd say the majority of the New World pictures have been shot in the United States. A minority have been shot overseas.

CF & TM: In many of your films, you have a weak central character— someone who is sort of a schlemiel . . .

RC: Of course, in things like *Little Shop of Horrors* and *Bucket of Blood* it was deliberate. In some of the other films, I'm not quite certain, I'm not positive. I think anybody who works in a creative way is conscious of what he's doing only to a certain extent. He's working a great deal out of his unconscious. It may be that I, personally, rebel. I've thought a little bit about this and I have no great thoughts on it, other than that I personally may rebel against the concept of the hero. It may be that I dislike the hero. And so I deliberately play up people other than the hero. I figure that if you've gone through school and the halfback is getting all the girls, and you get a chance to make films, and the format of the film is that the halfback gets the girl, you may deliberately undercut him.

CF & TM: Could you describe why you left AIP? Of course, you spent a little time with UA and Fox, and then set up your own company. Why?

RC: There's no particular split as such, because I still have some relations with AIP. I had lunch with Arkoff and Melamed[1] last week, as a matter of fact, talking about a few things As a matter of fact, I work quite closely with them in certain areas. It was just that I felt their subject matter and their budgets were limiting to me. So I deliberately went to the majors, with the hope of doing bigger and—quote—"more important" pictures. I found there were a great many limitations placed upon what I did from the majors. And I became more interested in doing films my way, and not thinking so much about the budgets.

So once I had come to that conclusion, the logical thing seemed to be to start my own company. Work with a low-budget type of operation, but at least have total control.

Certain things with the casting and cutting of my films for the majors, and specifically with the casting, and cutting, and story changes as

---

1. D. J. Melamed, AIP's treasurer

AIP . . . I finally said, "That's it." *Gas-s-s-s* was the final straw, really. I said, at that point, "I want to do my own films. If they succeed, fine. If they fail, I know who was responsible."

CF & TM: Can we expect to see another film directed by you coming along one of these days?
RC: Eventually. At the moment, I'm really caught up in this whole business of running this company, which is both production and distribution. And it's rather involved. It'll probably take at least another year to get really organized, but at that point, I'll probably start directing again.

CF & TM: What do you think are the key elements in selling a film? Some people might say intelligent distribution patterns, or word of mouth . . .
RC: I think the quality of the film is most important of all. That's probably not the answer you're looking for in relation to exploitation films or B films, but I think it's true, and I always base everything on that. I have always believed that the man who makes the best film will do the best with it commercially, providing the other aspects aren't completely thrown away. Subject matter is important, but the quality, I think, is the most important.

CF & TM: What do you think of the gimmicks people like William Castle use?
RC: I think they're great! I have nothing against them. We've used them a little bit. I don't work quite as flamboyantly as Bill Castle. But I think it's fine. You know the old word showmanship. Why not?

CF & TM: How do you maintain the quality of films you produce and distribute, but do not direct?
RC: I pick the best writers, the best directors, and the best actors available under the given circumstances, which, in low-budget films, has very often led us to new directors. On the basis of my theory that if you're dealing with a veteran filmmaker, in general, he should be doing more important work if he's really good. A man who is doing B pictures after thirty years might be very competent, and probably is, otherwise he wouldn't be working at all, but in general, what he will give you will be a competent B picture. And what I've always looked for is the B picture, the exploitation picture, that is better than that, that has some spark that will lift it out of its bracket. And that's why the Kershners, the Coppolas, the Bogdanoviches, and so forth.

CF & TM: We're interested to know if you have a strong sense of being a patron of the arts . . .

RC: A little bit. Because I am conscious that I am doing a little bit more of this than other people I know. In fact, the *Los Angeles Times* had an article on Sunday [September 2, 1973] about the American Film Institute. And they said something in it, that the American Film Institute wasn't doing as much as Roger Corman. The reason is, of course, that I have a distribution company, I am a producer, I have access to capital. And with my own company, I don't have to have someone to second-guess me. I can say, "OK, I think this young director is talented, I'll gamble with him." As I said, the Coppolas and Bogdanoviches and so forth have gone on to great fame and success.

We're working with some young directors now that we think are very, very good. Marty Scorsese is moving up very rapidly. Jonathan Kaplan is on his way. Steve Carver has just finished a picture for us in Rome, and even before he's back—he isn't due back in the United States for two weeks—AIP called me last week and wanted to know when he's due back. And it's his first picture! I told Sam Arkoff last week that I can't develop young directors fast enough to keep the American International production schedule going. In the past year, they've taken three directors from us, not even counting Marty Scorsese. Kaplan, Eddie Romero, and Jack Hill have all had successes with New World and have gone on to AIP. And, as I say, Carver's just on his first picture. They haven't even seen it! And they're already trying to find out what time he's due back in town!

CF & TM: There must be thousands of new Peter Bogdanoviches calling you on the phone or trying to see you, because they know that's what you do, to some extent.

RC: Yes.

CF & TM: How do they prove to you that they are really talented?

RC: It's very tough. For this reason: Bogdanovich and Coppola had been my assistants before I gave them their first chance at directing. I had great faith in them, and they knew my style of working—and they knew what was required. Some of the other young directors I've worked with, I have not had a chance to work with before giving them a chance at directing. I just talked with them. And it hasn't turned out to be quite that successful. They hadn't had this little, as it were, in-house training. So what we've been doing recently to make up for that, because I'm a believer to a large extent in the all-around filmmaker, we've been hiring them as cutters. And they'll work on one or two pictures as a cutter; and if I like what they've done as a cutter, I'll give them a chance to move on. For instance, Steve Carver cut for us for eight or ten months before he did his current film.

CF & TM: What do you feel is your most important contribution to film: your own work as a director, your innovations in the business, or, as we were saying, your sponsorship of new talents?

RC: I think it all goes together. I couldn't really pick any one aspect. Just as I think in terms of the all-around filmmaker, a director who is also an editor and who may well be a writer, I'd like to think of myself just as working in film. Francis Coppola used to try to call himself a filmmaker, not a director. I think of myself a little bit that way. It all has to do with the making of films.

Meeting with Roger Corman

Patrick Schupp / 1973

From *Séquences* 78 (October 1974): 20–24. Reprinted by permission of Yves Beauregard. Translated by Gregory Laufer.

Roger Corman is rather spare with his interviews. So *Séquences* seized the opportunity of his arrival in Montreal to preside over the 1973 Canadian Film Awards to ask a few questions of one of the masters of fantasy cinema.

PS: Mr. Corman, can you tell me how you started your series on Edgar Poe?
RC: I was working at the time for a studio that had us make groups of two films with a small budget—about $100,000 or $200,000—in black and white. We sold them as a group.

PS: *Attack of the Crab Monsters* and *Not of This Earth*?
RC: Exactly. But I was more inclined toward science fiction, and I didn't want to mix genres. All the films, however, had a common theme: horror. And then, one day, I was fed up with working like that, with a small budget and in black and white. I had been asked for two other films to be made in ten days, as usual. So I suggested that I make one instead, in color, and with fifteen days of filming, which was a lot more ambitious. I suggested a story by Poe that I like a lot, *The Fall of the House of Usher*. My studio, however, American International, a small company that had never done more than fifteen days of filming or put up a $200,000 budget, got scared. Finally, after several discussions, my bosses agreed and I started filming.

PS: *Usher*'s immediate success encouraged you to keep going, and probably the studio to keep paying. Poe was a goldmine, I believe. Based on his works, you directed *The Pit and the Pendulum, Premature Burial, Tales of Terror, The Raven, The Terror, The Haunted Palace* (which borrowed as much from Lovecraft as from Poe, if memory serves!), *Masque of the Red Death*, and *Tomb of Ligeia*. What connection have you drawn between films and books? I imagine that, in order to adequately translate the atmosphere created by Poe's language in cinematographic terms, you must have run into some difficulties?

RC: Indeed, that's an excellent question. We ran into some difficulties. First, there's the brevity of Poe's stories, which rarely go beyond a few pages. That meant that we had to explore Poe's psychology and recreate the atmosphere in which he worked as well as his themes. Then we went back to the story in order to check and to clarify. Do you want an example? In "The Pit and the Pendulum," Poe describes only the torture chamber itself. So in a sense we invented a prologue, a first and a second act. The characters end up in the chamber, that is, in the third act. What counts is in the chamber and that's where Poe's story begins. That, in fact, is one of our techniques: using Poe's story as the conclusion to a story whose premise we came up with.

The second point is that, in my view, Poe worked quite a bit in terms of the unconscious, in a middle world that Freud tried to explore in Austria in the nineteenth century. Poe in America, Dostoyevsky in Russia, Maupassant in France, even other artists, in literature, music, and painting, have followed the same path—the subjective exploration of the unconscious. You see, I firmly believe that the artistic and scientific fields are tightly interwoven, that numerous, apparently contradictory or opposing facets are in fact joined together, but in a context that is not always self-evident. And yet, since Poe's works are situated directly in terms of the unconscious, I've tried to recreate a completely imaginary world by using technical studio equipment. At that time, however, I tended to work in a more realistic manner, in the outdoors, etc. . . . I have no trouble saying that Poe brought me back to more intellectualized studio work. There, I had perfect control over the film's atmosphere with lighting, scenery, accessories, photos, etc. . . . And when we had to leave the studio for certain reasons . . .

PS: In the case of *Tomb of Ligeia*, I believe?

RC: Yes! *Tomb of Ligeia* was my last film about Poe, and in it I proved my theory! In fact, at the beginning, I wanted to maintain that imaginary world, except for some ocean shots. On that note, I have to talk to you about the ocean. There is a deep fascination in man with the sea, just like when you look at fire. There's a sort of hypnotism. So once I shot the ocean, and another time there was a fire in the Hollywood hills. And I reworked my schedule in order to go all the way to the burned area, to film and in that way to preserve a few scenes of a landscape with a supernatural atmosphere.

PS: So those are your outdoor shots. Burned land. Is that what you used in the opening sequences of *Haunted Palace*?

RC: No, *Usher*. But for *Haunted Palace*, I remade a similar set, inspired by that fire. I admit that that was a few years ago and my memory may cause me to overlook some details. I know that, for *Usher*, I went to the burned area, and in *Haunted Palace*, I used the shots of the ground where I remade a similar set. But that had had enough of an impact on me to make me want to reuse that impression of otherworldliness, of absolute desolation that only fire can offer.

PS: That, in effect, is the impression I had gotten. But the resulting atmosphere was remarkably accurate in comparison with Lovecraft's text, I mean in *Haunted Palace*. I am one of his great admirers, and I was wondering how the film would come out when I knew that it was in production with you.

RC: Me, too. I love Lovecraft, but I find Poe more interesting.

PS: Indeed, if only because of his themes . . .

RC: Lovecraft, however, is probably one of the best occult writers of the twentieth century. I worked only once on a script based on Lovecraft, in *Haunted Palace*. But my artistic director for the Poe films, Daniel Haller, directed *The Dunwich Horror*, which I financed.

PS: I really liked that film. Really well done. Especially the wave effect at the end.

RC: You see, there again we were using the idea of the sea!

PS: It was very effective, and magnificently offset the real by hinting at the invisibility of those unspeakable beings.

RC: In fact, we found ourselves in a world that was identical to Poe's, but contemporary.

PS: I wonder if Lovecraft is as popular with film directors as Edgar Poe! He's somewhat of an international craze. By the way, have you seen Alex-

andre Astruc's version of *The Pit and the Pendulum*? It was directed by the ORTF [Office de Radiodiffusion-Télévision Française] in 1968, I believe.
RC: No, but I heard a lot about it.

PS: I think that I preferred yours, probably because of those "acts" that precede Poe's story that you spoke to us about. Astruc has a totally different vision—more withdrawn, and more clinical.
RC: !!!

PS: I would like you to talk to us now about Vincent Price, who has appeared in almost all of your films, and whom you cast in spectacular fashion into a genre in which he will henceforth reign as an undisputed master. The link that exists between an actor and a director, in general, reached an exceptional level between you two, I believe.
RC: Indeed, you could say that! I chose Vincent for *House of Usher* first and foremost because I found him smart and distinguished. It also seems to me that Poe described himself or used certain aspects of his own personality in his characters, at the very least those that had a leading role. He never wrote an autobiographical story as such, but often used the first person. And so he was describing himself, if only to a certain point, of course. That is why I wanted an actor who was as smart as he was cultured. And there aren't too many, to tell the truth, who exhibit these two traits while at the same time looking the part. So it was totally natural for me to choose Vincent because, in addition to bringing a real dignity to his characters, not to mention a great talent for acting in keeping with a given time period, he conferred on them a raw and unaffected authenticity. Certain actors, as good as they may be, are used to acting "modern," and they have trouble "passing off" a character from the eighteenth or nineteenth century, which Vincent's flawless theater training overcame.

Furthermore, over the course of several conversations, Vincent and I came to agree that horror comes from the unconscious. In fact, for years we have had this theory, developed little by little over the course of our working together, that horror and fear are two quite distinct things. Horror is in part the reconstruction of childhood fantasies, and in part the anxiety from the world that surrounds us. You always fear someone bigger and stronger than you, who could hurt you, even if it's in your unconscious. Civilization advances, of course, and that fear is currently transforming into a fear / horror of a superior culture, one that is around us and watching over us, or that comes from a distant past that you can sense and that ordinary people don't suspect . . . And each time Vincent admirably knew how to express that ancestral fear that spurs horror.

PS: I remember seeing Price in *The Conqueror Worm*, an old film in which he was really poorly used.
RC: Yes. The director was English, I think. I saw part of it.

PS: Poor Vincent seemed pretty ill at ease and that made the variety and intelligence of his acting all the more striking in your films!

A word now, if you don't mind, on Floyd Crosby, the cameraman who shot most of your films.
RC: Of course. Floyd worked with me on almost all of my films—in fact, almost all those made in the United States—and I really like him. First of all, he's a charming man—you know that he's retired—and he was always an excellent colleague, and I remain very close to him.

In my view, he has two essential qualities: he was an excellent cameraman in technical terms, and he worked very quickly. Now, since all of my films were on a rather tight schedule (those made in the United States took only fifteen days or three weeks), we had to move quickly. Oh, I know that it's very easy to have an excellent cameraman, but he'll take his time and will do endless lighting tests, etc. . . . But in fifteen days, you don't have time to do all that. On the other hand, you can also find someone who works quickly, but then the lighting and workmanship get bungled. Floyd, however, the best cameraman I worked with, combined speed with technical precision.

PS: Let's turn now to one of your films, *Tomb of Ligeia*. The characters of Rowena and Ligeia are played by the same actress, Elizabeth Shepherd. Why?
RC: Well, I think that, in Poe's mind, these are just two sides of the same personality: one good, one bad. And so the same actress could easily—and logically—play both roles.

PS: An exciting job for Ms. Shepherd, especially since Rowena's makeup, starting out very pale, turned white as the film went on and indicated the personality shift and the increasingly profound taking of possession. Your directing and your relationship with Elizabeth Shepherd must have been very interesting in terms of the study and execution of this personality change.

So now we come to *Wild Angels*, from 1966, which marks a total turning point in your work.

RC: A necessary decision! While making the Poe films, I didn't think I was making a series! I made *House of Usher*. It worked out. I was asked to make others. Fine. And one of the reasons I chose *Ligeia* is because it gave me the chance to get out of the studio (we had filmed in an old abbey, near Norfolk, in England, which gave me the "gothic" atmosphere I wanted, as well as that sense of infinite space, which is impossible to recreate in the studio) and to drive home my own theories.

Also, after *Ligeia*, despite the studio's requests, I refused to keep going because it seemed to me that I had nothing left to say, that I was repeating myself. So I went off on a totally different path with *Wild Angels*, which had no historical references, period costumes, or spider webs. It was a tough and serious story bearing on an awfully contemporary problem, as a response, I suppose.

PS: Indeed. For that matter, *The St. Valentine's Day Massacre*, in 1968, and *The Trip*, in '69, are in the same vein, as is *Von Richthofen and Brown* in 1970. In *The Trip*, did you also want to address a problem that was as current and serious as it was sensitive? Or did you want to show the deleterious effects of the drug, LSD, as they were?

RC: No, not in the very least. I myself had taken LSD, as had Jack Nicholson and the screenwriter, and Peter Fonda as well. In fact, everyone who was involved in the production on every level did. You see, we believed in the potential of LSD and, when I made the film, I approved of drug use. But since I'm trying to be honest, I wanted to show the dramatic effects of a "bad" trip, even though my own experience may have been positive and pleasant. I owed it to myself to show both sides—the first part, euphoric, the second, agonizing—for the sake of fairness. In the end, the film was rather tough and seemed to me to go a bit too far. And since I left for Europe for another film as soon as filming for *The Trip* had ended, I didn't see the film before flying off. The studio made a few cuts, changed the ending and certain elements in the editing in order to give the impression of an antidrug film. But that absolutely wasn't my idea at the start.

PS: I see. Editing determines a film's impact in the end, and I could give you certain probative examples of tampering.

RC: I won't make you! It happened again with one of my last films, *Gas-s-s-s*, not so long ago.

PS: I've seen almost all the films you've directed, even the minor works from your early period, over the last fifteen years, let's say. Of all of them, I think that *Masque of the Red Death*, made in 1964, remains one of my favorites. I think that it also marks a turning point, or a significant stage in your understanding of the fantasy world. May I have your thoughts?
RC: In Hollywood, I was given three weeks to film and a rather small budget. I made *Masque* in England (it was the first film I made outside the United States) in five weeks, and with a much more substantial budget. But since English crews are a bit slower, let's say that it took four weeks to film with neither wasted time nor regrets.

The script, on the other hand, was heavily reworked. The first version was by Charles Beaumont. But I got the sense that, for the first time, he hadn't understood what I wanted with respect to Poe's works. So I reached out to Bob Campbell, who had never worked with Poe, and the two of us redid the whole script in two weeks. Because I had more money, I was able to build more complex sets, and because I had redone the script, I knew exactly where I was going with it, and I deliberately settled on that baroque vision, that look that is decadent in its opulence. So my perspective changed based on the circumstances, and that's what gave the film a different feel.

PS: In closing, may I ask about your projects? A science fiction film, I think . . .
RC: Correct. I have a few ideas in mind—some original—and two adaptations of novels.

PS: Would you consider Bradbury's *The Martian Chronicles*?
RC: No. That's indeed a novel that I like a lot and that I would have liked to have made for the screen, but I think that the rights have already been bought. No. There's *Stranger in a Strange Land*, by Robert Heinlein, which I almost made in co-production with Peter Fonda a few years ago, but those rights, too, had been set aside by someone else . . . Now it appears that I can buy those rights. There's also another novel that I'd like to make into a film. Here again, there's a question of ownership. If it doesn't work out, I'll write my own script.

PS: The only thing left is for me to thank you infinitely and to wish you good luck, and I look forward to seeing you soon on our screens.
RC: Thank you, and my regards to the readers.

Working with Young Directors

Roger Corman / 1974

From *The Journal of the Producers Guild of America* 16, no. 1 (1974): 13–15, 24. Reprinted by permission of the author.

Roger Corman is one of the more successful young film veterans who has offered opportunities to young film school graduates seeking careers as directors and producers. In addition to producing he is now actively engaged in distribution of films.

The position of the majority of young film school graduates looking for the opportunity to direct their first feature film is one with which I fully sympathize. I remember what it was like when I was first starting out, trying to gain a foothold in the motion picture industry and quickly discovering that there simply was no way to start from the bottom and work your way up to becoming a motion picture director. I worked at a number of jobs to build up as varied an apprenticeship as I could obtain at that time, including being a messenger boy in the mail department of a major studio, a driver, gopher, and grip. Then I wrote scripts, took a job with a literary agency, and no doubt alarmed my parents by considering my degree in engineering useful only in so far as elementary physics might help me to grasp the fundamentals of the motion picture camera, lighting, and lining up a shot. Nevertheless, nobody was at all anxious to give me a chance at directing, so I learned to become a producer first, raising the money to direct a film myself.

In many branches of the arts, and especially in the entertainment and communications media, the initial discouragement and frustration is the same—how do you acquire the professional experience to qualify yourself to function in your chosen field when no one will give you your first job? However, the plight of the aspiring film-maker is possibly the most difficult of all for the simple reason that the raw materials of his craft are more prohibitively expensive than those of any other. A writer, painter, musician, or actor is not dependent on thousands of dollars worth of equipment before he can begin to function. The aspiring writer, painter, or actor can with the minimum of personal expense and a reasonable amount of discipline and determination acquire some mastery of his craft and in so doing produce some evidence of his ability. For the young director, however promising his student work, however brilliantly incisive his criticism of the work of other directors, however assiduously he views and analyses films of all kinds, the only way he can prove himself a motion picture director is by actually getting out there and directing a film under professional circumstances.

When I was starting out there was virtually no possibility of directing a film outside the major studios and there was of course no likelihood of being hired as a first time director under the auspices of the majors. Despite the growth in recent years of independent production companies I know that it is still extraordinarily difficult to get that first assignment as a director, and this is one of the main reasons that I like to hire and work with new young directors.

It is, naturally, a source of some gratification to me that many of the young men who had their first shot at directing a feature film for me have subsequently gone on to do major work within the industry—including Peter Bogdanovich, Francis Coppola, Irvin Kershner, and Monte Hellman. From amongst the young directors I have worked with over the last couple of years, George Armitage, Jack Hill, Jonathan Kaplan, and Martin Scorsese have gone on to establish a track record of well-made and commercially successful films.

In the course of my meetings and talks with young film school students, or in conferences at film festivals and symposiums within the industry it has struck me that there is frequently some misunderstanding about my working relationships with young directors.

In fact, the relationship between a new young director and myself is based on an agreement that is quite simple and mutually beneficial. From the beginning it is understood between us that I as a producer (and now both as producer and president of a distribution company) am in the business of making feature films which are marketable within a highly competitive industry, and which are oriented towards the young film-going audience that, as analyses of the ticket-buying public continue to show us, still goes more frequently and regularly to the movies than any other age group. I believe that there is a definite advantage in hiring a young director to make a film to appeal to that audience. He is more in touch with their language and their aspirations, and particularly with their humor. On the other hand, however creative and hip he may be, the element of risk in hiring a new young director making his first feature film is always present. Conservative arguments can always be found for preferring a man who has already shown that he can shoot a film which cuts together, that he can handle an action scene, and so on. Consequently, I do expect that a first-time director will be willing to work for a lesser fee than he will subsequently command if he proves his competence. In the light of my foregoing remarks on the difficulty of securing that initial opportunity (largely because of the financial hazards involved if the producer's faith proves to be misplaced) it is not surprising that usually the would-be young director is happy to have the chance to make his first feature, even without the added expectation of making a lot of money from the undertaking.

On this basis I give a new young director the opportunity to direct a film on a subject and with a script approved by me as having good commercial potential, and to bring in as good a film as he can make within a firm budget and shooting schedule.

In many ways, working with young directors is a continual challenge to one's creativity as a producer. I deliberately choose a genre of film which I am pretty sure can be well made on a modest budget, and I exercise careful control over the development of the script to ensure that its story line is firmly rooted in visual and action elements. Wherever possible, I prefer that the young director also be closely involved in the development and writing of the project. As a veteran producer-director, I offer certain practical hints from my own experience during the preproduction period, but the major responsibility of choice in casting, locations, scheduling, designing of shots, etc., is the director's.

The one piece of advice I invariably give a young director is to prepare his shooting plan in advance and not be tempted into the assumption that he walk onto the set and wing it. I put particular emphasis on the value of having each day's work actually sketched out on paper, shot by shot, before he comes to the set in the morning. If he has laid down this basic guideline for himself, the young director stands a much better chance of being able to cope intelligently with the inevitable unforeseen crises and setbacks of actual shooting and can then improvise with some confidence, if necessity (or even on the spot inspiration) requires. To sum up, I would say that as a producer I have found that my best method of working with young directors is to be actively involved in the preparation of a project and then to retire to a suitably executive distance during the actual shooting so that the young director relies on his own authority and judgment on the set.

Since my experience in working with young directors has been good, and I have never had a total failure in performance from a first-time director, interest is quite often expressed in how I make my choices. Basically, I have followed two methods of singling out potential directors, with approximately equal success. The first, initially more experimental method, was to see how they worked as assistants to me in the rough and tumble of production. Coppola, Bogdanovich, Hill, and Hellman, amongst others, had all worked well for me in various categories including Second Unit direction before they got their first feature for me. Since I frequently functioned as a producer-director, and enjoyed working in natural locations, often with the minimum crew, my production assistants had considerable opportunity to work with initiative and creativity. Hellman and Hill were also excellent film editors, and Coppola first impressed me with his talent and originality as a screenwriter. Bogdanovich had also shown in a couple of writing assignments that he had a strongly developed cinematic sense.

The second method of selection which has worked well for me in recent years is to go directly to the film departments of the universities and meet the most outstanding graduates, assessing their work and personalities. In this way I have hired, among others, Bruce Clark from UCLA, Stephanie Rothman from USC, and Kaplan from NYU, who were all prize-winning students. It may seem to be a rather unadventurous case of hedging one's bets to narrow the field of choice to the top ten or so graduates of a film apartment, but since film has become an increasingly popular option at the college level it is surely a matter of common sense to pay most attention to young people who have already distinguished themselves among their contemporaries.

In conclusion, I should add that the energy, initiative, and aggression displayed by an aspiring director was often the determining factor that led to a feature film assignment. The energy and decisiveness of the director sets the pace of production and to quite a large extent of the finished film. Sheer physical and psychological stamina are essential to the director, so in assessing a young person's potential it is vital to balance his or her more academic qualifications and technical expertise with other, less tangible factors, among which persistence, ingenuity, and combativeness rate as high as sensitivity or brilliance in any one aspect of film-making.

Roger Corman Interview

Larry Salvato / 1975

From *Millimeter*, December 1975, 12–16, 48. Reprinted with permission from Penton Media.

Today Roger Corman, in the producer's role, is one of the most respect-ed men in Hollywood. Through the success of his own company, New World Pictures, he has proven to the film community that a small, inde-pendent company can wield a good deal of power in the movie market-place.

For Corman, the road to independence was not easy. In the fifties, high-brow critics laughed when they sat down to review any of the nu-merous low-budget films that he had directed in his early affiliation with American International Pictures. His name was more or less associated with everything that was cheap, vulgar, and exploitative in the cinema. But slowly, as the horizons of cinema began to expand and liberalize, Corman's filmography began to be re-evaluated and appreciated. His reputation as a director began to bloom in Europe, where he was the youngest director to be given a retrospective at the *Cinema Francais*. *The Little Shop of Horrors*, *Bucket of Blood*, *The Undead*, *Sorority Girl*, *Machine Gun Kelly*, and *Teenage Caveman* seem unlikely candidates for canoniza-tion in the cinema hall of fame, and as critic Michael Goodwin points out, "These films are characterized by a clean, minimal technical style, near-total lack of production values and a striking film noir ambiance."

In the early sixties, Corman directed an Edgar Allan Poe series plus a number of other horror films and, as the sixties closed, he explored the motorcycle / hipster genres (*The Wild Angels*, *The Trip*). By this time, Cor-man had gained enough respect to be entrusted with the direction of big-budget films for major studios: both of these ventures, *The St. Valen-tine's Day Massacre* and *Von Richthofen and Brown*, were atypical of his career style and didn't possess the economy and sharpness of vision found in his smaller, low-budget films.

After a disagreement with AIP over his picture, *Gas-s-s-s*, Corman ended his relationship with them and set up his own production company. He plunged into the administrative and production details of his company, and, as a direct result of that, he has not directed a film since. For the past five years, Corman has essentially been functioning as a producer. Independent of studio bureaucracy hassles, he has slowly been pushing the boundaries of exploitation films to where they have never been before: with higher budgets, more action, and better scripts. Moreover, the distribution arm of New World has garnered high esteem via their handling of such prestigious foreign films as Bergman's *Cries and Whispers* and Fellini's *Amarcord*.

With the help of Corman's super-efficient staff, an interview was finally arranged. As you might expect, a man with Corman's background could supply a wealth of information to any interviewer: questions about directing, questions about producing; the questions are almost endless. The irony of it is, that while Corman is a veritable library of information, he is also an extremely busy executive. I could have spent six hours talking with him, but his other responsibilities only allowed for a twenty-minute discussion. With Corman, however, twenty minutes is enough. He gets directly to the point without hemming or hawing and my questions were answered almost as fast as I could ask them.

Millimeter: When you left AIP, there was some talk that the reason you left was because of the way they handled *Gas-s-s-s*. I was wondering if you could elaborate on that.

Roger Corman: Yes, that was one of many reasons. They recut *Gas-s-s-s* after I finished it. Then I went to Europe to do *Von Richthofen and Brown* for United Artists. While I was there, they recut *Gas-s-s-s*, taking all the controversial points out of it. Now, the controversial points were the funny ones. For instance, one of the key characters was God. They cut God completely out of the picture, thus taking away not only the humor, but a lot of the meaning. And they cut the whole ending off. The ending of the picture, to me, was one of the best shots that I've ever done in my life. It was an incredible shot from the top of the Acoma Indian pueblo of a high school marching band, the Hell's Angels, and an Indian tribe; it was phenomenal. Everything I had in there, the whole picture was reprised at the top of the Indian pueblo, and they took that entire sequence out of the picture. And they did so many other things that the picture was simply emasculated.

MM: It wasn't your picture.
RC: It wasn't my picture at all, and it never showed anywhere.

MM: I saw it . . .
RC: I don't think there's a print in existence the way I made it. You saw their version. Because of *Gas-s-s-s*, and some problems with other pictures, I felt I would be better off having my own company. I was just beginning to work with larger budgets at that time, and having my own company meant I would have to drop back down to lower budgets, but I would have total control. For that reason, I don't regret the move, but possibly I do regret that the business of running New World Pictures has been so time consuming I've had to stop directing.

MM: When you started New World Pictures, did you find any surprises in running your own company?
RC: Yes, the biggest surprise was that it became so successful immediately. I did not think that we'd jump right in and grow the way we did. I anticipated a year of breaking even or losing a little bit of money and then kind of building up within the second year. When our first two pictures were hits, our company just took off faster than I had ever anticipated. I realized I was onto a successful formula, and if I gave the company more time, more than I planned originally, New World could become stronger and more successful. That was one surprise. The second surprise was the aggravation of distribution. It is not a pleasant business.

MM: You've spoken in the past about how the major studios are bogged down with their huge bureaucratic structure. Now that you're involved in trivia and a lot of details in your own company, have you changed your opinions about that?
RC: Some things go on at New World that I am not aware of. I'm beginning to welcome people making decisions on their own, because I'm no longer able to run every little detail of the business. Frankly, most of my work goes into production, and I hope distribution, advertising, accounting, and so forth can run themselves with only some supervision from me.

MM: Was starting your own company one of the reasons you stopped directing or was it that you just sort of sat out directing for a while?

RC: A combination of both. I made the decision to stop directing for a year or so after *Von Richthofen and Brown*. I had made so many pictures in such a short period of time that I felt I needed, essentially, a sabbatical. I didn't anticipate that it would be a five-year sabbatical. I may start directing again next year or I may not. I'm not certain; at the moment, I'm of two minds in that area.

MM: It must be a creative vent running this company.
RC: Yes, but in a slightly different way. As a matter of fact, as I said to somebody the other day, I'm currently developing the theory of producer as auteur. I believe a case can be made for the producer, as well as the director, as the auteur.

MM: There have been cases made in the past—like Val Lewton's films. No matter who directed them, it's a Val Lewton film.
RC: I think that if there is such a thing as an auteur, it's whoever is the dominant creative force on the film. On one film it can be the director; on another film it can be the writer; the contribution of the writer has been somewhat ignored, just as the contribution of the producer has been ignored. So what I believe at the moment is that the basic force behind the film is flexible, and you don't know who the force will be until you get into it and the different personalities come together. I think the ideal, the highest form of film, is when you're dealing with a writer-producer-director. For instance, Ingmar Bergman is a writer-producer-director. Most of the European directors are essentially producers as well. What they do is much of what the producer's function is in the United States. In Europe, the producer is really more of a banker. And for that reason, I think the European critics aren't really aware of the fact that in the American system most of the key decisions on every production are made by the producer, not the director. Essentially, the most important decision is what is going to be made and how it will be made. I've never heard of a case where the producer did not decide what picture he was going to make and how he was going to make it. He will then hire the director. The only case where that's changed is where the director is his own producer.

MM: I've noticed that, over the past few years, your budgets have gotten larger. Have you changed your attitudes about budgets?
RC: Yes, we've changed our attitudes over the period of the five years that we've been in business. We started in the area of $150,000 a picture, sometimes a little above, sometimes a little less. We've gotten up to the

point where we can spend—on a picture like *Death Race 2000*—approximately half-a-million dollars. *Big Bad Mama*, last year, cost us $400,000. And *Crazy Ladies* had a title change yesterday to *Crazy Mama* because of a conflict with an obscure book. We were threatened with a lawsuit; I liked the title *Crazy Ladies* better than *Crazy Mama*, but even though we thought we could win the lawsuit, I just didn't want to get into court. So we had a sneak preview last night which went very well, with the title *Crazy Ladies*, and this morning we're ripping out the main title and putting in *Crazy Mama*, because we start release printing soon.

MM: So why have the budgets been increasing?
RC: For two reasons . . . ah, for a variety of reasons. I shouldn't just say two reasons. One, we have more money available now. The company as such has been financed with my savings and when the company started, I was unable and / or unwilling to put out more than $150,000 on a picture. Now that we've had a few years of financial success, I'm willing to gamble a little bit more money. At the same time, by moving somewhat up in the budgets, it enables us to raise our sights as to the type of pictures we want to make. If you're going to make a picture for $150,000–$200,000 you have to be very careful of your subject matter. If you can gamble a little more, you can get into more interesting subject matter as you start to move up a little bit. So it's a combination of those factors.

MM: I was asking because a distributor I know, due to the advent of the multi-cinemas, has been able to book situations that were not drive-ins. I was wondering if that was sort of a quiet revolution that was affecting you?
RC: I would say that it is causing change and I would characterize it more as an evolution, rather than a revolution. We, in our first couple years, were heavily dependent upon drive-ins, although we have always played both indoors and drive-ins. But a larger percentage of revenues came from drive-ins in our first two years. In the last two years and now in the fifth year, the percentage from the indoors is rising.

MM: Do you feel that once you get into indoor spots you have to improve your production values for that audience?
RC: Indoor theaters do not necessarily require a higher-quality picture than drive-ins. The new theaters, indoor and drive-in, continually being built in suburban areas, play to a varied audience, making any generalization unrealistic.

MM: How do you decide to make a film? Do you do it by the seat of your pants or do you go in for the new demographics?

RC: We don't use formal demographics; I distrust them slightly. We do a fair amount of research and we do surveys of subject matter and titles at high schools and at theaters. So we do work with demographics to a certain extent. But at the same time, the final decision is mine and the original decision is mine. In other words, I will decide what types of pictures I want to do and then I'll do some research to see if there's a market for that. So we kind of blend both areas.

MM: On your distribution of foreign films, do you plan to do more of that?

RC: Yes.

MM: That's become a very successful area for you?

RC: We're very pleased with that. We started three years ago with Bergman's *Cries and Whispers*, then a year ago we had *Fantastic Planet*, which was a Special Prize winner at Cannes, and this year, Fellini's *Amarcord*. They've been very good for us for a variety of reasons. First, the obvious reason, we've made money on all of them. Second, they are a prestige item which helps the name of the company. And third, I particularly like to deal with that kind of picture; I think it's more a rewarding experience in distribution than some of the other pictures we might have.

MM: You seem to have both ends of the spectrum. You have Bergman's and Fellini's films, and, on the other hand, you have *The Big Doll House*. In each case, these films really appeal to small market pockets. Do you believe in that, that maybe this is what the independent must do, hit those little pockets the major studios let slip by?

RC: Yes, that's a deliberate choice and has been from the inception of the company. I determined I would hit a specific market; I would not try for the broad market. You can almost liken it a little bit to magazines. At one time you had *Life*, *Look*, *Saturday Evening Post*, and *Colliers*, which aimed for a broad market. All of those magazines are now out of business. And replacing them are specific magazines like *Time*, *Fortune*, *Sports Illustrated*, *Famous Monsters of Filmland*, whatever, something that aims for a smaller segment and that deliberately zeroes in on that segment.

MM: What do you think people are looking for in your markets? Do you have any concepts of what you always try to give them?

RC: I start with a theory of film that I worked with as a director, and that I continue to work with as both a producer and distributor and also as an occasional writer. And that is: that film is a visual medium. There must be something interesting to see in the film. The film must be conceived from a visual standpoint. Beyond that are our budgets; it must have something that can be exploited or advertised. Something that makes the picture a little different than the others. The one picture I will not make is the run-of-the-mill picture. I want each picture to be a little bit out of the ordinary, hopefully, a great deal out of the ordinary. Beyond that, I like to have a certain social viewpoint within the film itself, even if it's a light comedy, even if it's an exploitation film. I personally am somewhat to the liberal and / or left spectrum in my political thinking, and I want my films to reflect that, both because I want to express something of myself in my film and also because I think it helps the film; I think it gives the film a basis, a grounding from which you can work.

MM: You mentioned that you look for subject matter that can be advertised. Have there been any changes in this area? I once talked to a distributor who claimed he could sell anything with newspaper and TV time. Do you believe that? Do you think any film project can be sold effectively?

RC: Almost, almost. But you can only get them in for the first day or two; after the film has opened, the film itself must deliver. You can pretend that a film will deliver something and get them in for the first couple of days, but word of mouth takes over, and word of mouth is more important than any kind of advertising.

MM: You've given a lot of young directors their start in the business. What do you think you teach them? Now that you look back over some of your protégés winning Academy Awards and whatnot, do you have any conscious thoughts of, "I taught him how to do that, or he learned that from me?"

RC: Well, first let me say that if Francis Coppola wins an Academy Award, or if Peter Bogdanovich or Marty Scorsese or whoever does, it's primarily due to their own abilities. However, I do think I have taught them and other people some things. First, it's the viewpoint of film as a visual medium, and secondarily, it's working in a highly disciplined way. Particularly when you work on low budgets, you must be organized. If you have a ten- or fifteen-day shooting schedule, you must know what you're going to do before you go in, because there is no time to walk on a set of a ten-day picture and try to figure out what you're going to do. If you haven't planned in advance or are not prepared to carry out that plan efficiently, you can't make the picture under a ten- or fifteen-day schedule. But you can become a little less disciplined in this regard when you move up to higher budgets.

Now when I say you have to be disciplined, plan in advance, and carry out the plan, I recognize that you vary the plan. I'm not so rigid as to say that you plan every shot and shoot the film exactly that way. In the first place, we're all a little bit lazy and although we start out trying to plan every shot, I don't know anybody who has actually done it. If you can plan 60, 70, 80 percent of your shots, the rest will fall in line. When you do get on the set, you also must be prepared to shoot a particular scene, or you may find you're running out of time and have to shoot that sequence in one shot rather than three. So, as I say, planning is important, but I don't want to make it seem too rigid.

As a matter of fact, I played one of the senators in *The Godfather II*, and Francis came to my dressing room—this was a big-budget picture; I had a dressing room for this funny little part—and he said, "You will notice there's a lot of wasted time on this picture; it's not the way we used to work." And then what he said was very interesting; he said, "I could save this company a million dollars. I could take over a portion of the production manager's job and organize the company better and save them a million dollars in production, but I'm determined not to do that because, if I do that, it will take my mind away from functioning as a director. If the studio wants to save a million dollars, it's up to them to have their production managers and people work more efficiently, but I'm not going to do it for them. I'm going to think about what I'm doing as a director." And I think in the long run that Coppola's right in doing that.

MM: It seems like most of your protégés do bring their films in at budget.
RC: Yes, the director who's learned under smaller budgets and tight schedules develops an awareness of discipline and organization.

MM: Is it true that you once did seventy-five camera set-ups in one day?
RC: I think it was seventy-three; it's faded in my mind. It was a great day at Iwerson's; a lot of them were horse run-bys and we were shooting some chases, but nevertheless, it was seventy-three set-ups. I used to average forty to fifty set-ups per day.

MM: Do you miss the days when you could make a movie in five days for $60,000?

RC: To a certain extent. It was more fun then, because things were not as crucial. At any rate, when you spend more money, it becomes more important. I used to make films almost for the fun of it, as a joke. *Little Shop of Horrors* was essentially a gag to see if I could do it in two days and a night—and I did.

Filmmaking in Hollywood: The Changing Scene

Roger Corman / 1980

From *American Cinematographer*, August 1980. Reprinted by permission of Roger Corman and *American Cinematographer*.

The following has been excerpted from a luncheon speech delivered by Roger Corman on May 31 at the Thirteenth Annual Motion Picture Seminar of the Northwest, held in Seattle, Washington.

My subject today includes spotting new talent for the motion picture industry, which, to a certain extent, is a matter of being lucky enough to be in the right place at the right time and, on top of that, hopefully exercising some judgment.

I've just arbitrarily divided the subject up into four sections—those that I am the most familiar with and have dealt with most frequently: actors, writers, directors, and producers. However, Cal Bernstein, who spoke a little bit earlier, was talking about various cameramen and I realized that he and I had worked with some of the same cameramen, so I will mention them a bit, too.

Actually, I think there are four top cinematographers who either did their first feature for me or their first American film: Haskell Wexler, John Alonzo, Nestor Almendros, and Laszlo Kovacs. Vilmos Zsigmond and a number of others have worked with us, as well. As to how I chose these cinematographers, I'm not exactly certain. In some cases I looked at their film, but not in all cases. I never saw anything that Johnny Alonzo had done. He just came highly recommended to me. But usually it was a combination of looking at some film and really listening to other people's advice—taking recommendations and then talking with the person. I'm a very firm believer in really sitting down and talking with somebody. In that way you gain a certain insight into the person's ability and his temperament, as well as his willingness to work, particularly in low-budget films. But I feel that in any kind of filmmaking a person has to have not only ability, but also a certain stability, because this is a notoriously unstable field. You also have to be willing to work very, very hard. It's almost as if you had a dedication, in the true religious sense. It's almost a Catholic calling to a vocation, to work in films. Living in Southern California, if we simply wanted money we could all be working in real estate. We could make a lot of money more easily.

Now, breaking my subject down into actors, writers, directors, and producers, let me start with actors. You are on a little bit more solid ground in evaluating actors because you are able to look at film that they may have done previously, or to see them possibly on the stage. Then you can conduct interviews, which can be very misleading, because a person may come in and do very well in a cold reading or in an improvisation and either hang up on the set or be unable to go beyond that on the set.

I work on the basis of holding cold readings for actors when they come in. I explain the part to them a little bit, give them a script so that they can step into another room and look at it for a little while, and then ask them to come back and do the reading. I also work on the basis of improvisation, because you sometimes learn more from an improvisation than you do from a cold reading. All of these methods are imperfect, but they are the two ways in which I've found I could work the best. Plus, just talking with the actor and talking with other actors and other directors. We very seldom use screen tests, which are very good, but on our budgets, if I'm going to put together a crew for a day I'm not going to shoot a screen test; I'm going to shoot a day's work on the film. Beyond that there are intangibles; charisma and, unfortunately, looks for a lead do mean something, although they don't mean as much as they formerly did. We've had some success with the actors and actresses who have started with us.

In selecting writers you are on even more solid ground. We simply read what they have written before, but not necessarily screenplays. As a matter of fact, for our purposes, probably not screenplays, because working in a low-budget field we find that most of the established screenwriters are already beyond our budget limitations, so we must go elsewhere. We will go to film schools and find people who have written scripts or written and directed scripts in the course of their film training, or maybe written a script that has never been produced that we think has merit.

Very often we will go to novelists or short story writers who have been well reviewed. We subscribe to a number of literary journals and we read the reviews quite religiously, particularly of new novelists, new short story writers and a number of our best writers have come from that field. Bob Towne is a writer who won an Academy Award a couple of years ago and started with us and will be directing soon, as well. I might mention a number of the directors we have worked with who have been writers, as well, particularly Francis Coppola, Peter Bogdanovich, and Marty Scorsese. There is a unity between the work of the writer and the director, and the French, I know, refer continually to the auteur theory, although they have been referring to it a little bit less now than they formerly did. To me the true auteur is the writer-director-producer, the Ingmar Bergman, or somebody of that sort who combines all of those elements of the creative function in his hands. Now, as for directors, we have had some of our greatest success with directors such as Coppola, Bogdanovich, Scorsese, and Irv Kershner—I think someone mentioned a picture I had almost forgotten, *Stakeout on Dope Street*. The cameraman on that was Haskell Wexler, doing his first feature film, and the director was Irv Kershner, doing his first feature film.

Having been a director myself, I talk at great length to the director and listen to what he has to say. I look at previous film, particularly student films, more recently sometimes commercials. We have given first opportunities to many directors but we are not doing that quite as much as we have in the past because, like most other production companies, our budgets have risen and when I was making films for $50,000 or $100,000 or $150,000 it was not a difficult gamble to take somebody directly out of film school or somebody like Peter Bogdanovich, who had never even gone to film school, who just was a critic who had worked for me as an assistant and whom I felt was so bright that I could finance him in such a film.

Our films are now inching their way up to half-a-million, a million dollars. *Battle Beyond the Stars* will be close to $5 million, so we have become a little bit more cautious in those areas. As a matter of fact, speaking of *Battle Beyond the Stars*, we chose Jimmy Murakami as the director. He had never directed a feature film before, but was an Academy Award–winning animator and had worked for me as a second unit director and an art director in Ireland a number of years earlier and had been shooting some commercials in Europe. I chose Jimmy as the director of this film for a totally unrelated reason. We knew we were going to be shooting live action that would have to cut into special effects shots that might be shot six months later and, while I much appreciate the type of director who comes onto the set and becomes inspired and says, "I believe the camera should go there" (after an hour or so of deliberation) however, for the particular film I wanted a director who could storyboard the entire film, who could take a close-up of a pilot in a space ship with the camera right in front of him and, at a particular moment, that pilot looks in that direction to match a shot that will be filmed maybe ninety days later of another spaceship coming by. So Jimmy's qualities as an animator and as a director of TV commercials working off of storyboards became very important for that type of work.

As to some of the more intangible attributes of a director, intelligence, I think, is important above all. I have never met in my life a successful director who was not intelligent. Beyond that there is this intangible spark, the creativity, the mark of the poet to go with the intelligence and again, as I say, the dedication to film and the ability to work very hard, because directing pictures is physically very hard work. I think people sometimes forget that.

Speaking now of producers, I might mention that a lot of people are producer-directors, like Coppola, Bogdanovich, and so forth. I might also mention my wife, who has had the most successful production career of anybody I know. She's produced eight films and has had eight consecutive successes. I've had a couple of failures; everybody I know has had a couple of failures, but my wife is truly the only producer I've ever met who never had a failure. She may well support the family if *Battle Beyond the Stars* doesn't do it this summer.

The attributes of the producer, I think, are very, very close to those of the director: The same intelligence, the same ability to work very hard. There are some theories today on right and left brain in which the left brain is possibly a fraction more poetic. The right hemisphere of the brain, if I have these correct, is more logical. I would say the function of the producer and the director are almost the same, or the attributes are almost the same, except that I would say that while the director might lean a little more to the left brain, I would look for a little bit more logic on the part of the producer I was going to hire.

On the other hand, the producer doesn't generally get hired and you can underestimate what the producer does if you see what he is doing on the set, because if he's really done his job he doesn't do much on the set. His work is primarily accomplished before the picture goes into production. Most films start with an idea of a producer and then the decision is made to make that idea into a film. Now, that's the most important decision that will ever be made on the film. So the producer, who must then carry forward on a logical basis, at that moment is functioning on a creative basis, as well. As I say, putting all of this together you find, in general, that you are dealing with intelligent people who have learned the requisite technical skills, who are dedicated to the film medium and who are then willing to work very, very hard. Beyond that I don't know. There is a certain personal feeling I get talking with people and that conversation, or series of conversations, is extremely important because it determines whether or not I think I can work well with them. Somebody might very well be successful with another producer or some other company but might not work well with me because of my own personal ways of functioning and because of the budget limitations of New World. Now this is possibly not as specific as some of you might like it to be, but it's not a specific thing. It's kind of an informed guess—to talk to somebody and say, "Yes, I think you can do this job." That's particularly true when you are dealing with new people who have never done the job before.

Any questions?

Q: How much involvement do you permit a writer who works on one of your pictures?
A: When I work with a writer who is not a director, we try to keep the writer involved as much as possible. There are several recognized stages in the development of a screenplay, according to Writers Guild rules. There's the treatment, the first draft, the second draft, and the polish— and possibly more, but we try to hold it to that level. What I do as a producer is work with the writer through the treatment and the first draft. Then I bring the director in as part of a joint effort that involves the writer, producer, and director. This occurs at the time of the second draft or, at the latest, during the polishing stage, depending upon how well it is going. The director comes in so that he can contribute to the writing process. Then we have a certain amount of rehearsal and if the writer is available we like to have the writer come to the rehearsal and come to the set as much as possible. Then we like to have the writer's opinion of the various cuts of the picture—partially for just his thoughts on the cutting, partially on the basis that we may be looping or changing some lines or, if we are in trouble, maybe reshooting or adding a scene or two. So we try to keep the writer involved as long as the writer is willing to be involved, and most of the writers we've worked with want to stay with the film.

Q: What advice can you offer someone who wants to work in the film industry—preferably as a director?

A: My recommendation for someone who wants to work in the movie industry as a director is that, before coming to Hollywood, you would do best to get some directing experience. The most readily available opportunities for that experience today are in the film schools. Almost every major university has a film school. There are a million different routes, of course, and just as I am saying this there is probably somebody getting off a bus right now in Hollywood who has never done a thing and he's going to win a giant award next year. But from my own experience, I would say that it would be best to go to film school, or if you don't go to film school, to work in documentaries or commercials locally somewhere. You are more likely to get experience if you are from right here in Seattle, or in Minneapolis, if that's where you come from. In that way you build up a body of work. You build up a reel of film that you can show. Then, if you go to Hollywood—fine! But if you do, then my next statement would be to take whatever job is available. It is highly unlikely that you would be offered the job of director of a feature film today, or a TV series, or probably even a commercial, unless you had come with a record of having made commercials for a Hollywood commercial house or a New York commercial house. The main thing, I really think, is to get on the inside. I came out of Stanford with some honors and one thing and another. The only job I could get was as a messenger at Fox and I took it. I wanted to get inside the studio and I think that's the first thing, to get inside the filmmaking process on whatever basis, so that you can learn and so that you can also meet people. One of our brightest young guys advised to go to work as a grip on a picture. He did very well working as a grip on this film and was hired by the key grip on his next picture, so he's working around now. He'll spend about three or four months working as a grip and I've told him I will probably give him a shot as a second assistant director in the fall. Now, when he comes to be a second assistant director he will have invaluable experience, having worked as a grip. It's easy for me to say, as I get a little older, "You guys got to start at the bottom." But it is true. I think there are too many people at the top, whether they are writers, directors, or producers, who have not put in that work in the technical area. Francis Coppola started for me as an assistant editor and as a soundman. A number of others have started as grips and as editors. Several of our best young directors have started as editors.

Q: How deeply involved is your company in TV production?

A: We have not been particularly a TV-oriented company at all. We are doing a movie-of-the-week called *The Georgia Peaches*, which is actually a remake of a film we made as a feature and which we are doing for CBS. It's our first movie-of-the-week, as such. I have no track record in that area at all. All I can say is that our relationships with CBS have been very good. The only constraining factor is that they require a certain number of approvals and, having been the head of my own company for the last ten years and not having had to confer with anybody, it is a change of thought for me, but the experience so far has been good.

Q: Considering the subject matter of some of the low, low-budget, strictly commercial pictures you made when you were starting out, wasn't there a tendency on your part to not take them very seriously, to just dash them off?
A: No. There were directors I knew when I was starting who would take a commercially oriented film and say, "Well, it's just a cheap film. I'm going to knock it off." But most of those guys are not in the business anymore; they're not even directors anymore. Irvin Kershner started in the business with me and worked very, very hard—and he recently directed *The Empire Strikes Back*. At that time, my policy as a working young director was: "I will take almost any assignment offered to me, unless I can see that it is just hopeless." But if there was any spark, anything in the film whatsoever that I thought I could make interesting to myself or to an audience, I took the assignment. I then did my best to make that film, within the limits of budget and schedule, as well as I possibly could. If I could say anything to young directors, the most important thing would be: "Take every frame of film you shoot seriously and do the absolute best job you can. The minute you start talking down to your project, at that point you will have ceased being a director. Figuratively and literally you will not be a director much longer."

Q: How often do you fire a director of photography?
A: I don't. I'm sure somebody will be able to dig up an instance when I did, but I don't remember ever firing a director of photography, although I've come close a couple of times. I may have blocked one out, but to the best of my knowledge, I don't think I ever did. I choose the director of photography—and I touched on this a bit earlier—by looking at his previous work, by talking to the cameraman himself and by talking to the producers and directors (and very often the gaffers and grips) with whom he has worked in the past. In this way I can see an example of

the quality of his work and learn something about the way in which he works. For instance, there are a lot of cameramen who can photograph very rapidly, which is essential for us in low-budget work. However, their quality is not good. There is a slightly larger group of cameramen who can photograph very well, but will take all day to light the set. We are looking for the man who can do good work quickly—and that man is hard to find.

Q: Does your company finance its own film production?
A: A limited amount of financing is easy for us. We've had ten years of a fair amount of success, so we've built up what our accountants refer to as retained earnings. We do plow our retained earnings back. We reinvest our profits. However, we are finding that the low-budget films that we have been successful with three, four, five years ago are increasingly difficult to sell today, so we are moving into more expensive films and for those we must obtain some form of outside financing to go with our own. We are still financing our lower-budget films entirely in-house. Our bigger films involve increasingly some sort of pre-sale or co-production where we might sell out the foreign rights or sell out the TV rights. Today pay TV has become a very good market for us.

Q: Do you think the motion picture industry will weather the current recession in good shape?
A: I think it will. There is a saying that motion pictures are depression-proof, and that has been true to a certain extent, especially during the thirties when movies boomed in a full depression. More recently I've seen a series of graphs which indicate that movies dip a little bit in a recessionary period, but not as much as other aspects of the economy. Certainly not as much as automobiles at this time. So you'll see probably during the current recession a slight drop in the graphs, but the drop in the graphs for motion pictures will not be as heavy as for the economy in general. That will be harmful to the independent producer or director, although I'm sure there will be money available for good projects, as there always is.

Q: In the past few years women have become much more visible and important in the motion picture industry. Do you think that trend will continue?
A: The reason I smile is that I have a story to illustrate that point. I certainly believe that women have been becoming more active in motion

pictures and that the parts for actresses are becoming more important. You are seeing more women writers, directors, and producers. You are actually seeing more women on the crews. We find—and I didn't initiate this, but since I've hired so many women in positions of authority it may be filtering down the line—that we are seeing more women grips, women electricians, women assistant cameramen, and, specifically women editors. We built a studio recently and I changed the design—on the basis of having looked at our crews—to include a bigger women's room. It's happening, folks, so we thought we'd better allow for this in building the studio.

Motion Picture Production Considerations in the 1980s

Roger Corman / 1982

From *American Cinematographer*, April 1982. Reprinted by permission of Roger Corman and *American Cinematographer*.

What follows has been excerpted from the remarks of producer / director Roger Corman made during the symposium which he conducted at the Manila International Film Festival on the subject of "Motion Picture Production Considerations in the 1980s." Since Mr. Corman has effected several successful co-productions in the Philippines, and since his audience was composed largely of local filmmakers keenly interested in possible co-productions with foreign producers, his talk was heavily slanted in that direction.

For me, production starts right at the beginning. It is part of the creative process. For any method of motion picture production to be efficient, the aspects of the physical producing must be integrally tied into the financing, the screenwriting, the casting, and all of the other aspects of the making of the film.

One of the things I've seen go wrong on a number of films occurs when the producer has a certain set amount of financing available, and then, while he is working with the writer and the director, concepts come up that from the beginning could never have been done on that budget. This has given rise to a number of famous pictures over the last couple of years where, logically, the producer or production manager going in knew that the film could not be made for the agreed-upon budget. But the film was started anyway, with the kind of vague hope or faith that a miracle would take place. Sometimes a miracle does take place during shooting, but not very often.

I'm a strong, strong believer in pre-production planning. If there's anything I can contribute to your work based upon mine, it is that the most important aspect in making a film takes place before the camera rolls. The producer and the director must see eye-to-eye. This is essential. They must know the type of film they are going to make. They must be in agreement as to just how it is to be made, what the themes are, what the concepts are, even going so far as to know what the shooting style is. Such understandings are crucial for the producer and the director, whom I consider to be the most important people connected with the production of a film—not to negate the work of the writer, the actors, the cinematographer, and the other people involved—but it is the producer and the director who start from the beginning, to employ the services of the writer, to develop the script, then to cast it and go into pre-production planning.

As I say, I believe it is the pre-production planning that is the most important aspect of filmmaking. Based upon my own experience, I can tell you that my most successful films have been those that were made when I've been completely prepared gong in. I've got a pretty good track record, but I have had some failures, and almost every time I have made a film that has not done well, I can look back in the pre-production phase and say that I wasn't quite ready. I should have waited a few more weeks, another month, maybe even another couple of months to completely develop my project before I shot. Pre-planning is the essence of production.

As to the financing, you get into a number of things I can touch on, particularly in the area of co-production, which may be of interest to some of you, and which is an increasingly vital part of the filmmaking process. As the cost of making films soars higher and higher, it becomes more and more expedient for producers from different countries to combine their resources—to make bigger films, with each one of them contributing. I can give you some examples of the way I've worked here in Manila with Cirio Santiago, and the way I've worked in Europe and South America and in other parts of the world with other producers on a co-production basis.

My method is generally to start with the script. I develop the script myself, and usually, here in Manila, I will put up the script, the director, certain American actors, and a certain amount of money. The "below-the-line," or physical aspects of the production, are put up by, in this case, the Filipino producer.

The key to success here is pre-planning. I've seen a number of international co-productions fail because, in the planning stages, the film was created without anybody being quite certain about how it happened. An attempt was made, for example, to develop a script that would appeal to the American market, yet, at the same time appeal to the Southeast Asian market. But the finished picture didn't hit either market. Somewhere something got lost, and the result was a film that wasn't quite right for the American market, nor was it quite right for the Southeast Asian market.

The key to avoiding such a situation must be for each producer to understand what he needs within the production and make certain that the overall film fits into his particular market. For example, on several of the films we have done here in Manila, we have shot several additional scenes that might be used only in the Asian version of the film and other scenes that might be used only in the American version.

While the majority of scenes in the picture might be the same for both versions—let's say that in a one-hundred-minute film there might be a commonality of eighty to ninety minutes—there might also be ten to twenty minutes of differing interpretations of scenes, recognizing cultural differences in the respective countries. At other times we have been able to make a film which, in our opinion, would play exactly right for both markets with none of the scenes being different. So there are no set rules.

To illustrate that point, as I talk here I am telling you all the things I do the way I've been doing them for many years. And yet it's possible that I might walk out of here immediately afterwards, sit down with a producer to set up a co-production and do it in a different way, throwing out everything I'm telling you at the moment.

The main thing is to understand certain aspects of production and then be flexible—ready to vary the procedure when necessary. For instance—coming back to the physical production—when I talk about the importance of pre-production, it means knowing every possible aspect of the film, even down to the point of having the director sketch the majority of his shots. Obviously, certain things must be decided before you shoot. Your script is established. You have set your crew. You have worked out the details of your locations—or of your sets, if you are going to be shooting in the studio—or a combination thereof. You've worked out down to the last detail the props, wardrobe, set dressings—all of these elements. Music must be considered before you shoot the film, not as an afterthought.

When all of this has been done and you are ready to shoot, you must then realize that something happens during the shooting of the film. A film grows organically unto itself and you start to vary a little bit—and that's fine. If you have your framework well worked out and the director and the actors get ideas on the set, you should not be afraid to depart slightly from your agreed-upon program to take advantage of those ideas and situations that come up.

Where you can get into trouble is to function according to one of two extremes. One extreme is to stay so rigid to your pre-production planning that you strait-jacket the creative energies during shooting. You must be flexible enough to let new ideas come from shooting. The other danger is to be so open to those new ideas that the original idea gets lost. I've seen very good projects take such a different shape during shooting that the final shape varies too much from the original planning. So the main thing is to follow your planning, but be flexible enough to allow for slight variations and to take advantage of those moments of improvisation on the set—or those unexpected problems that sometimes make your pre-planning impossible to follow.

There is a classic situation in shooting low-budget films when you are on location and you know that you have to leave the location that day because you must be on another location. The sun is going behind the mountain in ten minutes and you have three more shots to get. The director had better be very fast and resourceful at a time like that. There are a number of things he could do, one of which might be moving the camera instead of making three separate set-ups. Hopefully such a thing won't happen, but it can occasionally happen and you must be prepared and flexible enough to deal with it.

I might mention one other thing in regard to co-productions. It is a technical thing, rather than a creative element, but recognizing it can save a lot of arguments later on, besides enabling you to make other films. There are various ways—and this really is part of the production process—of deciding in advance what will happen to the film after it has been completed. I believe that filmmaking starts at the very beginning of planning and continues until the picture is in the theater, or on television, or on a cassette. It is a mistake for the filmmaker to say: "I will just concern myself with this one narrow (production) aspect of the picture." I think you must follow your film from the beginning through to the end—and the end means being aware of the way in which the film is going to be distributed throughout the world.

One way is for the producers to pool their resources and agree that they will each take a certain percentage of the entire world market. Another way is for each producer to say, "I will take 100 percent of my own individual territory. For example, in Manila you might say to a Filipino producer, "You will get all of Asia." The American producer will possibly get all of the Western hemisphere, with some other division taking place as to the rest of the world.

This, too, is part of production planning—and it should be planned. It should be decided upon in advance as thoroughly as possible.

Roger Corman: Better to Be on the Set than in the Office

David Del Valle / 1984

From *Films and Filming*, November 1984, 15–20. Reprinted by permission of David Del Valle, Del Valle Archives.

David Del Valle: What was the concept of the Poe series? Did you initially just plan to make one film with *The House of Usher*, or did you see it as a series at the time?

Roger Corman: My original thought was simply to make *The Fall of the House of Usher*. I had been a great admirer of Poe since I'd been in school, and I'd always wanted to make that particular film and at that time I was making a series of low-budget pictures, generally black and white, on ten-day schedules, for about $100,000 or less for AIP (American International Pictures). Their policy at the time was to release two of these pictures together as a double-bill, two science fiction pictures, two horror pictures, whatever, sometimes two gangster films. They wanted me to do it again, and I felt we had been repeating ourselves too much, so I said "Instead of doing two black and white horror films for $100,000 each, let me do one fifteen-day color film for $200,000"—and it eventually became $250,000—and they agreed to do that, and that's how *The Fall of the House of Usher* was made.

DDV: Did you decide on Vincent Price from the outset?

RC: No. My original thought simply was to *The Fall of the House of Usher*. Once we had the script, I had several meetings with Jim Nicholson. We discussed a number of actors and we felt that Vincent Price would be the best; he was our first choice, the first man to whom we sent the script, and he accepted.

DDV: Was Daniel Haller the art director on that?
RC: Yes.

DDV: He did an incredible job, because the film has the look of a more expensive film. What was it like when that film first opened, and you started getting what for AIP must have been unusual critical attention.
RC: It was exciting. It truly was a wonderful moment. It was one of those rare films where we had both the critical acclaim and the box-office success, so we could kind of sit back and see it coming from all directions.

DDV: Sam Arkoff tells me that he was a bit reluctant at first to do a film that didn't have a monster in it, but legend has it you told him that the house would suffice.
RC: Right. The house would be the monster.

DDV: Did he go for that?
RC: He did. He knew—but Sam is very bright, I mean, you don't really put anything over on Sam. He knew that I was slightly conning him when I said that, but he also knew that it was kind of correct. Psychologically, or subtextually, the house is the monster, so it could be considered to be a correct statement.

DDV: How soon after *The Fall of the House of Usher* did you decide to make another Poe film?
RC: Very quickly. The film came out, it did well, I had a continuing relationship with AIP—I'd done a number of films with them—and Sam and Jim and I were having lunch and we simply decided over this lunch to do the next one and I suggested *The Pit and the Pendulum*. I had two choices. It was really interesting, because they asked me what I thought for the second one and I said, "Either *The Pit and the Pendulum* or *Masque of the Red Death*," and I think it was Jim who chose *The Pit and the Pendulum* or a joint choice at any rate. Each picture afterward, they would say, "What do you think?" and each time I would give them two choices, and one of them would be *Masque of the Red Death* and we kept staying away from it and staying away from it until late in the cycle, we finally did do it.

DDV: Did you have a hand in the script at the point that you did *The Pit and the Pendulum*?
RC: Yes, always.

DDV: So a script would be submitted to you, and then you would—
RC: No, it would come earlier than that. I would meet with Dick Matheson before doing the script, and we would discuss it. But when he did the script, I would leave him alone. In other words, he and I would have a discussion as to what we were looking for, and then he would do the script, totally on his own. I would get a first draft, we would discuss it, then second draft and so forth.

DDV: How did you meet Dick Matheson?
RC: Through Jim Nicholson. Dick was originally assigned by Jim to do *The Fall of the House of Usher*. Jim had read several of his other works. I had seen several pictures he had written, and knew some of his works in the fantasy field as a short story writer and novelist.

DDV: Did you make a conscious decision to introduce humor into the Poe films?
RC: It was a gradually developing thing and I've forgotten whose idea—it may have been Dick's—it was to work on it. Vincent was able to bring a great civilized and genteel air of horror with just a touch of humor that we began to play on a little bit more in each picture. There was little suggestions of it creeping in and I think it started with *Tales of Terror*, where one of them, and I think this was Dick's idea, *The Black Cat*, to do full-out as a comedy, and then from that, we did *The Raven*, where the entire picture was a comedy-horror film. The idea was that it would be sold—all of the films were sold as horror films, but increasing comedy crept into them, maybe because we enjoyed it and it added interest, and also it was a way to vary the series, because towards the end, I was beginning to feel that we were repeating ourselves, and going to comedy on *Masque of the Red Death*, then going to a full love story on *Tomb of Ligeia* were ways to vary the cycle so that you were not always doing the same thing.

DDV: When *The Pit and the Pendulum* was finished, did you then decide that it was going to be a series?
RC: It was never decided to do a series, because each time we said, "All right, we will do one more" until it became unwittingly, a series. Finally I said that I didn't want to do any more. I had done—I've forgotten—six or seven of them or something like that, and I said, "I've really done about all I can do; the shots are beginning to look very similar."

DDV: You couldn't face burning that house down again?

RC: Right! As a matter of fact, I did another horror film, *The Terror* with Boris Karloff in which we flooded the house. We flooded the house with a dam burst or something, and the water came through and drowned everybody and I did it only because I was so tired of burning the house down. I said, "What is the opposite of destroying a house by fire? It must be destroying a house by water. We're going to flood this place."

DDV: Did it amuse you that you were developing this cult following at the time?

RC: At the beginning, it did amuse me, but then you get used to it and you say, "Well, this is the way it should be."

DDV: After *The Pit and the Pendulum*, you did *Tales of Terror*, and that was the first one to use three different stories within a framework like an anthology. Now that was kind of a trend-setter too, because they started making them that way in England in color, those horror package, Amicus Films and so forth. *Tales of Terror* didn't do so well at box office. At that point did you think about not doing another one?

RC: Well, they were all successful, so when you say it didn't do so well in terms that the profit was less; in other words, the profit had dropped. I think, and this was a number of years ago and anything I say I might remember incorrectly—I've had interviews where I've actually forgotten the pictures. They'll say, "Do you remember so-and-so in this scene of this picture" and I'm thinking, "Did I make that picture; I don't remember" but I'll remember as closely as I can. I think this is correct. *Tales of Terror* did well, but not as well as the others and we felt it was because we had gone to the trilogy format. We did a little bit of research and we found in general, the multi-part films had not been a successful genre. Audiences did not want to see multi-part films, and particularly now in the age of television, when in those days, most television series were half-hour rather than an hour, they felt what they were seeing maybe, I don't know, were three half-hour television shows.

DDV: Were you shooting these films in fifteen days?

RC: Yes.

DDV: Including *Tales of Terror*?

RC: Yes, they were all fifteen. Except in England. The two English pictures were twenty-five days, we went from three weeks to five weeks, but

I wouldn't say in American terms, they were really twenty-five days, because the English crews did work a little slower.

DDV: Yes, they're notorious, aren't they?

RC: And I would say their twenty-five days were probably equivalent to maybe eighteen or nineteen or twenty of an American crew, so they were effectively a longer picture than the fifteen-day pictures in the United States, but not that much longer.

DDV: What was your first meeting with Peter Lorre like?

RC: It was great. I must say Peter Lorre is—was—one of the funniest people you will ever meet to talk with, and highly intelligent and very well-educated, so you're talking with a man who'd come up with great ideas for a full-out farce, and at the same time justify it intellectually and thematically in terms of Poe. It was just great. It was immensely stimulating working with him.

DDV: Which horror films influenced your work?

RC: I don't know. My favorite directors at the time had some features that might have lent themselves to horror films, particularly Bergman, *The Seventh Seal* comes like that. There was a mood that he created that could have been, had he wanted, moved in one direction towards horror. He didn't; he moved in a different direction. But Bergman, Eisenstein, and of course Hitchcock who did a kind of suspense-horror film, so in that field, those probably were the ones I liked the best.

DDV: I would think *Rebecca* would lend itself to the feel of the Poe films.

RC: Yes, very much so.

DDV: What was it like working with Vincent Price, Boris Karloff, and Peter Lorre?

RC: It was very interesting working with the three of them. First they were all good actors, and they were all simply good people to be around. That was one of the good things about the Poe pictures. There was a great spirit on the set that extended from the actors to the crew. Everybody was interested, because we were creating. The crew had opportunities to do things they would not normally do. The prop men would come up with ideas on the set, the special effects men were great at spinning webs and we gave them a lot of webs to spin, and they'd come up with ideas, and so there was a good spirit all around and the fact that these three

men were really such devils, I mean such good actors and such dedicated, hard-working actors, lent itself to a kind of a group enterprise. As to
how the three of them worked, which I think was the original question,
it was very interesting to me. Vincent Price was more the type of actor I
had traditionally worked with, which was a man who came in, fully prepared, who understood some of the method acting, which was the way I
had been trained, yet at the same time was able to improvise, was able to
work on a sub-textual level, and at the same time was fully prepared from
the script to understand the script and deliver the lines, and prepared to
be flexible and make those inevitable changes that occur on a set, sometimes because you have a better idea, and you can do it better, sometimes
simply because what's in the script for one reason or another does not
work and you must do it differently, so Vincent was that way. Peter Lorre
came in, really generally not knowing the lines. But he had a vague idea
of what the lines were, but he was so fast and so inventive as we would
rehearse, he would come up with just wonderful things. I would try to
integrate them into the script. I'd say, "That's great, Peter. Now let me
see, we'll do this and work it around" and it became very stimulating to
me to work from the script, work with Peter, and Vincent entered that
too, because Vincent was working from the text and trying to integrate
all this and come up with ideas of his own. Boris Karloff, a very fine actor, was more trained in an English tradition and really came in prepared
to do that script, line for line. It was a little bit more difficult for Boris
to adjust to the way in which Peter worked, and so we had, to a certain
extent, the kind of disciplined English actor, who came in knowing the
lines and knew the performance he was going to give, such as Boris, then
Peter, who has come in ready to create and is willing to be all over the
stage while he does it, and then the middle man, the man who would be
closest to my method of working, which would be Vincent, who comes
in knowing the script, prepared to do it, but who is also prepared to be
flexible and to see what we can do to improvise and play around with
the script. As a result, there were great times. Boris tried; I don't mean to
say that in any way he was rigid or didn't want to work that way, but he
simply had been trained in a different manner.

DDV: Well, he had been in retirement, hadn't he?
RC: Semi-retirement. He had been ill and he worked, but did not work
much.

DDV: I always felt that *Premature Burial* never really got the attention it
deserved. Why wasn't Vincent Price in that one?

RC: Ah, it started off being done for a different company. I have forgotten exactly how these things happen and there were some contractual points of difference.

DDV: Was it something to do with your contract?

RC: It was my contract, yes in conjunction with Pathé. Now they were always my company in conjunction or partnership with AIP, and there was some, as will happen, some discussion as to exactly how profits were to have been allocated on some previous films, at which point I moved slightly away from AIP and started *Premature Burial* with Ray Milland for Pathé. Vincent, I believe, actually at that time had an exclusive contract with AIP, so I made the contract with Ray and I remember while this was going on, Sam Arkoff, as I said earlier, it was very difficult to move around Sam, had been talking with Pathé, which was primarily a laboratory that wanted to get into a distribution company and on the first day of shooting, Sam and Jim Nicholson showed up on the set. Well, I thought, "This is very nice, since we've had a little bit of an argument, they're here to wish me well," which I really had not anticipated in any way, and they came over and shook my hand and let me know that we were all partners together again, that they had bought out Pathé and instead of my being in partnership with Pathé, I was in partnership with AIP once again. It was all right with me, because we then settled all our previous difficulties and kept on going again.

DDV: How did you come to cast Jack Nicholson in *The Raven*?

RC: He was a friend and he was a good actor, whom I'd known for a number of years and who had done a number of films for me, and I always thought that Jack was a good actor and did have great potential. Actually, about that time, I began to wonder a little bit that I was the only guy around who was hiring him, and I thought, you know, either everybody else is right or I am but it cannot be both.

DDV: He always lent himself to costume, I think.

RC: Well, he's somewhat of a contemporary actor. However, he was very good, knowing that he has contemporary quality. I always liked what he did in *The Raven* and he was very good with Peter. And Peter played it very well, because Peter immediately decided that he was going to be ashamed of his son. He was going to be terribly ashamed of Jack, at which point Jack and I discussed this and that together and decided that Jack's motivation would be that if Peter was going to try to disown his son and didn't want to have anything to do with him because he was such an obvious fumbler that Jack's motivation would be to win the approval of his father and the scenes took on—and this is not in the script, there may have been one or two lines but not really this—a great added dimension as we played them, as Jack was essentially saying, "Father, I will do anything for you," and Peter was saying, "You idiot, you get away from me here," and it really played very well.

DDV: Hazel Court told me you ordered her from the set one day because she was breaking up so much. She said it wasn't like going to work at all. She said, "We all had very early hours; we were there quite early in the morning and sometimes quite late at night and everyone was trying to keep Boris's health in mind," but she said there would be times when Vincent would be about to give her a line and then he'd pull a parrot out of his cloak or something. She said it was impossible. She said, "Roger just one day said, 'Get out, go away, you're of no use to me' because—" And there's actually a scene in *The Raven* where she is just visibly cracking up.
RC: On the edge.

DDV: On the edge, teetering on the brink.
RC: But Hazel was very good.

DDV: Was there ever a chance that Peter Cushing or Christopher Lee would have gotten into the Poe series?
RC: I had talked to Christopher Lee at one time, but we really had become identified with Vincent Price, so specifically at that point except for the one which we did with Ray Milland.

DDV: He would have been quite interesting in a couple of them. I don't think you could have done comedies with him at that point in his career.
RC: Christopher is a good actor and he has moved away from horror things. He wants to broaden his image and apparently he's done it successfully.

DDV: Along with *The Raven* and *Premature Burial*, you also did a very bizarre movie called *The Haunted Palace*, which is far more H. P. Lovecraft than Poe. How did that come about?
RC: That actually started because we wanted to do another one, and this was late in the series, when I was saying that I'm beginning to repeat and so forth. I just said that I didn't want to do a Poe film and Jim Nicholson

and I both liked the work of Lovecraft, who I think is very, very good. For me, Poe is fractionally more interesting, and a more complex writer, but I think Lovecraft is very good in that field and so we decided to do a Lovecraft film, and then I don't remember exactly how this happened—it's all very weird—Somewhere late in the game, Jim felt that somehow we should combine the Lovecraft story with Poe, but the script had already been written. I made some gestures towards bringing some Poe into it so that it could be sold, I think, as Poe and Lovecraft, but it was really primarily Lovecraft and it was slightly misleading advertising.

DDV: It's an interesting film though.

RC: I think it was the first film in which I used zoom lenses. They had recently been developed and they were much slower than the normal fixed lens, and as a result you simply needed more light; you had to pour in the light on the set in order to reach an intensity that a zoom lens could photograph. It's possible with all the lights crowded in closer really to heat up the set for the zoom lenses.

DDV: When you were shooting these films, did you kind of edit as you went along?

RC: I always did as much as possible. I don't know exactly how you'd use the phrase "edit as you go along" but I always planned my work very carefully. I was always about to have every shot worked out before I started. I was never quite able to get to that level, but I would generally have at least two-thirds to three-fourths of the shots sketched in my script before I started the film, so I felt secure that I had the basic scenes planned leaving some room for improvisation within that, and that brought me to a semi-editing position, because if you're going to do that much planning, you really are editing in front.

DDV: I have got some stills from *Tales of Terror*, showing Valdemar in Hades. That isn't in the film.

RC: Right, we had that sequence taken out. It didn't work. I don't remember why. I shot it, I put it together and for whatever reason I made the decision to take it out. It was a shot sequence; it was not a long sequence. I was just dissatisfied with it and I don't even remember why.

DDV: Did you have any other instances where sequences were done that were not included in any of the films?

RC: Well, there would always be, like, brief moments of scenes or sometimes occasionally there would be one whole dialogue scene that ran two or three pages. That was the only time I remember actually a whole sequence. But even then, the sequence was no more than four or five minutes and it may have been for this reason. These pictures really were rather low-budget films. We tried to make them look more expensive than they were, but they really were quite low-budget. And I think when I really looked at the Hades sequence, for five minutes I felt that it, you know, it really didn't look right. I felt it didn't fit in the mold.

DDV: When did you decide to shoot *Masque of the Red Death* in England?
RC: That decision was made by Jim and Sam. The films had been quite successful in England. They had a co-production deal with Anglo Amalgamated, who were the distributors in England, and Anglo suggested that we go there, and as I said, *Masque of the Red Death* had been one I had wanted to do for a long time, but it was really a little bit bigger than what we had been doing and required simply more money and more time and therefore *Masque of the Red Death* became a logical film to do as the first one in England, where we were going to be given five weeks. I did not realize that five weeks was not really that great an amount of time.

DDV: Was Nicholas Roeg brought in as part of the English package?
RC: Yes. I had approval on all of that, so they suggested him as the cameraman and I talked with him and saw some of his work and I said, "Fine." He's a good guy and I liked the quality of his work, so there was no problem.

DDV: The sequence with Hazel Court when she said, "I just gave myself up" and apparently she was completely nude in that sequence, or at least she appeared to be and the British censors were kind of strict about that. Did all of the Poe films get X ratings?
RC: In England? I'm not certain.

DDV: I think that all horror films were given an X over there.
RC: Very possibly. There was no actual nudity in any of them. It was a different age. With Hazel, I think she was nude under a diaphanous gown and they probably felt that there was too much showing through. Today that would play six o'clock television and nobody would worry in any way.

DDV: *The Tomb of Ligeia* is my personal favorite, except for *The Pit* which is a lot of fun to watch. What is it about?

RC: All right. Now, it became extremely complex at the end. As a matter of fact, I remember I had written into the back of my script a little chart of the changes, and I hate to say I don't remember exactly but there was a concept where—was her name Rowena?—would lose possession of her body and the Lady Ligeia would return to take possession, then Rowena would regain possession of her body. So it was a tale of Ligeia coming from the grave, to reclaim her previous life and her husband through the current wife. And what became very complex was the rapidity and method in which Ligeia would return to take over the body of Rowena. I remember I actually had to have a chart that I wrote down one night as I was in the middle of one scene. I said, "Exactly where are we?" And I had to stop for a minute and look back at the script to rechart what was going on.

DDV: Was it ever going to be called *The House at the End of the World*?
RC: It was always *Ligeia* because that was the title of the Poe story.

DDV: Now Daniel Haller did do the art direction on that, or at least he told me he was there.
RC: He was there. Although we had to have an English art director on both pictures, Dan was with me on both films. He stayed, as a matter of fact he and his wife had a flat and I stayed with them, in Knightsbridge when we did *Masque of the Red Death* and it was a great camaraderie on the set which came home to our flat. On *The Tomb of Ligeia*, Dan did not stay for the whole film. He came over for a few weeks and did the sketches and preparatory work, and by that time, I had already worked in England once and we were able to trust work, then the carrying out of the work, to the English art director.

DDV: Were you aware, when you were shooting *Ligeia*, that that was going to be the last Poe film, or was there ever talk of another one?
RC: Yes, they wanted me to do another one, and I felt when I was doing *Ligeia* that this would be the last one, although I wasn't certain, because I'd felt that on a couple of the previous ones, that I was just wearing out on this series. I just decided, after it was over, that I did not want to do any more, and they had all been profitable, so they wanted to do more, so they simply stopped them for a year, figuring I would change my mind and I said, because I had other things to do. We talked again a year later and I really still did not want to do any more. I felt I had done all I wanted to do or could do with that genre at that time. So they did a couple more Poe films with other directors.

DDV: When you did *Ligeia*, I have always been impressed with the way you got a particular kind of performance out of Vincent which is not, as I well know, easy to do sometimes. Did you have talks with him about the fact that you really wanted a straightforward kind of performance?

RC: Of course. Obviously, as an actor and a director do when working, we discussed the roles in some detail. In that one, just as in *The Raven*, where I was moving to make it part horror, part comedy, in this one I was moving to make it part horror, part love story, really. We discussed and we were in arrangement on that so that it would come out that he was playing a leading man, where you would not say he had actually been a classical leading man in the other films.

DDV: In these films—he told me—I've known Vincent about ten years, but I've never discussed the Poe films with him, except in bits and pieces, and he told me one day that the thing he liked about *Ligeia* was that he got to take off the facial hair. He said, "I looked in the mirror and Vincent Price doesn't look back." It was such a feeling of achievement. He said, "With Roger, he was always pleased that I brought little bits of makeup and ideas to the character," Roderick Usher being his favorite.

RC: That was great, because what we did with the hair was wonderful.

DDV: Well, he looked like a death's head, and you always manage—your opening shot of him was always being thrust through a door or something and I often told him that these films would be referred to as his Late Wife movies, because you can bet your money that if he's in it, his wife, if she isn't already dead, she's well on her way.

RC: Right.

DDV: Finally, how did you come to make *The Terror*?

RC: What happened with *The Terror* was I shot the basic picture *The Terror* in two days, on sets that were left over from *The Raven*. Anyway, they were sets left over from one of the Poe pictures—I think it was *The Raven* as a matter of fact—and they were sitting up at the studio and I never had a script for *The Terror*. Actually, it all happened—*The Terror* would never have been made had it not rained on a Sunday. I had planned to play tennis on this Sunday and it rained and I was sitting around the house and I thought "You know, all those great sets are going to be torn down in a week. What I should do is go out and get a script or develop a script—"And I called Leo Gordon, who was a friend of mine and a writer and also an actor, and I said, "I've got an idea for a horror film. What I really need—and I have to shoot it in the week—" This was on a Sunday, and we were going to finish in five days. I called the head of the studio and asked, "Could I have the set for two days of the next week" and he said, "Sure" and I made a deal. All of the lights were up, it was lit, the set decorations, the props, everything was there and I just walked in and shot it!

Cautionary Fables:
An Interview with Roger Corman

Ed Naha / 1984

From Danny Peary, ed., *Omni's Screen Flights / Screen Fantasies: The Future According to Science Fiction Cinema* (New York: Doubleday, 1984). Reprinted by permission of Ed Naha.

Ed Naha: You first dabbled in futuristic fiction in the mid-fifties, beginning with your fourth film as director, *The Day the World Ended* (1955). This was a cautionary film about the aftermath of nuclear war. Were you first attracted to the science fiction genre because you felt it would allow you the opportunity to say something meaningful to movie audiences?

Roger Corman: I think I was trying to find an area of film that interested me and where, within the contexts of the action movie, I could possibly portray some of my ideas concerning the future. I had always been interested in science fiction—when growing up, I had been an avid reader of science fiction literature and had, of course, seen many science fiction films over the years. I found the science fiction genre intriguing to me as a filmmaker in several ways. First, it's an unlimited breeding ground for imagination and ideas. You can let your innermost beliefs and desires run more freely in science fiction films than you can in the somewhat limited structure offered by "realistic" pictures. Also, you can use the film medium in wilder ways. For instance, you certainly can experiment with special effects. So it's a freer type of film, visually and intellectually.

EN: Was there anything you wanted to "say" in your early science fiction films?

RC: There was no *one* specific thing that I tried to get across in my science fiction films. But ideas were important.

130

EN: In movies such as *The Day the World Ended* and *Teenage Caveman* (1958), you were restricted by pretty tight low-budget exploitation movie formulas. Did you find that confining in terms of editorializing?

RC: To a certain extent, but not completely. In *The Day the World Ended*, I was locked into a story that American International Pictures assigned to me about a post-nuclear world filled with radiation and mutants. I did some work on it, and I think we managed to make a pretty scary movie that included a few thought-provoking situations.

Now, *Teenage Caveman* was a different story entirely. By the way, I never *made* a movie called *Teenage Caveman*. The movie I shot was called *Prehistoric World*. AIP re-titled it for awhile, but, thank goodness, they went back to the original title shortly thereafter.

Prehistoric World was an example of my being able to work within the low-budget formula and improve upon it by using a little imagination. All American International wanted to do was film a prehistoric picture. So they said, "Make a prehistoric picture for $80,000 in ten days."

Bob Campbell, my writer, and I came up with the idea of taking the prehistoric storyline and laying it in the future after civilization had been destroyed by nuclear war. We created a religion for the cave dwellers that was based around the remnants of their previous world, our contemporary world. We placed those remnants in a radioactive area, which became a forbidden zone to these tribesmen.

What I like about *Prehistoric World* is that, for nearly the entire picture, you really think you're watching a nice little prehistoric movie about superstitious elders and a rebellious teenage warrior (Robert Vaughn) . . . until the last few minutes. It has an ending that is very similar to the one that was used years later in *Planet of the Apes* (1968).

I enjoyed the movie a lot more than *The Day the World Ended*. This was partially because the ideas in it were mine, but also because there were *more* ideas in it.

EN: What about *The Last Woman on Earth* (1961)?

RC: Basically, it was the story of the last three survivors on Earth following a nuclear war: two men (Antony Carbone and Edward Wain, actually writer Robert Towne) and a woman (Betsy Jones-Moreland). Of course, a three-sided romance evolves and, of course, it does not make for a happy existence.

The Last Woman on Earth was an offbeat little movie. I produced it for my own company, so I had total control over it. But it was never really what it could have been. We really tried to do something thought-provoking, but we were pretty much done in our small budget. We were shooting it back to back with another film, and we were so rushed that we never actually had a finished script during production. The script was written as we filmed. We got pages every day. We never knew on any given day exactly what we were going to film. We finished the whole movie in two weeks. Still, we tried our best.

My writer was Robert Towne (who later did the screenplay for *China-town*). We tried to depict the aftermath of an atomic war in a realistic way. I was, and still am, very much interested in the concept of nuclear holocaust. I think the possibility for it happening is there. Personally, I don't think it's going to occur, but I think that, through film, we should keep on cautioning and warning people that it *might.*

EN: What moved you to portray an almost existential future in the movie *Gas-s-s* (1970), a film that combined elements of the 1960s youth culture with germ warfare, the ghost of Edgar Allan Poe, and motorcycle gangs?
RC: *Gas-s-s* was a pretty personal statement. This was made towards the end of the great counter-culture cycle of the late 1960s. I had been something of a supporter of the youth culture, although I certainly was past my youth at the time. I had geared a few of my movies, such as *The Wild Angels* (1966) and *The Trip* (1967), toward a sympathetic portrayal of the counter-culture.

In *Gas-s-s,* it was apparent that I was beginning to get a little disillusioned. I intended that the picture be sympathetic toward our lead gang of kids yet, at the same time, I wanted to show that I was beginning to suspect that all of the ideas being spouted by the counter-culture and all of the dreams were not totally rooted in reality. In the picture, I wanted to literally *give* youth the world they desired and, then, make a cautionary statement about how youth might not be able to handle it as perfectly as they anticipated.

In the film, a cask of experimental nerve gas ruptures, and fumes spread into the atmosphere. Everyone over the age of twenty-five dies, and, suddenly, the world is run by kids. Nobody knows what to do. Once I established that premise, I got pretty wild. I had Poe, Martin Luther King, Che Guevara, and even God in the movie. After I had finished it, however, American International Pictures took it and recut it. They were a little nervous about this vision of the future and trimmed the movie pretty heavily. One of my biggest disappointments was that they cut God out of the picture. He had all the best lines.

EN: Were you more optimistic about the future then?

RC: I was most optimistic about the future during the mid-1960s. By the late 1960s, I was beginning to ease off a little. The transition for me happened about 1969–1970. I don't think I've become pessimistic since then. I've pretty much stayed on an even keel. I'm hopeful about the future but I'm not starry-eyed about it.

EN: Do you try to portray the future in terms of technology or with a more humanistic slate?

RC: I don't think you can separate the two. They interrelate. I think it's a mistake to say there is the technological world and there's the human one. They work together. They have to, don't they?

EN: What elements are necessary to interest you in a science fiction film you'd consider producing?

RC: The main idea must be interesting. Hopefully, it will be meaningful as well. Secondarily, I am concerned whether or not that idea can be told in an imaginative *visual* manner. I used to hate going to see a science fiction film and watch scene after scene of two scientists talking to one another.

EN: Do you see room for humor in futuristic editorializing?

RC: Definitely. But humor is a very tricky business. The humor in *Battle Beyond the Stars* (1980) is a good example of how I like to treat humor in science fiction. That film had a serious story, but had humorous undertones running through it. The humor was always there to underscore a statement, to further a point.

Before you can try anything else your story has to be accepted as being realistic. The comedy can then be introduced to reinforce the plot. Unfortunately, many directors can't handle drama and comedy simultaneously. We had problems making that movie because there is always the tendency, when confronted with both drama and comedy, to go for the comedy. Not only that, but to go for the comedy in a broad way. It's fun to do. It's easy to do. But . . . it also undermines the story.

EN: Are you frustrated now, as a producer, by budgetary constraints that keep you from realizing the sprawling futures seen in, let's say, the *Star Wars* films?

RC: Yes. That's a major frustration. In one paragraph, a writer can demand $50 million worth of production costs and there's nothing you can do about it, except, perhaps, weep openly. Budgetarily, you just can't film it. If you're creative, you find ways to *suggest* it but it gets very trying when you have to do that more than a few times during a picture.

Not even George Lucas's money can match the imagination that was seen in the pulp science fiction of the 1930s and 1940s: you would need an infinite budget to get all that on the screen.

EN: Why do you think it's respectable to make a science fiction film now when back in the days when you were directing, it was considered no more than an exercise in Saturday matinee mayhem?

RC: It's quite a legitimate genre today for several reasons. I think science fiction, as literature, is a lot more accepted today because the kids who used to read it are now adults and they *still* read it. It's been around longer so it's become more respectable. Plus, there are new generations of readers who are not ashamed to be seen carrying science fiction books around. Science fiction literature has a much broader base of appeal today. There are more science fiction books and magazines being published today, hence, more readers.

At the same time, I think people started seeing the advantages of editorializing through science fiction films in the 1960s and 1970s. Movies like *Planet of the Apes*, *The Andromeda Strain* (1971), and *2001: A Space Odyssey* (1968) could not be called kid stuff by any stretch of the imagination.

George Lucas, I think, has to be considered a pivotal figure in the current science fiction boom. He made the first giant commercial success in science fiction and he made it well. That he made it well added respectability to the genre. The fact that it earned hundreds of millions of dollars didn't hurt the cause either. In Hollywood, a profitable film automatically becomes respectable.

EN: Is there any science fiction story left out there that you would like to film?

RC: The one I always wanted to do and actually tried to get an option on at one time has just been filmed . . . *Dune* (1984). I even had a treatment written on my own a few years ago when I thought I could get the option. But that option never came through.

Dune, to me, is the ultimate futuristic story. It combines adventures with ideas. There are comments on society, on politics, on human relations throughout the plot. Yet, on an entertainment level it just barrels right along with space warfare and nasty villains.

If I could find a story set in the future that impresses me as much as *Dune*, I'd love to return to the genre.

The Orson Welles of the Z Picture: An Interview with Roger Corman

Wheeler Winston Dixon / 1986

From *Post Script* 8, no. 1 (Fall 1988): 2–15. Reprinted by permission of Wheeler Winston Dixon.

On 21 April 1986, I invited producer-director Roger Corman to the University of Nebraska for a detailed public question-and-answer session as part of a week-long retrospective on Corman's career as a filmmaker. Our interview actually began in the cellar of the theater where we were screening *Cries and Whispers*; a tornado siren sent the entire audience under cover, and ever conscious of time and money, Roger insisted that we begin the interview then and there.

Wheeler Winston Dixon: One of the films that we're running here in the retrospective, *Little Shop of Horrors*, was shot in two days and one night. You were shooting roughly forty-five pages of script a day. You used two cameras on that film?
Roger Corman: Yes.

WWD: Is that unusual for you?
RC: Yes. It's the only time I ever did that during dialogue scenes. We simply *had* to; we had no time. It's customary to use several cameras during action scenes, if you're going to cover it. But on that film, if I had a dialogue scene, I'd have a camera over on the left photographing one actor and a camera over there on the right photographing the other actor, and I might even—this is before the widespread use of zoom lenses—be on a dolly. Now I'd probably use a zoom. I might start on an over-shoulder shot, going into a close-up, and then an over-shoulder shot on the re-

verse angle, dollying into a close-up, so I would have effectively four different angles to cut on the scene. It saves time.

WWD: How much rehearsal did you actually have with the actors?
RC: I had a fair amount of rehearsal because what I did—this was a standing set at the studio—I made an arrangement to use it for two days; but I got the head of the studio to give me the set, use of the stage, not to shoot on for three days but to rehearse. You have to know the union rules. Screen Actors Guild charges more if you hire an actor for a day; if you do that, it costs more than one-fifth of a week—for obvious reasons. So I hired the actors for a two-day shoot on a five-day week. I hired them for five days, rehearsed for three, and shot for two.

WWD: Were they presold to the theaters with deficit financing (presales to theaters)? How did AIP generate the cash to make these films?
RC: It was a complicated matter, different for every film. Sometimes they were presold to the theaters, that is, to the theater circuits. Sometimes they were financed out of cash flow. AIP, although a small company, was rather successful. Their budgets were limited because of the money available, but they always did seem to have *some* money available.

WWD: Did AIP put out two black-and-white films on one double bill so they would control the entire double bill, so they wouldn't have to give away the top or bottom half to another film?
RC: Sometimes they did that. That wasn't the regular practice, but in a period of time, it became normal procedure.

WWD: What led into the production of the color films, such as the later Edgar Allan Poe cycle?
RD: The first Poe film, *The Fall of the House of Usher*, had about a $250,000 budget. I was making black-and-white films generally on an eight-, nine-, or ten-day schedule for about 70, 80, 90, sometimes $100,000, and they would put them together as a kind of theme double bill, two horror films, two science-fiction films, something like that. And it was rather successful. Then AIP came to me and wanted two more black-and-white horror films, and I was simply growing a little bit tired of this. And also I felt that we were beginning to repeat ourselves and that other people were beginning to copy the concept. So I suggested that, instead of doing two black-and-white films on a ten-day schedule, that I do just one film

on a fifteen-day schedule in color, and I suggested *The Fall of the House of Usher* as the property. After some period of discussion, they agreed, and it was something of a breakthrough for them because they had never spent $250,000 for a film, and I never had a fifteen-day schedule. I felt I was, to a certain extent, in the big time with that. The film was something of a critical success and was commercially the most successful film they ever had. So it was a move forward for both AIP and for me.

WWD: And it was also the first film that AIP made that didn't have a monster per se in the film. You had a difficult time trying to convince Sam Arkoff, the head of AIP, that the House of Usher was the monster.
RC: Sam said, "What's a horror film without a monster?" And I said, "Sam, the *house* is the monster." And when we were shooting, there's one line where Vincent Price says "the house *lives*." He didn't know what this was all about. I explained this to him, and he immediately understood—it really made the film.

WWD: *The Pit and the Pendulum* was the next film?
RC: Yes. And it was very successful, both critically and commercially.

WWD: And then you shot *The Raven*. *The Raven* gave birth to a very peculiar sort of side-bar film, as it were. I understand that you finished *The Raven* two days early and then went home and whipped up a script for a film that became known as *The Terror*, which was shot on the existing sets of *The Raven* in two days, with the services of Boris Karloff.
RC: That's vaguely correct. This story got a little distorted over time. *The Raven* had the normal fifteen-day schedule, and after the first two weeks we had one more week to go. I was going to play tennis on a Sunday afternoon, and it rained. And I was sitting around the house, and I thought, "You know, these sets are pretty good." In fact, they were *very* good. I thought I could do another film on them, so I started fooling around, and I wrote a story outline that afternoon. The next day on the set, we had Vincent Price, Boris Karloff, and Peter Lorre, and I suggested to Vincent that I might come back and do another one. But Vincent, who is something of an art critic, was going on a lecture tour and was unavailable. So I spoke to Boris, and Boris said, fine, he'd do it. So I made a deal with Boris to shoot two days. The two days seemed to be my standard. I figured you can't do anything in less than two days. And I got this guy who was a friend of mine, Leo Gordon, and we worked from the outline I'd written. We wrote only those scenes that Boris was in for two

days. I got my good friend Jack Nicholson to come along, and Jack came for the two days. I told Jack, "Boris will work the two days with you and I'll write the rest of the picture, and you'll be the *star* of the picture." Jack thought that was great. And that's exactly what we did.

WWD: Jack Nicholson, at the time, was not a very well known actor.
RC: No. He got a little less then than he gets today (laughs). And we did indeed shoot all that in two days. Then I shut down and wrote the rest of the picture. I calculated that I was financing this by myself and didn't have enough money to finish doing it because I was tied to the Directors Guild and a number of other things. The only way to finish the film was to go non-union. I couldn't do this as a member of the Directors Guild, so I got my ace assistant, Francis Ford Coppola, to come along. I told Francis to go out and shoot the rest of this thing, and he said, "Fine." He went up to Big Sur and shot a portion of it with Jack, and then he came back, and he was offered a contract at Warner's to direct a film called *You're a Big Boy Now*. He came to me and said, "Look, I got a great deal here at Warner's. This is the start of my career." I said, "Okay," and then I had Monte Hellman for a little bit. There were four or five directors, and finally Jack came to me—and we had one more day of shooting—and Jack said, with some justification, "Every idiot in town has directed part of this film. Let me direct the final day." I said, "Fine, Jack, you do it." So Jack directed the final day. We then cut all this together, and the film did not make a great deal of sense. It also wasn't particularly interesting, but by that time I was working on another Poe film. I had some sets again, so I asked Jack and Dick Miller to help me finish it. I told them, "When I finish shooting one day, I'm going to hold the crew over, and you guys come to the set around seven o'clock at night, and we're going to shoot a couple of new scenes fast and tie all this together." So we shot the sequence in which Dick played Boris Karloff's assistant or manservant or something, and Jack was the young officer who had taken refuge in the castle. So Jack grabs Dick, throws him against the wall and says, "I've been lied to ever since I've come to the castle. Tell me what's going on." And Dick told Jack the entire plot, tying all of this stuff together. The picture didn't have much of a twist at the end. Boris, according to the original story, had played Baron von Leppe. In order to get a little bit of a twist in my final rewrite, I decided that Boris was an impostor who had killed the Baron von Leppe and taken his place. That became the story Dick told Jack against the wall of the set. Weirdly enough, this film was fairly successful.

WWD: In the middle of all of these films for American International, you went off on your own and, with your own money, on location, you made a film called *The Intruder*.

RC: It was a film I wanted to do. At that time, things were going very well, and I had never had a failure. I think I directed seventeen or eighteen films, and they were all successful. So at that point, any idea I came up with independent distributors would back me on. We never missed, so I bought this novel having to do with integration of schools in the South. This is around 1960. And I prepared the script with Chuck Beaumont, the writer of the novel. And to my great surprise I was a little more naïve than I am now. All the companies that had agreed to back me on any kind of idea I came up with turned me down on this one. So I decided to back it myself, and it's one of those things that sounds as if it's very logical, but it wasn't logical. I only worked with a couple of professional actors. Almost everybody in the film were local townspeople, and I wanted to shoot in the Mid South, which was where most of the integration problems were taking place. But I didn't want to be in a southern state. I wanted to have, in my own mind, the protection of a Midwestern state and the laws there. Looking at a map of the U.S., I found what's called the bootheel of Missouri, which runs along the Mississippi River in a little kind of wedge south of Missouri proper, between Arkansas and Tennessee or Kentucky, something like that. There I was able to get a southern look and southern accents for the townspeople. All of that worked right. But I was thrown out of two towns with flat-out threats from the sheriff of one county and the chief of police in another. Being in Missouri really didn't make any difference. The sheriff actually told me, "If you're in town when the sun sets, you're in jail. And don't ever come back." The final sequence of the film took place in a schoolyard, and we had shot in East Prairie, Missouri. The first day or two days of this final sequence went OK, and then the sheriff told me to get out of town. We couldn't go back, so I shot some swings in a part in Charleston for half of the next day, and the chief of police kicked me out of Charleston, and we ended up shooting at a country schoolyard. It was summer, and we were out in the country, where there were no police or anybody to see that we were there, and we finished the sequence. Nobody has ever noticed, but the size of the swings varies slightly from shot to shot because they were in three different areas. Luckily people were more interested in the scene itself.

WWD: There is a great sequence in that film where William Shatner, as Adam Cramer, an avid racist, delivers an impassioned pro-segregation speech, which really stirs up the townspeople. You told me that many of the people who were at that rally were really pro-segregation, and they thought Shatner was the hero of the film.

RC: Oh, they loved him! They *believed* him! I recruited these guys out of the public park. They had great faces, and I said, "This is the man who is coming to town, and I want you to be part of this group." When Shatner said, "This country shall be free and white," they cheered, and they believed him all the way. Some of them were heartbroken at the end of the film when they realized that Cramer was the bad guy. It was a great shock to them.

WWD: You continued working for American International as the Poe cycle ended. AIP wanted you to make additional Poe films, but you decided to opt out, feeling that the series had run its course. Then you made *The Wild Angels*, which was one of the first Hell's Angels motorcycle pictures, then *The Trip*, which was one of the very first drug pictures. And then after *Gas-s-s-s*, which you made in 1969, was totally recut by AIP, you left the company. You had lots of interference on that, I understand. AIP eliminated the main character called God. *Gas-s-s-s* has never really been released in this country, if I'm correct.

RC: It had some limited release but not a major release. I was very unhappy with what AIP did to it.

WWD: Then you went over to Twentieth Century-Fox and did *The St. Valentine's Day Massacre.*

RC: Yes.

WWD: How was it working for a major studio after you had worked for AIP?

RC: I really didn't have any problems. At that time, Dick Zanuck was running Fox, and I got along fairly well with Dick. There were a couple of differences. One, the ease of production was much greater. There was more money, and I had a very good crew. On the other hand, the crews worked slower. I became a little bit impatient at the slowness of the pace, but it wasn't a major factor. There was a little bit more interference in the casting. I did not get the cast I wanted.

WWD: Is it true that you wanted Orson Welles to play Al Capone?

RC: I *had* him! I wanted to do a gangster film with a very distinguished cast, so I wanted Orson Welles to play Al Capone and Jason Robards to play Bugsy Moran. Essentially, I had them, and Dick Zanuck rightly or wrongly said, "Nobody can work with Welles. You just *can't*. He'll scream and yell and try to take over. He's driven every director he's ever worked with crazy. The only time he works is when he directs himself. If he isn't the director, he's going to be the director by the second day." So we switched and moved Jason to Al Capone, and Ralph Meeker played Bugsy Moran. They were quite good, but Jason really was better fitted for Bugsy Moran, and Welles—I had made a deal with him through his agent without meeting him. I met him later on, and he said he was very disappointed he had not played this part.

WWD: After a brief period then at Twentieth Century-Fox, you decided to set up your own company, New World, which was the most successful new studio and distribution outfit launched in the 1970s in the United States. A lot of people at that time were saying that you were never going to get it off the ground. Could you briefly describe why you decided to go into this, with such an enormous amount of risk involved, building up a studio and a distribution network as well?

RC: I was really just tired of directing. I had directed so many films. I directed something like fifty or sixty films in thirteen or fourteen years, something like that. The last film I did was for United Artists, a picture called *Von Richthofen and Brown* in Ireland. We were shooting in an airport outside of Dublin, and I was living in an apartment in that city. And each day I would drive out to the airport, and the road would fork. One road would go to the airport, and the other would go, I think, to Dingo Bay on the west of Ireland, and every day I was tempted to go the other way and just drive through the rest of Ireland. I barely made it through the film. I was exhausted. So I just felt that I would stop directing for a year. I would quit and take a sabbatical, save a little bit of money, and start my own distribution company, work on it for a year, and then turn it over to somebody else and go back to directing. I started the company, and the first film, *Student Nurses* (1970), was very successful. And the second film was a success. We did three pictures in six months, and they were all successful. And we just kept going, and I never got back to directing. I couldn't really find anybody to run New World in what I thought was an efficient manner, so I just stayed with the company.

WWD: You work with your wife, Julie, on many of your projects. How does the responsibility break down? Do you ever coproduce?

RC: On the films my wife produces, she is a total producer, doing it herself. She has complete charge of her own films and functions as an independent producer. I do the same on my films. Julie started producing in the early 1970s.

WWD: As New World moved along, you began to develop an enormous amount of new talent. That's something you've done throughout your career. At AIP, you discovered Francis Ford Coppola and gave him his first chance to direct with *Dementia 13* on a twenty-thousand-dollar budget, for an ax-murder movie shot in Ireland.

RC: It grew a little bit over twenty, but Francis was pretty close to the budget.

WWD: And when you started New World, you picked up people like Joe Dante, who went on to direct *Gremlins*, and numerous other people. How did you continue to find or develop these people? Would you watch student films, or go to local playhouses? How did you manage to keep on top of this?

RC: I watched some student films, and some people applied to the company. Others are recommended by certain people, people whose opinion I trust. Having been a writer and a director myself, I might be a little more qualified to judge on writers and directors. We had a kind of training program that not everybody goes through, but Joe Dante is a good example. Joe started as an assistant editor, went on to be a trailer editor, then a feature editor, then a second director, and finally a director. So by the time he was a director, he had learned our style of work.

WWD: Was his first film *Hollywood Boulevard?*

RC: Yes, he and Allan Arkush, also a good director, codirected that. Jon Davison was the producer. I was the executive producer, or whatever. They were all from the NYU Film School. For a little while, everyone came from UCLA, USC, and NYU.

WWD: Recently you sold New World. Now you're setting up an organization called New Horizons, which is the production company, and Concorde, which is the distribution arm. What are your projects now? Do you foresee a return to direction?

RC: I will not direct this year, but I am thinking about directing again next year. Just as I've gotten tired of directing, now I'm getting a little tired of sitting behind a desk. But it won't be until next year, *if* I direct. The pictures will probably start to be a little big bigger. We're finding that the very low-budget films that were working for us very well in the 1970s are not working as well now. They're doing all right, but the theater public seems to want bigger films, and that's understandable. So we'll be starting with some of the bigger films.

Audience Member: Do you think it would be as easy today to start a new independent film distribution company as it was in the early seventies, when things were a little bit tougher for the major studios?
RC: It's a somewhat complicated answer. Overall, it's easier. For theatrical distribution, it's a little big tougher, however, because as I say, the lower-budget pictures aren't doing as well. However, with the rise of videocassettes it's easier because you can get most of your money back from video alone today. So it's a *somewhat* safer investment and an easier operation.

WWD: You told me you were adopting a pattern for New Horizons where you would have two groups of pictures. One would go straight to the theaters, and one would bypass theaters and be sold directly on videocassette.
RC: Yes. I haven't done this as yet, but I think it's going to be the plan. We'll have two different types of films.

AM: Is one of the reasons low-budget films aren't doing so well the demise of the drive-in theaters?
RC: It's partially that. It's a number of other things. It's very difficult to get somebody to spend five dollars or six dollars a ticket to see a one-hundred-thousand-dollar, or even a million-dollar film, when they can wait and see it on television for nothing, or for the same five dollars they can see a twenty-million-dollar film, or for one or two dollars a night they can rent a videocassette. The economics are working against low-budget films, and the demise of the drive-in is part of that. But these other factors are as important or more important. That doesn't mean that there won't be any successful low-budget films. There will always be, at least for the near future, somebody who—either out of luck or skill or both—will break through with a low-budget film. But as a regular program of successful films, I think it's extremely difficult today.

AM: Does it concern you as a producer that the cost of film stock and getting everything done has risen so much in film? Do you think students are better off shooting in 16mm color negative, or is video perhaps the way to go?

RC: Video might very well be a way to go if you're not aiming directly for theaters. If you feel your film is going to television or to videocassette, I would recommend that you go video. It's clearly cheaper and faster. You've got it right there. It doesn't have to go to a lab. You can do your opticals, your effects—nothing against the camera—but it can be done very quickly. If you stay with film do what I do, and go to a lab in Canada. They're cheaper and will undercut the American labs by quite a bit.

AM: You worked with Richard Matheson a lot on the Poe films. How closely did you work with him on writing the scripts? A lot of them didn't follow the Poe stories too closely.

RC: I worked reasonably closely with Dick. One of the reasons that the scripts didn't follow the Poe stories faithfully was because many of those stories were no more than ten or twelve pages long; they were really short stories. In a sense, they were fragments, and there wasn't really enough there for a feature script. We would very often take the Poe story and use it as a climax. For instance, in *The Pit and the Pendulum*, Poe's story took place entirely in the room where the pit and the pendulum were located. It was the *experience* of the man under the pendulum, and we invented a story, which became the first two acts of the film, to get us to that point. Later on, we started taking even greater liberties. *The Raven* became a comedy. And at that point, I said, "We've done enough Poe films. It's time for something new."

AM: What do you think of special effects in today's movies? And with the audience of network TV shrinking, don't you think it would be more profitable if you did a series for, like WTBS or HBO or something like that and not NBC or one of the traditional networks?

RC: In regard to the first part of the question, special effects are getting better, and they're also becoming more expensive. But the audience expects them now. I think really the turning point was *Star Wars*. I've done science-fiction films all my working life. We had a certain level of technical expertise, which was acceptable at the time. But *Star Wars* really moved everything onto a different level, and since *Star Wars*, the audience will not accept the simpler type of special effects. So we're forced, really, into more expensive films. This touches on an earlier thing I mentioned—to spend more money and get better special effects to get an audience into the theater. I have my own special-effects facility, and I find that works very well.

Regarding the second part of the question, it is indeed true that the percentage of the viewing audience held by the networks is diminishing. But it's diminishing at a very slow rate. It's easing one percent a year or maybe two percent a year. So for the near future, the big money in television will continue to be with the networks. Public television is a possibility, and pay cable services, such as Showtime and HBO are possibilities, but they're shrinking more than the networks. The most important medium in the last couple of years is the rise of home video. And the segment that's been hurt most by home video has been pay television. Motion pictures have been hurt a little bit; free television has been hurt a little bit, but pay television, pay cable, has been hurt dramatically. People can go and rent whatever they want: Why should they use a pay cable service?

AM: Would you like to go back to the old days of double features? Is that completely uneconomical, or is it to do with audience concentration, or perhaps the cultural shift towards TV viewing at home?
RC: All of the above. It is, to a certain extent, economic. The cost of films is so great today that you really can't go with double bills. You can't afford to divide up the box-office dollar. You've got to take the entire amount of money to survive. In the few places where they *do* show double bills, the second feature has to be just that. It has to be clearly a second feature, a failed film that tried to be a first feature, or a reissue of a first feature. As Thomas Wolfe said, "You can't go home." Times change. It's probably better now to concentrate on the one film and try to do one film better.

AM: What are some of your secrets for producing a film so quickly? I imagine other people aren't able to do things as quickly as you're doing them.
RC: The main secret is preproduction. It's not particularly a secret. Preproduction planning is the core of everything. If you're going to move quickly and efficiently, you have to be as prepared as you possibly can be going in. And even if you're going to move slowly on a big budget, it's better to go in with full preproduction planning. Now, I might add that you must be flexible. You never shoot the picture exactly the way it was planned. About the only director who had a reputation for shooting exactly as planned was Alfred Hitchcock, who had planned every single

shot beforehand and almost never varied, although maybe he occasionally would change a shot. My technique is to plan as much as I can and then vary it a little bit during shooting. Sometimes something I shot as planned simply won't work. And you have to change it. Or you may get a better idea on the set. But at least if it was planned and done in advance, you have the core of it. You have something—the skeleton, as it were—that you can move a little bit from.

AM: We just saw *Cries and Whispers*, which you distributed and coproduced, and it's a film that obviously you were attracted to for a number of reasons. I'm just wondering how you can make the shift from Bergman's *Cries and Whispers* to something like *The Wasp Woman*, which you directed. When you make a *Wasp Woman*, do you think, "Oh, I'm just making another B movie and throwing it out into the world," or do you care about what you're making, as a film, and perhaps as a work of art?
RC: That's a multipart question, and I'll try to deal with it as well as I can. First, you find from experience that certain films and certain genres, as it were, work best at the box office. We referred earlier to *The Intruder*. When I made that, I had never made a film that lost money. With *The Intruder*, I did a film that I believe was very good, and it got wonderful reviews. One of the New York papers called the film a major credit to the entire American motion picture industry. It won a number of film-festival awards, but it was the first film that I ever made that lost money, which taught me something. *The public simply didn't want to see that particular kind of film.* So you learn fairly early on that, unless you are as good as Bergman or a [Federico] Fellini, you can't do what you please. I think I was a pretty good director, but I had no illusions that I was working on that level. Unless you're that good, you have to stay fairly close to a commercial subject. After *The Intruder*, I tried to do a film that would work on two levels. This is really the core of my filmmaking philosophy, without getting too grandiose about it. On the surface level would be an entertainment film, a genre film, an exciting film of a certain type, and on a deeper subtextual level would be a film that would have some meaning to me. It didn't always work out that way. Sometimes it has a meaning to me, but nobody else will find any meaning in there at all. But at least for me there was something there, and that type of filmmaking seemed to be a type of filmmaking that worked for me and was successful. So I got some satisfaction out of it, and the films themselves were a commercial success.

An Interview with Roger Corman

Robert Benayoun, Jean-Pierre Berthomé,
and Michel Ciment / 1990

From *Positif* 348 (February 1990): 20–25. Reprinted by permission of Michel Ciment.
Translated by Gregory Laufer and Constantine Nasr.

Q: When you worked with American International Pictures, the company established a style of films intended for teenagers. How responsible were you for this concept?

A: It was the joint decision of James Nicholson, Samuel Z. Arkoff, and myself. AIP was a small company at the time that started up without a lot of money, and we were struck by the fact that most people we saw in the theaters were very young audiences the major studios didn't seem to be paying the least attention to. The stars had become fairly old, so well known that their names had become a trademark equivalent to Coca-Cola, and it was always these fifty- or sixty-year-old guys that were treating themselves to love scenes with enchanting young women. I used to go see their films with my friends, and we didn't like that. No young guy wants to see the pretty girl leave with a sixty-year-old. He wants her for himself. I decided that what we needed were young actors in the roles of young people. AIP immediately adopted the idea, and right away we realized that it was working out very well, particularly at the drive-in. From there we came out with titles like *I was a Teenage Werewolf* and *Teenage Caveman*, realizing that teenagers made up the bulk of audiences at the time.

Q: What was your status at American International Pictures? Certainly more than just a simple director under contract.

A: I was never associated with AIP's activities as a company, either as a stockholder or as a salaried employee, or anything of that kind. I worked with them film by film. I had produced the first film they distributed,

148

and I got along so well with them that we decided to produce more to-gether, and this agreement continued, film after film, because we had an amicable relationship and because the arrangement was as beneficial to me as it was for them. Towards the end of my career as a director my films became more important, and AIP could not afford to do them, so I began wandering, working for other studios, but between the bigger films, I always came back to them. I would go to have lunch with Jim Nicholson and Sam Arkoff, and inevitably it always ended the same way: "Why don't we make a film together?" "Sure, I'm not doing anything over the next two months. I'll make another one for you."

Q: Who had the idea of involving AIP in the production of horror films in England?

A: AIP films achieved great success in England, particularly my series of adaptations of Edgar Allan Poe, and it was Nat Cohen, who led Anglo-Amalgamated, who suggested to Jim and Sam that they collaborate to-gether to produce another Poe adaptation in England. I was delighted by this godsend because it gave me the chance to accomplish something greater. All of my American Poe films had been shot in three weeks, while I was given five for the first in England, *The Masque of the Red Death*. I also had the opportunity to use the resources of the big studios, to make use of the sets or parts of the sets of films such as *Becket* or *A Man for All Seasons*, which gave my films a richer atmosphere. The arrangement worked out very well. The only thing that bothered me, and it was not really crucial, was that the English crews were less flexible and worked a little more slowly than American ones, which probably made my five weeks working in England the equivalent of four in Hollywood. That was still progress. And that's again what I had for the following film, *The Tomb of Ligeia*.

Q: Was your decision to leave AIP and found New World Pictures linked to the way that your last films, *The Wild Angels*, *Gas-s-s-s*, *Bloody Mama*, or *The Trip*, had been altered by the studio without your approval?

A: Yes, and it is to a certain extent a consequence of the sixties. I had always had a politically liberal bent, and I was becoming a little more radical, while, conversely, AIP, which had grown a lot and gone public, was becoming more conservative. In my last films, I was starting to put in a few more radical things that disturbed the established order, and they began cutting them out. In *The Trip* and *Gas-s-s-s* in particular, they made some cuts that made me furious. Taking a step back, I can understand their reasons even if I still do not agree with them, but in the end it pushed me to create my own company, combined with the fact that after *Von Richthofen and Brown*, I was really tired.

I was shooting the film in Ireland and every morning, I came to the outskirts of Dublin faced with the same choice: to the right, there was Shannon Airport, where I had to film, and to the left, there was Galway Bay and rest. I struggled to finish the film, and at the end, I simply arrived at the conclusion that I had made so many films in so little time—fifty films in sixteen years—that I needed some fresh air. And I decided to take a year off, to stop directing for one year, but to use that time to create my own production and distribution company, so as to not cut myself off from filmmaking during that time. I really thought I'd return to directing at the end of one year, but New World's success was much greater than I'd had planned, and I continued to lead the company, year after year, telling myself over and over every year that I would return to directing the following year. And I never did.

Q: Is that because you were focusing only on New World's financial concerns, because you were tired of directing, or because you preferred seeing young film directors take over?
A: There was some of all of that, and with success a kind of inertia set in. I was doing something that I liked, perhaps not as much as directing, but I got a lot of satisfaction from it, and also a lot of benefits. I was working with good people, everything was coming along nicely, and I was telling myself that I would return to directing the following year, or else the year after that.

Q: Speaking with those who worked with you at New World, one gets the impression that you kept a very close watch on their work and did not hesitate to give your point of view as a producer on what should be in the film.
A: That was the most important part. When I was directing for other companies, I was perfectly aware of the fact that they were the ones putting up the money and that they had a certain degree of control over the film. I probably had more independence at that time than most other American directors, but I was well aware that I was working for somebody else. You get a lot of satisfaction working for yourself and in knowing that, for better or for worse, succeed or fail, you are the only one responsible and nobody tells you what to do.

Q: From New World emerged directors such as Joe Dante, Allan Arkush, Jonathan Kaplan, Ron Howard, and Paul Bartel. How did they come to you?

A: They came from various places. One of the first who came to work with me at that time was Jonathan Kaplan, who had been recommended to me by Martin Scorsese, who had had him as a student at New York University. So Jonathan came to direct a film, and Jon Davison, who went on to become the producer of *Robocop* and a lot of other blockbusters, also hitchhiked his way across America and arrived in my office sporting a card with my name on it, explaining that he knew that Jonathan was going to work for me and that he also had gone to NYU, where he had made his way by organizing pirated screenings of my films for students, which had earned him quite a bit of money. I thought that the guy had nerve, that he was the type of guy we needed in the company, and I hired him as my assistant. He then said that he knew one or two guys at NYU who could help us in the editing department. And that's how Joe Dante and Allan Arkush came to us and how we quickly found ourselves with a tight core of young filmmakers from New York University, whereas before most of our young folks had come from UCLA and USC. These three schools are, I think, the most important in the United States.

And then other people arrived from other places. Ron Howard, for instance, was the star of *Eat My Dust*, a car-chase comedy that was a big hit. I remember that the film opened one Friday and that it immediately broke the opening records in several theaters. When I got the ticket-sale numbers on Monday morning, I called Ron, who had a percentage of the profits, right away to tell him the news and offer him a sequel. And he said to me, "I've been waiting next to my phone since nine o'clock in the morning. It's after eleven. What took you so long?" I told him to come by and see me, and he gave me his pitch: "Somebody who makes a hit wants more money. I'll do the sequel for exactly the same price. Not more money, not a bigger percentage. And on top of that, I'll make another film for nothing." "Perfect. What more do you want to do for nothing?" "I want to direct the film." And I immediately said to him, "Ron, I always thought that you were born to be a director." It was after his performance in *American Graffiti*, I knew he had studied directing at USC, and *Eat My Dust* was such as success that I had to somehow keep Ron. And that is how he wrote, directed, and produced *Grand Theft Auto*, which resulted in a great success and established Ron's career as a film director, for which he stopped acting and became an excellent full-time film director.

Jonathan Demme was in charge of promotion for United Artists, and it was in Ireland that I met him. We saw each other again in New York; it was there that I hired him with his partner Joe Viola to write and direct a film for me. They worked on several films, and Jonathan suggested that he would really like to direct something. And they made *Caged Heat*, which was followed by two others. It was one of the reasons that I stayed with the company. It was a business, and a profitable business, but it was also like an evolving club. Each person brought his friends. Someone was doing a job and wanted to try another one. It was very informal and very invigorating all at once. A lot of people with enormous talent worked with us during that period.

Q: How did you feel when they left you to make more important films elsewhere?

A: Ron Howard always says that I told him, when he was getting ready to make his first film: "Ron, if you prepare this film well, if you work hard and what you make is good, then you'll never have to work for me again." And it's partly true. I'm aware that my films are small or medium budgets, because I finance them myself and because that's all the money I have. I can't produce a thirty-million dollar film. In my view, a good movie director who does a good job can only go on to a more important film. It's inevitable, and it doesn't sadden me in the least. It's only fair. In New World's time, the average cost of one of my films was around three or four hundred thousand dollars.

With my new company, Concorde, it's surpassed around one million, principally because of inflation: a film that cost four hundred thousand dollars costs a million now. But, in fact, I also try to increase my budgets and to put more earnestness into the company. I always like informality and creativity, people who laugh, who shout and who toss out ideas from their heads, but I try to move towards more ambitious films, even if the most important thing is to have talented guys I like to work with and who like to work with me. Let's say that instead of being a simple film school, now we've gone on to become a university. I try to have more time for filming. In the seventies, the average was about three weeks. Now the films we make in the United States take about four weeks, and they go up to five for those we make abroad, particularly in Asia and South America.

Q: Do you see a difference in mentality between those young people who worked with you in the seventies and those who did it in the sixties, such as Coppola, Scorsese, or Monte Hellman?

A: There are more similarities than differences, but I think that in the sixties, young film directors were more aware of the world beyond film and were, in that regard, more serious filmmakers. When Francis Coppola went to study cinema at UCLA, he also studied theater, literature, and history, and he approached filmmaking with a more comprehensive vision, as did Hellman and Scorsese. The next generation of film directors concentrated more exclusively on filmmaking, and their films are perhaps a little more entertaining, but they sometimes miss the depth of their predecessors. Don't quote me on this, but I think that this is a tendency not only for those who began with me but for many other film directors from the eighties.

On top of that, I think that every artist blends his own experience and the inspiration that he takes from the society and the culture that surround him. The sixties were a period of malaise and social upheaval in the United States. Profound changes were underway; the Vietnam War was extremely unpopular in the United States and led to great unrest. This violent turmoil gave birth to directors who were more socially committed and concerned with addressing real-world problems. For better or worse, the political world and the culture of the eighties are more even-tempered, just like the presidency of Ronald Reagan. We are no longer involved in a war, there are no more big changes, things are rather calm, and the new film directors are a reflection of these circumstances. In a sense, it's a good thing. It is better to live in an age of peace than an age of war. And at the same time, perhaps the artist needs that kind of stimulation.

It goes hand in hand with the evolution of the market, which influences the creator as much as the creator influences it himself. In the sixties, audiences wanted a more radical cinema, and so did the filmmaker. In the eighties, they seem to want a more conservative type of movie, pure entertainment, and that's what movie directors are striving for. Every decade has its culture. Who knows what's in store for us in the nineties!

Q: Do you have the impression that changes in the industry, the disappearance of the studio system, have moved it closer to what you used to do?

A: The big studios still dominate the system thanks to their distribution channels, but they no longer have as much control over production. Now there are many more independent producers in Hollywood than there were when I was making my films. It was Vincent Canby, I believe, who wrote in his review of *Jaws* for the *New York Times*: "What is *Jaws* but a Roger Corman film with a big budget?" It was a joke, but there is a half-truth: the major studios now produce the kinds of films that I use to make. They make them bigger, and, I have to admit, better, but there is a real similarity in their conception. Twenty years ago, I was taken for a young rebel. I became, in the words of a recent publication, "Hollywood's established rebel." I don't know what an "official rebel" could be, but that's how they see me now.

Q: Why did New World venture into the distribution of reputedly difficult European films such as *Cries and Whispers*, *Amarcord*, or *Mon Oncle D'Amerique*?

A: Because I felt like it. I liked the work of these filmmakers. I felt that they didn't succeed in reaching their potential audiences in the United States, and it seemed to me that, since I had a distribution structure, I could do something to fix that. I had no illusions about the money I could make in doing so because it wasn't a very lucrative niche, but I felt like helping these filmmakers and I managed to do so. The films I distributed reached a much wider audience than that which could have been reached ordinarily. They made more money than they would have otherwise, and I made a small profit in addition to getting immense satisfaction.

Q: You had distribution. How did you find theaters?

A: The first film I distributed, in fact, was Ingmar Bergman's *Cries and Whispers* which was released in art houses in New York, Los Angeles, Chicago, etc., where his films where shown anyway. After that, we succeeded in getting the film shown in purely commercial theaters that had never screened this type of film. We even showed a Bergman film in two or three drive-ins, against the advice of all the experts who foretold disaster. Surprisingly, the film finished a completely normal run, to the satisfaction of the theater owners, for whom the film didn't matter as long as it didn't fail at the box office. And I received a letter from Bergman, absolutely delighted that his film was shown in drive-ins.

In this way, we also distributed many films by Truffaut, Resnais, Fellini, Schlöndorff, Bergman, Kurosawa, and many others. We were very selective and did not take more than two or three per year, but many of them saw real success, and during that time when we were distributing these "difficult" films, we accepted more Oscars for Best Foreign Film than all of the other companies combined.

Q: Why did you leave New World and create a new company, Concorde?
A: Because they made me an offer I couldn't refuse. The company was doing very well—it wasn't for sale—but a group of lawyers contacted me to buy it, with the support of an investment group in Chicago. They wanted to get into distribution and get into it with an already-established company that was well known by theater owners and endowed with a network of international partners, in order to be able to get started immediately. What interested them, in fact, was to issue stock and raise capital right away. I didn't want to sell but, month after month, they tried again with increasingly irresistible offers, and I ended up telling myself that if they were ready to give me so much money for the company, they might as well have it. But I didn't sell them my films, or any of the rights to them, just the name and distribution structure.

For me, it made no difference. I sold them New World one evening, late at night as it always seems to be. We cracked open some champagne, and the next day at 9:00 A.M. I was at my desk, working on the same projects as the day before, at the head of Concorde, my new company. The contract provided that I would stay on awhile as an advisor, but that I could continue producing my own films. So I briefly stayed on to advise them, but what really interested them was the financial aspect, raising capital. They really hit upon a lot of money, but unfortunately lost quite a bit and ended up reselling the whole company rather quickly.

Q: As a result, you kept the rights to *The Little Shop of Horrors*, which was remade as a musical, and then as a new filmed version.
A: Yes, and I sold them only the adaptation and remake rights by keeping all those of the original. In fact, at the end of the summer, I'm probably going to produce a film whose temporary title is *Son of the Little Shop of Horrors*, and that Chuck Griffith, who wrote the first version, will both write and direct. He's already made several films for me and is a very good movie director.

Q: Did you keep up the same production pace of a dozen films per year with Concorde as you did with New World?
A: No, we increased it, and these last two years Concorde produced more films than any of the major companies in Hollywood. Twenty films in 1987, twenty-two in 1988. These are huge figures, and I think that last year, Warner Bros. came in second with nineteen films. We produced ev-

erything: Horror films, science fiction, crime, comedies, film noir, musicals, swashbuckling and sorcery films. We created a medieval character of the Death Stalker, who is returning in his third film . . . but we lowered production this year. Twenty-two films is a bit too much, and at the end of the year, we were all really very tired.

Q: Do you always look for young people from film school?
A: Yes, and I think that we have a new generation of very good filmmakers out there. People like Harry Brand; Katt Shea, a young, very talented woman; Mary-Ann Fisher, who's just made her first film, *Lords of the Deep*, which was released last week to great acclaim; Jim Wynorski; Steve Burnett; and, going beyond the United States, Terry Notts, who comes from Geneva and went through Stanford University where I myself studied, then through the film department at USC, and last fall made *The Terror Within* for us, which has had great reviews and great commercial success; Lucio Viosa, a Peruvian who has already made two films for us and is one of the best film directors I have worked with; Sirius Santiago, who produces action films in the Philippines; Hector Oliviera, a very good Argentine filmmaker. They were trained in their own countries.

Q: What about your technicians? Do you have a permanent team you use film after film and do you always recruit them after they leave film school?
A: We have a permanent team of about ten people, mostly editors, post-production technicians, and those in charge of the studio, while the rest—and we do not use more than about twenty people on average on a film—are hired from film to film. But in a sense we do try to perpetuate the type of "family" teams I had in the past, people who are not only committed to the film, but who work together and know that they have quite a lot of job security with us. As for their training, if, for example, we take chief cameramen fresh from school, it is only after they have spent a year or two getting their bearings in the real world, proving themselves by making commercials or else second-tier scenes with us or elsewhere. We don't hire chief cameramen right out of school.

Q: Do you still distribute European films?
A: No, we produce and distribute our films but we don't distribute European films anymore. And it's mainly because the American market for them grew to a point where, in my opinion, the major companies invested too much money in them. In fact, I'm convinced that they

spend more money to have the best European films than they will ever get back. I don't know why they do it, but I'm not going to compete with them under these circumstances.

Q: How did you come to produce *Saint Jack* for Peter Bogdanovich, who had long ago left you for bigger companies?
A: As you know, he started with me with *Targets*. He went on to a bright career for the big guys, but he and I always stayed friends. He was at a difficult point in his career when he took an option on that book, *Saint Jack*, and showed it to me saying that he wanted to adapt it. It seemed to me that we could make a good film, and, moreover, the action was located in Singapore, and I was used to filming in Southeast Asia, mainly in the Philippines and Hong Kong. So we collaborated to make this film, which was a real success and which we liked very much.

Q: You didn't want to give filming opportunities to people like John Cassavetes, who always had problems financing his films and made them on very tight budgets?
A: No. I knew John well, and he worked with me as an actor, but he had a very personal and independent style of directing that really didn't agree with what I was trying to do. I have a lot of admiration for his films, but we didn't have the same work styles.

Q: What was your reaction to Wim Wenders' offer to give you a role in *The State of Things*?
A: I was amused and delighted. As a producer, I spend too much time in offices and not enough on sets. I have my small studio near Venice Beach, and several people pointed out to me that I always seemed to smile more when I went on set. I had never thought about it, but it's true. It's in the studio, not in the office, that I feel at home, and I'm happy there. When Wenders invited me to go on set, I told myself that we were going to have a good time.

And then there was the fact that the film was shot exactly how I used to make my small-budget films. Wenders was supposed to shoot in Century City, a big office complex, and the cost of the shooting permits to film there was too much for his budget. He said to me, "We're just going to go there on a Sunday afternoon when the offices are closed. We'll get out of the car, we'll set up the cameras and we'll shoot very quickly, without permission, and then we'll leave right away." I said to him, "Great. That's exactly how I had shot the scene in front of the Arc de Triomphe in *The*

Young Racers. The French told us how much it was going to cost us, and we gave up on permits. We just pitched the camera in front of the Arc de Triomphe and filmed quickly before running off. I'd be delighted to work on your film." I've never seen the film. My friend John Boorman told me that I looked like I had an inner dread, so I saw no reason to go check.

But we had a really good time. Wim gave me the freedom to come up with my own character, but he still had his views on how it should be and told me what he wanted. And that's what I did: I wasn't about to argue with the director!

Q: You also took on several roles for friends like Joe Dante and Francis Coppola . . .
A: And now Robert Towne, who just offered me one. I knew him when I began directing. I came out of college with a degree in engineering, and after a few films, I realized that I knew nothing about directing actors. So I enrolled in an acting school to study it from a director's point of view, and it was there that I met Bob Towne, who was there studying from a screenwriter's point of view. We became friends, he wrote his first two or three scripts for me, and he went on to a very bright career. He's going to make the sequel to *Chinatown* soon with Jack Nicholson again in the role of Jake Gittes, and two days before I left for Europe, Jack called me to say that he and Bob had a role for me in the film. They have a scene where Jack, who returns in his role as a private detective, destroys an honest lawyer by testifying in court with tampered evidence. And they want me to play this honest lawyer. I accepted, but I think that when they start filming I'll be directing my own film, my first in many years, which means that I am probably going to have to turn down a good role.

Roger Corman: A Mini-Mogul Directs Again

Gregory Solman / 1990

From *Millimeter*, May 1990, 111–24. Reprinted with permission from Penton Media.

Like Mary Shelley's Frankenstein monster, Roger Corman's directorial career wore a death mask for the last two decades. But beneath the surface appearance, it was very much alive and spiritually kindred to the work that haunted those dark, echoing memory chambers of the 1960s, and later, to the films it had inspired—and, in a real sense, created—by its earlier manifestation. From the beginning of his career, Corman has lived this seminal myth. As film theorist Leo Braudy points out, it's a common metaphor for the act of filmmaking, "bring[ing] scientist and magician together in a typically cinematic conflation."

Corman saw the myth's possibilities as a cinematic figuration from the beginning, in the spurned impresario of teeny-hopper talent in *Carnival Rock* (1957), in the mad scientist *X: The Man with X-Ray Eyes* (1963), and in the more explicit dualism of Peter Fonda and the brutish biker called Frankenstein in *The Wild Angels* (1966)—a work with which the creator seeded a new genre of American movies. So, while the film awaiting release by 20th Century-Fox may be titled *Roger Corman's Frankenstein Unbound*, the real story is about a director who has been reborn.

Millimeter: Why have you started directing again?

Corman: I never really intended to stop permanently. I just became tired during the shooting of *Von Richthofen and Brown* (1971), the last film I directed. I had directed fifty pictures in the last fifteen years, and that was just too many. I remember shooting at an airport in Ireland, and each morning on the drive to the airport, I would pass a junction. To the left was the road to the airport, to the right, Galway Bay. And every morning I was tempted to wing the car to the right, watch the Atlantic Ocean, and say, "To hell with it." I never did that. I went to the airport dutifully and shot the film. But I knew halfway through the film that I had to stop. My plan was to take the traditional sabbatical—one year off. But during that year, I started New World, and the company grew. Each year I thought I'd spend another year or so at it, then go back to directing, and one thing soon led to another, and it all kind of faded away. But I never thought I would never direct again.

MM: During the shooting of *Roger Corman's Frankenstein Unbound,* did you ever say to yourself, "Now I remember why I quit directing?"
Corman: That didn't really occur. I enjoyed the actual directing. The work with the actors and the camera was quite enjoyable after such a long period off. There were some production problems that hampered the making of the film, though I wasn't responsible for the production as much. From a standpoint of production management of a bigger-budget film, it bothered me a great deal to see money being wasted on things that were not going to show up on the screen. And there was an attempt to save money on things that were. In other words, I felt I wasn't getting the full use of the budget, that it was going into various areas that weren't going to affect the film in any way.

MM: In the last twenty years, many people have noted the shift from below-the-line budget to above-the-line, for instance.
Corman: I think that's true, and this film bore that out. But I don't offer strong criticism because everyone was trying very hard. They were just used to a different type of production. There was, for instance, an American production manager and an Italian production manager, and there may have been problems communicating between them. I think some things could have been done better. We had a very big office in Milan, for instance. I think we could have had more people on the set, and fewer people in the production office. But, in general, the film went well. I got substantially the picture I was looking for.

MM: Would you allow that this is not your first Frankenstein movie, that this is a story you've told many times?
Corman: I've been fascinated with the Frankenstein story all my life. And it grows ever more pertinent. Mary Shelley's nineteenth-century novel has been consistently underestimated. It's a brilliant, prophetic science fiction / horror / fantasy. It is not a pure horror story, and that's the way I describe the film.

MM: So, when you were doing what I've called those concealed Franken-steins, it didn't really relate to any particular generation, era, or event?

Corman: I think the theme is universal. It's various manifestations re-flect the culture of the time in which the newest version is made. In fact, my version starts in the twenty-first century, moves back to the nine-teenth, and then jumps two thousand years into the future. I try to adapt the Frankenstein story—it's almost become a myth by now—to those particular times.

MM: How does it exist as myth today?

Corman: It relates to a man's quest for scientific knowledge and God at the same time. These quests have been with us always.

MM: In your directing career, there is a certain progression in your tech-nique from the simple narrative structure of movies in an era when color television was new, to the late 1960s when you show an expanded for-mal consciousness.

Corman: It was possibly a reaction to the world around me, the break-ing up of the traditional forms of the sixties. And partially, it was inter-nal. For instance, I have a degree in engineering, but never went to film school. So unlike most directors today, I did my learning on the job. I really think of those first two or three years of work as film school.

MM: What do you think are your gifts as a director?

Corman: I'm not certain I know what gifts, if any, I have. But it might be the ability to relate my inner psychological life to the culture of the time. So that a film I make reflects and interprets the culture, but is a film of my own. I would combine that with my training as an engineer, so that on a more mechanical or craftsman-like level, I think I work efficiently.

MM: Is that quality admired in today's business?

Corman: It is admired, and is a necessity in our company. I don't know that it's admired or recognized in the industry at large. I don't think anybody has anything against efficiency; it's just not at the top of their priorities.

MM: Did anything get out of your control during *Frankenstein*, for in-stance, special effects? In *Tales of Terror*, you created a cat's point of view by simply printing a spherical shot anamorphically. Clever and inexpen-sive. I'm assuming that most of your special-effects budgets were a small part of even your sci-fi and horror films, correct?

Corman: Yes. The budget for special effects was not particularly high. For instance, in *X*, where Ray Milland is able to see through buildings, we did something very simple. Before shooting, there were certain buildings under construction. So we photographed the framework. A month or two later, when we were in postproduction, we came back to re-photograph the same buildings, on which the shell was now on the outside. Then we simply reversed the order, so he sees the shell, then the framework.

MM: When you got to the special effects in *Frankenstein*, were you surprised by what's happened in twenty years?
Corman: No, I was aware of it. I was producing them, and we've had our own special-effects facility. When I did *Battle Beyond the Stars*, which was a $2 million picture, I went to a number of special-effects houses, which were giving me quotes of $2 or $3 million. I said, "Fellas, that's larger than the budget for my entire picture." Then I determined that I could start my own special-effects facility for about $200,000. My number-one piece of equipment was an Elicon, which won the Academy Award that year for being the most advanced motion-control unit.

MM: Was this shop open to outside clients?
Corman: Yes. In fact, we did the special effects for *John Carpenter's Escape from New York*. We did the glider landing on top of the World Trade Center. I remember that one in particular because someone sent me a review of one of the New York critics who commented on the skill of the glider pilot. (Laughs) I thought, my God, does this man actually believe that somebody landed a glider atop the World Trade Center? Well, I guess our effects were pretty realistic.

MM: What is your current thinking about production design and mise-en-scene? In your early career, in films such as *Little Shop of Horrors*, your response to placing characters on scene borders on counterculture filmmaking. But by the time we get to *Pit and the Pendulum*, you seem much more interested in an authenticity of context.
Corman: Well, you might say that I was possibly more interested. But frankly, the simpler and more practical reason was that *Little Shop* was shot for $30,000 in two days. We didn't have money to build sets. In other pictures we did. Most of *Frankenstein* was set along the shores of Lake Geneva, and there are too many modern buildings there. So we ended up at Lake Como in northern Italy. It's not completely correct, but if you

shoot carefully and pick your angles, you can shoot some of the towns there to pass for the nineteenth century.

MM: I think it was Martin Scorsese who said you required sex or violence every so many pages of script. Is that true?
Corman: (Laughs) Those stories have grown better with each retelling. There were no actual formulas as such.

MM: As a director, did you hold yourself to your own producing standards on *Frankenstein Unbound*?
Corman: Pretty much. The picture had a seven-week schedule and I shot it, to the day, in seven weeks. It's a $9 million budget, but it will actually cost less than that in the end. It fits very nicely in between the brackets.

MM: This film was due out in April or May, then delayed indefinitely. How are we to interpret this?
Corman: Very simply, the opticals are not finished. We were in complete agreement from the beginning that this is not a summer film, that it simply can't compete against those budgets. We felt that late April, early May was right. [In fact, our own films are fully booked until late May.] Then someone at Fox determined that April 13 came on a Friday and I think they're planning a *Friday the 13th* type of film. But at this point, there is no date to book in May. So, by everyone's consent, there's no firm release date. A film of this size can make a lot of money, if it does decent business.

MM: When you became a producer, did you function more as the Arkoff/Nicholson team did for you, or have you been more a producer/director?
Corman: Somewhere in between. My style as a producer was to be primarily involved in the preproduction process. Secondarily, postproduction and minimal involvement in the actual shooting. Most of the stories were made with my original ideas. I would then hire a writer and work with him on the development of the script. Sometimes he would be a writer/director, but more often just a writer. I would bring the director in on the second draft, so I would have a structure that I was happy with. Together we'd develop the final draft. I would have meetings with the director to discuss the theme of the picture and how we planned to shoot it. Once we were in agreement [which we always were, to my

knowledge, *before* shooting], there was very little reason for me to go to the set. Because I had been a director myself, I found out on the first few films I produced that too often the cast and crew would start to look to me, which would take away some of the director's power. As soon as I realized that, I made it a habit to only go to the set on the opening day, to see it was off to a decent start. After that, I would look at the rushes, but go to the set very seldom.

MM: What about post-production?

Corman: I would then come back into the process. I think it's in the DGA rules that the director is entitled to a first cut. I do more than that. I generally give the director two complete cuts, and sometimes three, then we'll discuss possible changes. I've never had major problems with a director on the editing because, in most cases, the solution to the editing process is obvious. It's an equation, and the answer is clear. And unless I feel strongly, I defer to the editor's judgment. Very seldom have I insisted that it should go a certain way [and then, it will go that way, because it's my company], but that's hardly ever happened. We've had good relationships with directors, and if they don't have that big jump forward to the major studios, they always seem happy to work with us again.

MM: Since you raised the subject, I must ask you about some of the most famous directors you've started (Coppola, Scorsese, Penn, Kaplan, Demme, Bogdanovich, Towne) all of whom never made films for you again. Is that implicit in the Faustian agreement they struck with you, or are they simply disloyal?

Corman: No. My feeling is this: I was giving them a chance. And they in turn were working for a low salary. And I think it was a fair trade-off. If they did well and jumped to big-money spots, I wished them well. On that basis, I've remained friendly with all the directors who started with us. There's no disloyalty involved. If I'm paying a director $10,000, $15,000, or $20,000 to do his first film, and he then gets an offer of $100,000, or a half million or more for his second, it's only logical he take it. I've understood that, and it's been kind of unwritten that this would happen.

MM: Do those rules still apply?

Corman: As my company has grown in the last few years, I've started to take an option on one picture with our new directors: "I will pay you this amount of money for this picture, but I have an option on the second, because I started you and gambled money behind you. If you've done well, I want to have one more film, but at a raise in salary before you go on to the majors." And we've not had any problems with that arrangement. Beyond that, I think it would be taking undue advantage of a director who is so eager to do his first film that he's very likely to sign anything in sight.

MM: Does this new business arrangement derive from your experience of how much it takes to start someone's career?
Corman: Yes. It takes more money. Francis Coppola did his first film (*Dementia 13*) for me for $40,000 or something like that. Now we will spend as much as $1 million on the first film of a director, and since we are self-financed and privately held—meaning we back our films with our own money—that's a sizable gamble. So I think it's only fair that if he does a good job, we have a chance to go one more time with him. That's been working quite well for the past year or so.

MM: Did you hold yourself to those budgets as a director?
Corman: Yes, almost all of my films were under $100,000 until well into the sixties.

MM: It seems that you opened up a market for independent directors, which really came to fruition in the 1970s, after you had stopped directing.
Corman: I regret that a little bit, that I wasn't directing myself at that time. But your career takes unplanned turns.

MM: What I mean is, after the collapse of the studio system, you didn't seem to be a beneficiary of the new system in the sense that a Coppola was.
Corman: No, that's true. Coppola, as an independent producer/director with studio financing, moved immediately to high-budget films. I stayed with my own company and financed them myself. But I have no regrets.

MM: How has Concorde (Corman's new company) worked out for you?
Corman: The company has been successful. For the past three years—and this is a little surprising to most people—Concorde has made more English-language feature films than any other company in the world, including all of the majors. And we will probably be first this year.

MM: Was that kind of product volume part of the business plan, or are there really that many good ideas?

Corman: Well, that's the problem, I don't have that many good ideas, and I find we are repeating ourselves. We are doing Parts II and III of successful films, which is what everyone else is accustomed to doing, but which I never did before. When *Death Race 2000* (directed by Paul Bartel, 1975) succeeded, I didn't do a Part II, but a variation called *Deathsport* (directed by Allan Arkush and Henry Suso, 1978), a new picture on a similar theme. When Ron Howard starred in *Eat My Dust*, a big success for us, we didn't do a II, but Ron came back to direct and star in *Grand Theft Auto*, which was similar. Now, however, we've had success with *Slumber Party Massacre*, and we did a Part II and III.

MM: Do you mind being called a studio?

Corman: We do have a studio, in Venice. This is one of the reasons for the success of Concorde. We're the only independent that has its own studio, its own theatrical distribution offices, and its own sources of independent financing. So we can finance, produce, and distribute a film, all out of the same shop.

MM: What's the distribution game like these days?

Corman: When I sold New World, I went out of distribution for several years. When I came back into distribution as Concorde, distribution had changed. It had become much more difficult. The concept of the giant major studio releases of one thousand to two thousand prints simultaneously, with a $5 million or $10 million ad campaign, really damaged independent film distribution. This had started before I sold New World. In the interim period, it had become the norm and taken over. As you know, that's what happened to the independent distribution companies—Cannon, De Laurentiis, New World itself—almost all of these companies had great moments but lost, between them, more than a billion dollars, which is a huge amount of money for independent motion-picture companies. They simply could not compete with that kind of spending and power from the major studios.

MM: So, what has been your strategy at Concorde? You were once a great distributor of foreign films . . .

Corman: When I came back in, I resolved to be extremely cautious. So we've stayed with the more commercially oriented films, and we distribute regionally. In other words, we'll take a hundred prints, move them into Miami, then Dallas, then Houston, and go very cautiously. Now it may be that inherent caution has kept us away from distributing foreign films. I've been thinking about going back into it. But the little knowledge that I have is that the people who are doing it are not doing that well.

MM: How are Concorde films viewed by theater chains?
Corman: The exhibitors like us, because we are almost the sole remaining alternative to the major studios; they want and need a reasonable supply of medium-budget films because they have these six- , eight- , and ten-plex theaters—a lot of screens around the country. It's comforting for them to know that a company like Concorde has a good supply of playable films.

MM: How typically will your films be booked?
Corman: A major film opens with a giant ad budget, so it does well its first week, but it starts to slip. The theater may have planned that film to go two months. They know there is a place to go to fill that slot. They don't expect our films to gross like *The Hunt for Red October*, for instance, but they know we can be counted on for decent business. There comes a time when a circuit has a thousand screens, and would like to have a film that can go into twenty or thirty of them.

MM: Is the strategy of the major studios to retain hegemony by inundating advertising and publicity in lieu of vertically owning theater chains?
Corman: Weirdly enough, I'm buying into a theater circuit. I expect to close the deal in May, so I can't say more about it yet, but I will be one of three partners in a rather large theater circuit.

MM: Then by summer you'll have a near-complete integration. Have you considered cassette sales too?
Corman: We had a choice. We were thinking about starting our own videocassette company. I discussed it with Brian Krevoy (vice president of business affairs). But I'll always remember a lunch I had with MGM/UA when one of their vice presidents said casually, "The lion still roars," I remembered that. We know that MGM is not as strong as they formerly were, but to the public they are the lion. If our films go on the Concorde label as videocassettes, they are little films. If they go out through MGM, they are MGM films.

MM: Your abstinence from television is odd. But wasn't *Target: Harry* (1968) something like made for TV?

Corman: Yes, that was the only film. It was a movie of the week for ABC, before there was such a thing. I've never really worked in TV before, apart from selling films to it. But, for the first time, I'm thinking of going into television—probably late. I was never particularly interested in it, but it's very possible that we will do something for television this year.

MM: For awhile there was a rumor that you had never lost money on a film. True?

Corman: No. I have lost money several times, but I'd say over 90 percent of the films have made money.

MM: Even your exploitation films tended to be leftist efforts, weren't they?

Corman: They were clearly leftist efforts, and still are. My sympathies are still solidly to the liberal side. It is strange that many of the people I knew in the sixties and seventies turned to the middle of the road, or conservative. There's not many of us left hanging in there.

California Gothic:
The Corman/Haller Collaboration

Lawrence French / 2006

From *Video Watchdog*, April 2008, 14–42. This extended version of the interview is published here for the first time with the gracious permission of the author.

The following interview with Roger Corman, Daniel Haller, and Joe Dante began as an afterthought while I was doing research for the book *Visions of Deaths* (Gauntlet Press), which contains Richard Matheson's complete shooting scripts for both *House of Usher* and *The Pit and the Pendulum*, along with my articles detailing the making of both films. Since I was going to be visiting with Richard Matheson to discuss his work for Roger Corman I thought it would be a good idea to get Matheson and Corman together to reminisce about their days at American International Pictures. Joe Dante, who had worked with both men and is also a big fan of the Poe pictures, quickly agreed to join in the celebration. Then, I thought "why not also invite Daniel Haller," the inventive production designer of all of the Poe movies? By a strange coincidence, Daniel Haller actually lives only a few blocks from Richard Matheson in the Woodland Hills area of Los Angeles. So after a few phone calls, I had everyone confirmed for a luncheon meeting at a restaurant near Matheson's house, since Richard had recently undergone heart surgery. Unfortunately, the day after I met with Richard to discuss his Poe scripts, he was suffering from severe back pain and had to cancel. So while Mr. Matheson's comments were "devoutly to be wished," they did not come to pass. However, I think the interview manages to capture a great deal of the lively interplay and great friendship between Roger Corman and Daniel Haller. It was recorded July 2006 in Sherman Oaks, California.

Lawrence French: Roger, you've said Daniel Haller's work as production designer was a very important factor in making all the Poe films so successful.

Roger Corman: Yes, I think Dan was a major contributor to all of those films. His work was exceptionally good, especially when you realize the small amount of money he had to work with. Dan was ingeniously able to adapt standing sets and flats we pulled out of the scene docks at the studios where we were shooting the pictures and also rented a lot of set pieces from Universal. Dan then moved on to become a director of several films I produced for AIP and later on, for pictures we made for my own company, New World Pictures.

Joe Dante: What was your first picture as art director for Roger?

Daniel Haller: I think it was the *War of the Satellites*. Harry Reif was the set decorator on that film, as well as on *The House of Usher*. Harry had worked on Herbert Biberman's *Salt of the Earth* and was very left wing, but he did everything he could to save a buck for everybody. On *War of the Satellites* he brought in these damn lounge chairs and I said, "Harry, what hell are you thinking about, this is supposed to be a spaceship!" Harry said, "Oh this is the newest thing." Well, we were shooting that day, so what could we do?

RC: We had space recliners, with anti-gravity features.

DH: What saved us on that was that Sputnik had just been launched, right when the picture came out.

RC: No, what happened with that was after Sputnik had gone up in 1957, the very next morning I was in Steve Broidy's office, the president of Allied Artists. I said to him, "I can have a picture on *Satellites* in the theaters in ninety days if you give me a commitment now." At the time I had no story, but I had several writer friends so I knew we could do it. But for the special effects I had hired Jack Rabin, and as happened so many times with Jack, he and his partner, Irving Block, would come up with these beautiful drawings, and I'd sign them on the basis of the drawings they had done. Then, what they eventually came up with had no relationship whatsoever to their original drawings!

JD: So you used potatoes wrapped in tinfoil. I liked Jack Rabin, though, because when I used to work for you at New World, Jack would come into the editing room and he'd be snookered by 1:00 P.M.! Jack was not a small guy, and he'd say, "You can lose a lot of weight if you don't eat anything all day and just drink." (Laughter) Now we all know the story about how you asked Jim Nicholson and Sam Arkoff to make one color film instead of two black and white pictures in 1959, but whose idea was it to actually make the first Poe film, *The House of Usher?*

RC: Mine! Now for some reason, I've heard Sam Arkoff claimed it was his idea. But he was the vice-president of business affairs and he was a lawyer and I don't think any picture ever made by AIP was Sam's idea!

JD: Sam said a lot of things after Jim Nicholson died, making it seem like he was the guy responsible for many films made at AIP.

RC: Which is not really correct. Jim Nicholson was the head of production, the idea man, and just as importantly the title man and the poster man. He had been a theater owner and ran double-bills where he had learned from experience what would work. Jim realized that if you put two low-budget black and white films on a similar theme together, more people would come. For instance, two science-fiction films, two horror films, two gangster films, or two teenage-gang films, which were very popular at the time. You would think that you might appeal to two different audiences if you put a science-fiction picture with a romantic picture, but Jim simply found from experience that what audiences wanted was two of the same kinds of pictures, that went straight to the core audience. That whole idea is what really made AIP a success. Actually, two things made AIP. First, both Jim and Sam were very smart, but secondly, Jim came up with the idea of selling two films together, which was picked up by Allied Artists, and I was making pictures for both companies. I had done a number of these combinations for both AIP and AA, and they were extremely successful.

Then a couple of things happened. Jim and Sam asked me to do two more horror films, on ten-day shooting schedules, for under $100,000 each, and I said, "no" for a number of reasons. Firstly, I was getting tired of them, so a lot of the changes in the films were for no other reason than I was bored with what I was doing and I wanted to do something else. Secondly, we had gone to the well too many times. A number of cities were playing two pictures I had made for AIP and two I had done for AA simultaneously, so the returns were beginning to drop off. I had a percentage of the profits, so I could see we weren't making as much money as we had earlier—so it was not a good commercial plan if AIP wanted to move forward. So I said to Jim and Sam, "instead of doing two ten-day black and white films, let's make one fifteen-day picture in color for $200,000." At that time, AIP had never had a fifteen-day schedule and had only shot in color a few times. They were very leery of color, because it was more expensive. They asked me what I wanted to do, and I said *The Fall of the House of Usher*. It was a classic story I had read in high school and always loved. I had no thoughts of a Poe series at the time; it was just a picture I wanted to make. It was really a gamble for them, because AIP was a very small company at the time. At first, there was a little resistance, but I was finally able to convince them. I remember Jim agreed immediately, but Sam was very cautious. He was worried because there was no monster in the picture and generally there had always been a monster in AIP's horror and science-fiction pictures. I had no real answer for Sam, so I thought for a minute and said the first thing that came into my mind, which was the house itself would be the monster. Sam thought about it a minute and said, "okay." So they agreed to make the picture on that basis.

DH: The way I remember it was that I had just done a picture, *The Ghost of Dragstrip Hollow*, and it was Jim and Sam's idea to build a set for that show, and then use it for *House of Usher*. I didn't go along with that idea, but Jim and Sam went to Europe on a buying spree. At the same time, they still owed Roger some dough and Roger was kind of pissed-off at them. So Roger said to me, "Let's really spend some money and make this a good film." Then I told Roger about what Jim and Sam wanted me to do, which was to re-use the old sets, which I thought would look really shitty. Roger said, "All right, let's pull out all the stops. Spend $5,000!" So I went over to Universal and for $2,000 we were able to rent three horse trucks full of scenery and eventually were able to piece it all together and make it into something that looked fairly good. That's how I remember it.

RC: I said to spend more, but I don't know if I said to spend double.

DH: No, but I think we brought the picture in for about $150,000.

LF: Except you've always claimed that the budget for *House of Usher* was around $270,000.

RC: Well, as I recall, it was a little over $200,000 with everything in. I don't know if it was as high as $270,000, but I don't remember the exact figure.

LF: So when you started the picture, AIP had given you $5,000 for the sets and $5,000 for Richard Matheson's script.

DH: And $5,000 for Vinny.

RC: That's $5,000 we wasted on the script and the sets. (Laughter)

LF: What I find so bizarre is that when I talked to Sam Arkoff, although he claimed *House of Usher* was his idea, he actually printed Roger's version of the story in his autobiography!

RC: Well, I haven't read Sam's autobiography, but as I said I've heard from other people that he claimed it was his idea to make *House of Usher*. But you say in his autobiography he says that I brought the idea to AIP?

LF: Yes, and he even printed the story about you telling him that the house would be the monster.

RC: Well, then his autobiography is correct. Sam is a lawyer, and you'll notice that being a lawyer, he would put the correct story in writing. (Laughter)

DH: When we first started the film, Roger wanted to make a really good picture, but we saw right away we were going to go way over what AIP had initially approved for the budget. So we worked twenty-four-hour days. What we would do is shoot all day long, and then we'd stop and Roger and I would go out to dinner.

RC: Along with Jack Bohrer (the assistant director). It was the three of us.

DH: Right. Then afterwards, we'd go back on the set and stay there until we had the next day's work all planned out. We'd go over all the shots and say, "Where would John Ford put the camera?" or "Where would Alfred Hitchcock put the camera?" Sometimes we'd stay as late as midnight or 1:00 A.M. so I always knew what Roger was planning to do the next day. Then I was able to get with the grips and let them know what we needed for the upcoming shots. That was especially good when we needed cranes or anything else that would require a lot of advance set-up time. So whenever Roger finished a shot and said "Print," we were already in position and ready to go on to the next shot.

RC: That was really the most efficient way of shooting I've ever seen. It was also the most enjoyable, because we were all good friends. We shot the first two Poe films at California Studios, and then for *The Premature Burial* we used Producers Studio, a rental studio on Melrose Avenue. Danny, Jack Bohrer, and I would go over to Nickodell's on Melrose, right across from the studio and have dinner and drinks, which we'd charge to AIP. I'd have a Martini and a glass of wine, which at the time, was really big drinking for me. It was all very pleasant, telling jokes and talking about what happened during the day, and then we'd just walk back to the studio and spend time going over the shots for the next day's shooting schedule. We'd re-adjust the props and the sets, taking objects from one set and moving them over to another and making different compositions to fill the scene. We worked very hard on the sets and the set dressings, and as Dan says, we'd not only work out the shots, we'd also plan out the next day's schedule. As I tell young directors now, it isn't enough to know the shot you're doing and what the next shot is going to be, but you really have to know what you'll need in two hours, which we were able to do. We'd be able to say, "Look, we need a crane at 3:00 P.M. this afternoon." Now, you can't say you're really efficient if you're only thinking one or two shots ahead, knowing it's going to take two hours to get a crane on to the set. So we really shot very efficiently, especially since Vincent was a really good guy and everyone liked each other. Then, on the later films, Peter Lorre was great fun. So there was this great spirit of camaraderie on the set. Everyone on the crew was very good and they rose above the level of technique, to help with the artistic endeavor as a whole.

JD: One of the big appeals that the Poe movies had for kids, was that it wasn't just a horror picture, but it was a classy horror picture. You could go to see the movie and not read the story and do a book report on *House of Usher*. So it was cool for kids.

LF: That actually caused some concerns at AIP. Didn't James Nicholson object to using Edgar Allan Poe, since he felt teenagers might not want to go see a movie that was based on an author they were forced to read in school?

RC: That's right. It's interesting that you mentioned that, because I had completely forgotten that. Initially, both Jim and Sam had some doubts, but after we had a couple of meetings they finally agreed to make it.

JD: What was the story behind Burt Schoenberg, the artist who painted the portraits in *House of Usher*?

RC: Burt Schoenberg was an acquaintance and sometimes friend of mine back then, who was sort of a wild-man painter. At the time it was still the beatnik period, before the hippies, and I had just done *Bucket of Blood* and there were all these coffee houses up and down Sunset Boulevard. Burt had done all these weird and strange paintings, so I thought for *House of Usher* he would be the ideal guy to do the Usher portraits. He was noted for doing that type of expressionistic portraiture and was fairly well known around Hollywood. I chose him specifically for the particular look we got. I think he very nicely conveyed the image of the Usher ancestors—in which we are shown a recognizable person, but through a distorted vision. And I think it's possible that the artist who painted the Usher portraits may have been picking up the distortion from the evil in the minds of the people that he was painting.

LF: Do you mean Burt Schoenberg was picking up the distortion, or that the artist who supposedly painted the portraits in the movie was picking up the distortion?

RC: The artist in the movie. Burt had his own problems. He was a good guy, and he probably projected something of himself into the paintings, as well, but the idea was that the people in the paintings were so insane that their personality somehow moved the mind of the artist who had painted them. I really thought they were amazing paintings and I remember at the end of the picture, Vincent and I where each going to take one of those paintings home, but somehow they vanished. I had them taken to my office at the studio where we were shooting, but they all disappeared. I guess somebody liked them more than I did and just grabbed them. That bothered me, because I really liked those paintings.

LF: Vincent Price told me he also admired them; he thought they really captured that Poe feeling of agony, so it's too bad he never got to keep one of them. Do you remember which portrait Vincent wanted?

RC: I think Vincent wanted the portrait of the evil sea Captain (Captain David Usher).

JD: Those painting were great, but I heard rumors about Burt meeting a bad end. He went insane or ended up in a sanitarium?

RC: Yes, the word "went" insane isn't really correct. He was pretty crazy to start with.

DH: I was the person who had to go over to his studio, which I think was over on Fairfax, and deal with him. He was a nice guy, but he was way out there on the astral plane. He was always talking about being on the astral plane. I will say that the first time I directed was on *The House of Usher*. As I said, I knew everything Roger was going to do, because we had gone over it all the night before. So on the last day of filming, the final shot was an effects shot, where all the debris is falling down on Vincent Price.

RC: Yes, I remember that.

DH: Well, we only had about five minutes left before we would run into overtime and for some reason Floyd (Crosby) wanted to pull a light from above. That meant we'd have to open the stage doors and clear out all the smoke with these big wind machines. So I told Roger it was going to take us about five minutes to clear the stage and get it ready for the final shot. Well, that meant we'd go into overtime, so Roger took his hat off and threw it on the ground and stormed out to get a breath of fresh air. Then suddenly, almost as soon as Roger walked out the door, for some reason the stage just cleared, like that. Then without anyone saying anything because the crew all knew what the situation was, they just locked the doors, the bell went off, the soundman rolled and everyone was looking for Roger. Finally Floyd looked at me and said, "Come on Dan, say 'Action!'" So I said, "Action!" and Vinny went ahead with the scene, which had been rehearsed beforehand, and we got the last shot and I said, "print it." Then Roger came back in. He couldn't come in before, because the stage doors had been locked, and he said, "who said 'Action?'" I told him, "I did," and he said, "Did you print it?" and I said, "Yeah, I printed it." He said, "Good work, Dan—we didn't go into overtime."

RC: That was Dan's first time as a director.

DH: Yes, we had some really good times. Like Roger said, they were the best of times.

LF: How did you decide on adapting Poe's "The Pit and the Pendulum" as the follow-up film to *House of Usher*?

RC: *House of Usher* had been a big success, bringing in over $2 million for AIP, so Jim and Sam asked me to do another Poe picture. I had always liked "The Pit and the Pendulum," so I said, "all right." At that point it wasn't evident that I was going to do a whole series of Poe pictures; I simply thought, "Now there will be two Poe films, instead of one." Then, as each succeeding film became successful, I simply thought I was doing one more Poe picture.

LF: Of all the Poe films *House of Usher* was probably the closest you stayed to the original Poe story. Richard Matheson said *The Pit and the Pendulum* was really a completely original story he had to devise, using some of Poe's ideas.

RC: That's right, and actually *The Pit and the Pendulum* was one of the most difficult of the Poe pictures to write, because Poe's original story had almost no characterization at all, whereas in *The Fall of the House of Usher* there was at least enough characterization to build a screenplay from the story. So although we tried whenever we could to be faithful to Poe, we had to vary them to a large extent. Otherwise the picture would only be twenty-five minutes long, because most of Poe's stories were only five or ten pages. With *The Pit and the Pendulum*, the original story was about a man in a room being tortured. So we simply utilized that, by having John Kerr come to Vincent Price's castle and then putting him under the pendulum for the climax of the film. You could think of it as our creating a two-act prologue that leads up to the third act— which would be the actual Poe story. But in creating the first two acts, Dick Matheson attempted to use concepts and themes that Poe developed in his other stories. For example, the idea of Vincent Price walling up his unfaithful wife was something Poe had used in his other stories, particularly in "The Cask of Amontillado." So, although we were inventing a story of our own, we generally tried to maintain a consistency of thought towards Poe's work, by incorporating similar ideas taken from his other stories.

JD: After you made *The Pit and the Pendulum*, you had your adventure shooting *The Intruder* in the south.

DH: For obvious reasons, that was a film that didn't play well in the south.

JD: No, but it was a terrific movie that was way ahead of its time. Here's an article I brought along from the *Los Angeles Times* in 1963. It was two years after you shot the picture and you were still looking for a distributor! Then for whatever reason, after the success of *The Pit and the Pendulum*, you decided to make your next Poe film for Pathé labs.

RC: Yes. The reason for that was because I had a dispute with AIP over the profits on *The Pit and the Pendulum*.

LF: Richard Matheson said he also never saw any profit payments from AIP for *The Pit and the Pendulum* and that film obviously made a lot of money for AIP.

RC: Yes, I could go into details, but since this is for publication . . . but basically, depending on who you were, they had multiple statements. The same thing happened on *Bloody Mama*. I was getting solid profit participation payments and Shelley Winters was saying, "This picture is playing everywhere, it didn't cost very much to make, I can't believe it's never gone into profit." I figured, "I don't really want to get into this," so I didn't say anything to Shelley about it.

JD: You were seeing the future of Hollywood accounting practices.

RC: Yes, exactly. Because of that, after *The Pit and the Pendulum*, I said, "To hell with this!" So I hired Chuck Beaumont to write *The Premature Burial* and went to Pathé labs who agreed to co-finance the picture with me. Vincent Price was already signed to a contract with AIP where he couldn't do a Poe film for anyone else, so I signed Ray Milland for the lead. I still remember on the morning of the first day of shooting, Sam and Jim walked on to the soundstage and I thought, "what is all this about." They were both smiling, so I thought, "oh, they're coming to wish me well." Then Sam came up to me and shook my hand and said, "Congratulations Roger, our partnership continues." It turned out that the night before they had brought out Pathé's interest in the picture. Sam was a funny guy who did a little bit of self-aggrandizement in taking credit for Jim's ideas, but I liked them both.

JD: The interesting thing is, although *The Premature Burial* wasn't going to be an AIP picture, it looks just like all the other Poe movies. It's got the same style and looks just as if they made it.

RC: Well, "they" was essentially us. I was directing, Dan was the art director. Floyd was the cameraman.

DH: The thing was, I was also under contract to AIP at the time. Roger said he was going to make this picture, and I said, "Well, we've got a little problem here, because I'm under contract to AIP, so I don't think I can do it." So what I did was go to talk with Jim and Sam to see if they'd let me do the picture. This was only a couple of weeks before Roger was going to start shooting. They thought about it and they agreed to let me do it. They probably already knew they were going to take the picture over from Pathé, anyway.

RC: Yes, I think it was already in their minds. But it was essentially exactly the same crew.

JD: So the big difference was using Ray Milland, instead of Vincent Price.

RC: Yes, and Ray worked very hard and he gave a very good performance. Having Ray as the lead in *The Premature Burial* was an interesting switch, because he had been a romantic leading man in the forties, so he brought that persona with him, and he played the part with a little more charm and romance. Vincent, on the other hand, was more of a character actor, who brought a certain quirky aberration to the roles. They were both really great gentleman, and both were very good actors.

LF: The first time you veered into comedy was in *Tales of Terror*. What was the thinking behind that?

RC: There was a feeling in my mind, and to a certain extent in Dick Matheson's mind, that we were in danger of repeating ourselves. I was starting to set up shots too closely to the way I set shots up in the previous pictures. Even some sequences would start to become too similar to what I had done before. So, to make the films different we decided to vary the approach. We felt a nice way to vary them was with comedy. Since we were doing a trilogy of Poe stories we decided to break things up a bit and bring something totally different into the film. So *The Black Cat* is a full comedy. Actually, I shouldn't say full comedy; it's really a comedy with horror, where the other films might be horror with some comedy.

JD: It seems from a production standpoint it would be more difficult and more expensive to shoot three different stories, rather than just one.

RC: Yes, but on the other hand Dan was reworking the same sets.

DH: That's all we ever did! (Laughter) The thing was, we had to rent soundstages at a studio, so what we would do is have three crews. Three construction crews, three painter crews and three grip crews. So if we were shooting on one stage, we were constructing on another stage to save money. So we were going twenty-four hours a day, and we would use the same pieces over again, and just juggle them together.

RC: Dan was really great with perspective. He really made the sets look much bigger than they were.

DH: But we didn't draw a lot of the sets out. I'd just do a sketch for the construction foreman on a cocktail napkin and we'd work it all out. But I had a twenty-four-hour day, while Roger got to go home and go to sleep in his own bed! I had to have a dressing room on the stage, so I'd be able to go in and take a nap in this portable dressing room.

RC: Yes, and I remember during our dinners at the Nickodell, Dan would draw the sets out on the back of a cocktail napkin. Then after doing that, I went over to 20th Century-Fox, and they had this big drafting department drawing up intricate plans for all the sets. I said, "Why?" This isn't a house that's going to stand, we know roughly what the set is going to be like, and so a sketch is truly good enough. Danny would sketch all the sets in some detail, so I knew what they would look like, but if a set is supposed to be twenty feet long, it makes no true difference if it only goes out nineteen feet. It's not tied to any posts or anything to support a second floor; it's just a backdrop really. Also, the set will change with every lens you use anyway.

JD: For some reason all the Poe films have dreams sequences, or if they aren't dream sequences, they're flashbacks, and they're all done in this interesting Butler-Glouner kind of way. Was that something you just liked in *House of Usher* and wanted to continue using in all the subsequent Poe films?

RC: Yes, that was in Dick Matheson's script, but then Dan and I worked it all out. It was a chance to experiment and really do whatever we wanted. I loved shooting the dream sequences, as did the cast and crew, and eventually they became signature segments in all of the Poe pictures. I think we put a dream sequence into almost every Poe film. What went into those dream sequences and how I expressed them would usually be based on certain theories of my own. One idea I had was to dispense with everything other than the purely visual, so they were all shot silent and in black and white. I thought of them as exercises in cinema technique, where we could depart from reality, by using special lenses, surreal sets, gels, and afterwards a lot of optical printing. From a theoretical standpoint, they were pure cinema. Actually; quite a bit of the dream sequences were Danny's thoughts on how to do it, as well, because after I shot them in black and white, Dan got together with Larry Butler and Don Glouner.

DH: Yeah, we used a kodalith film, which is a film you use for lettering and it actually wasn't Larry Butler who did the color work, but another guy we used, who was over by Allied Artists. Of course, his studio is no longer there.

RC: It wasn't Jack Rabin, it was too good to be Jack. Dan also did all the compositing work, once I had shot the picture.

DH: I think it was Ray Mercer, and I was able to sit there with Ray and we'd add the colors and effects and we go over it until we got what we thought was right.

JD: Les Baxter did the score for most of the Poe films. Did you use temp scores in those days?

RC: No, we didn't.

JD: So you'd just run the picture for Les Baxter and he'd go away and come back with the score?

RC: Yes. I never worked that closely with composers on classical scores. On more contemporary scores, like *The Wild Angels* and *The Trip*, yes, but on classical scores all I ever did was discuss the mood I was looking for and where I wanted the music to go. I figured he knows and I don't know, so as long as he knew the mood I was looking for, that was enough.

JD: Was there ever a situation where the music came back and you thought, "Jesus, this isn't quite what I wanted, this doesn't work." I'm remembering back to Paul Chihara's *Death Race 2000* score.

RC: No, I generally accepted the score, because once you've paid for the composer and the score, you'd have to use that score. I don't remember so much the score on *Death Race* being a problem, but it was the sound. It was the only picture I've ever made where the soundman did not have the complete sound job done when we went in to do the final mix. Paul Bartel was in the mixing room at Ryder Sound, and I was next door with two new sound editors, and we were cutting things in and working like crazy while Paul was in the next room. I was checking back to see where Paul was at, because he might only have ten more minutes left, and I finally said to Paul, "Push it over the edge. Just push sound over everything."

LF: Right after you wrapped shooting on *The Raven*, you immediately started another film, *The Terror*.

RC: Yes and *The Terror* had the greatest list of un-credited directors on any film I ever made. I started shooting it on the sets we had used for *The Raven*, then Francis Coppola took over. Francis got another job and then Monte Hellman took over. When Monte Hellman left, Jack Hill took over.

DH: Roger even offered it to me, but I already had taken another job.

RC: Oh, that's right. Dan turned it down and Francis Coppola accepted it! So Francis was my second choice for *The Terror* (Laughter). What actually happened was Dan had done such great sets for *The Raven*, during the last week of shooting on *The Raven* I said to Dan, "It's really a shame we have to tear these sets down." I had a little bit of money, enough for two days of shooting, so I decided to try and come up with a story outline for another horror picture we could shoot in only two days. So I called up Leo Gordon, a friend of mine who had written *The Wasp Woman* and asked him if he could write scenes for a picture using the castle sets Dan had done for *The Raven*.

LF: Boris Karloff was apparently a bit upset when you actually went ahead and shot his scenes for *The Terror* in only two days.

RC: What happened was that at the end of shooting on *The Raven* I talked to Boris to see if he would agree to work for two days on another picture. Boris looked at the script—except at that point all I had was an outline and a few of Boris's scenes written—and I said, "Boris, this is going to be a tough one. We're going to have to shoot it in only two days," and he agreed to make it. I think it must have been in the back of his mind that I wasn't really going to do it in two days. You know how people sometimes say they're going to do something, but they never really do it. Well, we had to do it in two days, because that was all the money I had. So Boris knew what he was getting into, although I don't think he realized it meant he'd be working steadily from the time he got on the set in the morning, until the end of the day. Actors don't normally work that way, which is why Boris was somewhat upset.

LF: What's also interesting about *The Terror* is that you flooded the house, instead of burning it down.

RC: Yes, I had used fire consciously in a number of the Poe films, but I felt there was beginning to be a certain amount of repetition, so I finally said, "That's it! I can't burn down another house." So in *The Terror*, I destroyed the house by flooding it. That was a conscious decision on my part. I felt I had destroyed enough houses by fire, so I said, "What is the opposite of fire? The opposite is water, so this house will be destroyed by water. I just cannot burn another house down." In retrospect, fire was better. When I look at the films, clearly the fire sequences are better than the water sequences. Then, because we didn't have that much water on the set, I asked a friend of Francis Coppola's, Dennis Jakob, who had gone to UCLA film school with Francis, to drive up to Hoover Dam and get all the shots he could of water rushing over the dam. I had a Volkswagen bus that Francis and (key grip) Chuck Hannawalt had built, that we used in Europe for *The Young Racers*. It was built with racks for all the camera equipment before that became the normal thing to do. This was before the Cinemobile, so we really should have developed that business. Anyway, after I shot for two days with Boris, I told Dennis Jakob to drive to Hoover dam and get shots of water rushing over the dam. So we ended up cutting together all this water footage into the climax of the picture. Then, Francis directed Jack Nicholson on locations up at Big Sur before he left for another job.

LF: *The Terror* is also the only time Francis Coppola has directed Jack Nicholson.

RC: Yes, I think that's right. Of course, it wasn't until last year that Jack and Marty (Scorsese) finally worked together on *The Departed*. Anyway, what finally pulled *The Terror* together was several months later I started shooting *The Haunted Palace*. On the last day of shooting I paid Floyd and everybody else a little bit extra to stay on, and after we finished shooting with Vincent Price, Vincent went home and Dick Miller and Jack Nicholson came in and I shot them on the sets of *The Haunted Palace*. I had Jack grab Dick Miller and throw him against a wall and say, "I've been lied to ever since I came to this castle. Now tell me the truth."

JD: Not only does Dick explain everything, he makes it so complicated it's rather difficult to understand. It turns out that Boris Karloff, who is supposed to be the Baron Von Leppe, is actually an impostor. He thinks he's the Baron, but he's actually Eric.

RC: That's right. Eric killed the Baron and took his place. That came about on the last day of shooting because I was thinking this picture is really kind of dull. I was wondering what kind of twist we could put into the picture to make it more interesting. The thing we came up with was to have Dick Miller explain to Jack that the Baron was not really the Baron.

LF: Did Chuck Griffith have any input on the script for *The Terror*?

RC: No, it was Leo Gordon who wrote *The Terror*.

LF: So it was convenient to have Leo Gordon acting for you in *The Haunted Palace*; he was right there when you needed to write the new ending for *The Terror*! Of course, *The Haunted Palace* was not really based on a Poe story, but a novel by H. P. Lovecraft. How did that come about?

RC: What happened there was we were running out of good Poe stories to use, and I wanted to take a break from Poe, anyway. Jim Nicholson knew Lovecraft's stories and really liked his work. I thought that Lovecraft was a good writer, but I didn't think he was of the same complexity and nuance that Poe was, but I felt *The Case of Charles Dexter Ward* would be fine for a movie. Then, after the picture was finished, Jim and Sam changed their minds and decided they somehow wanted to integrate the picture into the Poe series. I always felt calling it a Poe picture made absolutely no sense. It was really something that was done simply for box-office appeal, because all the Poe pictures had made a lot of money for AIP.

LF: Apparently Charles Beaumont used some elements from another of Lovecraft's stories, *The Shadow Over Innsmouth* in his script—specifically the idea of mating Debra Paget with the amphibious frog-like creature in the pit.

RC: That's right. We decided we could give the picture more depth by incorporating ideas from other Lovecraft stories and *The Shadow Over Innsmouth* was one of them. That was Chuck's idea, because he was very much an admirer of H. P. Lovecraft's work.

JD: The early sixties was really a very creative period in Southern California. Richard Matheson and Charles Beaumont were doing all these *Twilight Zone* episodes, then Richard did the first two Poe movies and Chuck Beaumont wrote *The Intruder* and *The Premature Burial* for you.

DH: Chuck Beaumont and Richard Matheson were really good friends.

JD: Yes, and there was this whole group of writers, including Ray Bradbury and Robert Bloch. All of those guys made it a very exciting time. But when Chuck got ill, his friends were sort of covering for him. He had some great credits with you like *The Haunted Palace* and *Masque of the Red Death*. Do you think he wrote all those scripts himself?

RC: I think he did. I think it was at the beginning of his illness, and the more serious stages of his illness came later on. But Chuck had an incredible illness, which accelerated aging. I'm sure there's a technical word for it, but that's essentially what it was. He was growing old very, very rapidly. However, even though Chuck's scripts were very good, because he was ill, he couldn't do any re-writing. So I had Francis Coppola, who was my all-around assistant at the time, do a dialogue polish on *The Haunted Palace*. It amounted to very minor changes, because by that time Chuck was quite ill.

LF: Did Charles Beaumont and R. Wright Campbell actually collaborate on the script for *The Masque of the Red Death*?

RC: No, they didn't. Chuck Beaumont had written the first draft of *Masque*, but I was not totally satisfied with it. By this time Chuck was in the later stages of his illness, plus I was off in Europe. I was shooting *The Secret Invasion* in Yugoslavia for United Artists and Bob Campbell who had written it was there with me. One day while we were talking I showed Bob Chuck's script for *The Masque of the Red Death* and said, "I don't think it's quite right." So I asked Bob to come to London with me where we worked on the re-write of *The Masque of the Red Death*. I always thought Bob did an excellent job on the re-write.

LF: From Charles Beaumont's previous work, I imagine he came up with the idea of making Prince Prospero a Satanist.

RC: Yes, that was in Chuck's first draft and then Bob Campbell introduced the sub-plot of the dwarf from another Poe story, *Hop-Frog*. That was Bob's idea, which I thought was good because it gave an additional dimension to the picture.

JD: Why did you go to England to make *The Masque of the Red Death*? Since it was all shot in the studio, couldn't you have just as easily made it in Hollywood?

RC: That was simply a matter of economics. AIP had a co-production deal with Anglo-Amalgamated in England, so Jim and Sam suggested we go to England to make *The Masque of the Red Death*. All the Poe films had done extremely well in England and there was also a subsidy from the British government called the Eady plan. That was before any other country had a subsidy. I think there was a tax on theater admissions and that money was reserved for pictures that were made in England. We were quite happy to go over, because it meant we would be able to increase our budget for *The Masque of the Red Death* which was going to require more time and money than we had spent on any of the earlier Poe pictures. The budget is determined so much by your schedule and for *The Masque of the Red Death* we had five weeks. In Hollywood, from the beginning to the end of the cycle, all of the Poe pictures were done in three weeks. With twenty-five days I got a bigger look, but I'd say that five weeks in England was the equivalent to four weeks in the United States, simply because the English crews worked slower. They did very good work, but were very slow in comparison to American crews. We broke at eleven in the morning and also at mid-afternoon for tea, so while it was very civilized, we didn't get quite as much work done.

DH: The subsidy meant you got about 20 percent of your costs back, but you could only bring in the director and one star. Everyone else had to be British. I went over there, but I had to work on it as a producer. We had Nicolas Roeg as our cameraman, who had been the camera operator on *Lawrence of Arabia*, and after he did *Masque of the Red Death* they were going to give him the cameraman's job on *Doctor Zhivago*. But at the last minute they pulled back. *Zhivago* was such a big show they had every piece of electrical equipment in Europe shipped to Spain. It was a big, big production.

LF: So for *Masque of the Red Death* Danny designed all of the sets, even though you had to give the credit to an English art director?

RC: That's right. I had Dan come over and Dan's wife Kinta had rented a really nice house in Knightsbridge and I lived with them while we were shooting *Masque of the Red Death*. We had some really great times there. We'd have dinners and people would come floating in from the set, Vincent and all of the actors. Bob Campbell who had worked on the script was also there, so it was a sort of general meeting place, like the Hemingway thing, a movable feast, except it was just moving from day to day but always staying in the same house. But when Dan and I first went to the studio, we went through it and found we could adapt some of the sets left over from major English historical pictures. Dan was able to adapt and build our sets around existing flats that really gave us the best look we ever had, because we had sets from multi-million dollar pictures. What were they, *Becket* and *A Man for All Seasons*?

DH: I think it was *Becket*. Actually, we were quite lucky, because due to union rules what they would normally do is to take all of the scenery after they finished a big show like *Becket* and put it out in a big field and then run over it with tractors, so you couldn't have a scene dock. But somehow we were able to get all those big sets and re-use them for *Masque of the Red Death*. We also ran into trouble when we tried to hire the best people for our crew. In Hollywood, because we were one of the first of the independents, we'd offer to pay the crew a little bit over-scale. We'd get grips and electricians and pay them slightly over-scale, so we'd have really good studio technicians who usually worked at the majors. On *House of Usher* I think we had five grips, and Chuck Hannawalt would tell one of them to go and work with me and we'd put down the dolly track for the camera. So when we first came to England, I suggested to Roger that we pay the crew over-scale. The scale at that time was so low, it didn't really matter. An art director only got $125 a week. But the unions wouldn't let us do it, because they said the crew would have allegiance to the wrong people. Then the studio we were working at wouldn't let us do it, because they said, "everybody will want that." So we were screwed and we had to take whoever they gave us. In fact, during set construction they might only have one table saw and there would be four guys standing in line to use it!

RC: Yes, the English crews were bound very rigidly by union rules. It was also a major problem to get overtime. You had to tell them before two in the afternoon if you wanted overtime and then they had to call a union meeting to decide whether or not you were going to get it. I got it every time I asked for it, but they still had to call a meeting. I've heard of directors who asked for overtime and the crew would hold a meeting and say "no!" I got along pretty well with the crew, although they knew I was somewhat critical of the slower pace. It became something of a slight sore joke.

LF: Did Danny also work uncredited on *Tomb of Ligeia*?

DH: I just scouted locations for *Tomb of Ligeia*. After that I had another show to do, so I left. But on *Masque of the Red Death* I was there the whole time, although I worked with an English art director.

RC: Yes, on *Tomb of Ligeia* Dan just set it up, drew some sketches and then told the art director what he wanted. Then the English art director took over. As a matter of fact, I think Dan left because he was going to start his first official directing job: *The Haunted Palace*, based on a Lovecraft story.

DH: No, it was *Die, Monster, Die*, based on *The Color Out of Space*.

RC: Oh, that's right. I didn't mean *The Haunted Palace*, but after so many years all of the titles start to run together.

JD: Later on, you both did another Lovercraft film for AIP, *The Dunwich Horror*.

RC: Yes and AIP had originally asked me to direct *The Dunwich Horror* and I said to them, "No, I don't want to direct it, but I'll produce it, instead." I then asked Dan to direct it, so that became our second Lovecraft picture together.

JD: After scouting locations for *Tomb of Ligeia* did you go on to direct *Die, Monster, Die* with Boris Karloff?

DH: No, I came back to American first and then I went back to England to make *Die, Monster, Die*. By that time, Boris couldn't walk very well, so we had him in a wheelchair for most of the movie. Boris had a flat on Cadogan Square that had two floors, but he couldn't navigate the stairway. I remember we used to share a car that drove us to the studio in the mornings and he'd get in the car with the newspaper, open it up and look at the obituaries and say, "Well, my name isn't there, so I guess I can go to work." (Laughter)

RC: I also remember on *The Raven*, Dan had designed this beautiful long staircase and Boris was supposed to appear at the top of the staircase and walk down it to meet Vincent and Peter at the bottom. Boris was very frail so he came to me and said, "Roger, I can't walk down that staircase." I said, "All right, here's what we'll do. I'll have two guys off camera to help you and just take two steps and then I'll cut away to a reaction shot of Jack Nicholson." Then we'll bring you down to the bottom of the stairs, and we'll do the same thing, just take two steps at the bottom of the staircase and we'll continue the scene with Vincent and Peter.

LF: That may be why Karloff was so upset about making *The Terror*. He said you had him in a tank of cold water for the climax of the movie.

RC: Yes, that bothered me as well, because I didn't realize how difficult it was going to be on Boris. We had him in the water, but I figured being in water up to your waist couldn't be that bad, but he complained to me about it and I got him out right away and after that we used a double.

LF: Christopher Lee told me he would have loved to act in one of the Poe films with Vincent Price and said when he first came to Hollywood he made a special point of finding you at Columbia and introducing himself to you. Do you remember that?

RC: Yes, I do. A few years later we were also on the jury of a film festival in Spain. I would certainly have liked to use Christopher Lee in a picture, but now after doing *Lord of the Rings* and *Star Wars* I think he probably gets too much money.

JD: The interesting thing is when you were doing the Poe pictures these guys had a certain iconography. There was such a thing as a Vincent Price movie, so you could make a picture like *Theater of Blood* or *Dr. Phibes* and it made sense because Vincent was in it. Then, after he died, they were trying to re-make *Theater of Blood*, but who were you going to put in it? Robin Williams? There isn't anybody. You can't get what you got from using Vincent Price or Christopher Lee. These guys had a whole history behind them and as a result a whole kind of movie is now gone. Once Christopher Lee is gone, there is nobody else who has that association. So you can't make vehicles for classy horror stars anymore. Of course, now they're all about teenagers anyway.

RC: And the special effects have become the stars.

JD: Yes, and as you've said, the "B" movies have become "A" movies. The kind of movies AIP made in the fifties are now being made by Warner Bros and Paramount for zillions of dollars with huge special effects.

LF: Actually, I think Roger has worked with more horror stars than probably any other director: Vincent Price, Boris Karloff, Peter Lorre, Basil Rathbone, Lon Chaney, Barbara Steele, Hazel Court, Beverly Garland. Practically everyone, with the exception of Christopher Lee and Peter Cushing.

JD: And John Carradine.

RC: No, I used John Carradine in *Boxcar Bertha*.

JD: That's right!

LF: When you used horror stars like Boris Karloff and Basil Rathbone were you also a fan of their past movies?

RC: Yes, very much so. I thought Boris as the original monster in Frankenstein gave one of the defining performances in motion picture history. Both Boris and Basil were very intelligent actors who I enjoyed working with. They would come in knowing their lines to the letter, with an interpretation and we would discuss their parts just a little bit. These were both consummate professional actors, who knew we would discuss before the film began the approach they'd be taking and they came in prepared to give fully realized performances.

LF: Vincent Price told me before doing *Tomb of Ligeia*, he had talked over with you his idea of using a ruin for a Poe picture.

RC: That may be true, but actually we used the abbey for a variety of different reasons. Originally, *Ligeia* was going to be made away from AIP and for less money, so I thought we could do it less expensively if I shot it on location in the countryside. Also, as Bob Towne began writing the script, it became clear it was developing more into an exterior picture. The previous Poe films had all used stylized sets to follow my theory about the unconscious mind. My theory was that Poe was working with the concept of the unconscious mind shortly before Freud was, both from a scientific and an artistic standpoint. It was almost as if the world was ready for this type of thinking. Now, if Poe were writing largely from his unconscious, his unconscious mind would not be aware of the exterior world. All the sight and sounds of the world come through the eyes and ears to the conscious mind, so the unconscious mind is not aware of what the outside world looks like. On that basis, I decided to build all the sets for the Poe films as interiors, on studio soundstages, since I wanted to express the interior world of the mind. I did this consistently on all the Poe films, trying to make the sets very stylized. But on *Ligeia*, although I still believed in my theory, I realized it was becoming more of an exterior picture, so I decided to vary the series by going out on location. So we shot in the English countryside in natural daylight for the first time.

LF: So Danny was trying to create sets that expressed the unconscious mind of Poe!

DH: Actually, if you look at the films, a lot of the sets were just thrown together. We'd have liked to be able to build everything new, but you just couldn't do it on those budgets. I'd start a couple of days beforehand and I'd get together with the grips and just construct the sets from units we knew we had on hand. I didn't do that many drawings. I'd just go and put a chalk line on the floor and we'd take the stock units we had rented and I'd say, "Put this here, and put that one over there." The construction foreman and his crew would assemble them, then the electricians would know what we were doing and Floyd would know not to put lights on something that had holes in it.

JD: *Tomb of Ligeia* is one of my favorite Poe films because it's so darn arty.

LF: That's why Sam Arkoff didn't like it. He said it was too arty and not as scary as the earlier Poe films, but most importantly it didn't make any money for AIP!

RC: Actually, all of the Poe films made money, but *Tomb of Ligeia* made the least amount. I think it was because the series was just running out of steam and also because it was overly complicated.

DH: Sam told me and I'm sure he told Roger this, when you drill a well and strike oil, you don't stop drilling, you drill again and you keep drilling until the oil is no longer there.

JD: Well, Sam kept drilling, because after Roger left he kept making Poe pictures and they had less and less to do with Poe, and frankly, they're kind of dull. But when you said you were going to make *Tomb of Ligeia* away from AIP, who was going to finance it, Anglo-Amalgamated?

RC: Yes, probably, or myself, because by that time I had a certain amount of money and I could finance pictures on my own.

LF: Wasn't your original idea to use Richard Chamberlain as the lead?

RC: Yes, because Vincent was really too old for the part, but when AIP came back into the deal, they insisted on using Vincent even though he was really wrong for the role.

LF: Vincent Price told me the abbey you used in *Ligeia* was a beautifully preserved twelfth-century Cluniac monastery, so I made a special point to visit it when I was in England. It's an English Heritage site called Castle Acre Priory and it still looks exactly as it did when you shot the movie there in 1964. How did you find that location?

RC: While I was in England preparing the film I talked to some society for the preservation of old homes and castles and I got their notes for all of England. On a Friday I rented a little mini-coupe with unlimited mileage from a company in London and on the weekend I went to Wales, a portion of Cornwall and all the way up to North Umberland and the Scottish border. I was checking castles and abbeys all over England and was back in London on Monday morning. I gave them back the car and when the guy looked at the speedometer he said it was the all-time record! No one had ever driven that much in three days before. I hardly slept, just a couple of hours each night, because I was on the road the whole time. It was really a great trip and I ran into someone who was a Duke, who had this old house with an abbey attached. He showed me his abbey and served me tea and he had all of this unusual reading material on the table. Newspapers I had never even heard of, so I asked him pleasantly about them and he said all the newspapers and magazines in England were communist: *The Times, The Guardian, The New Statesman*—all of them. Then he gave me a paper to take with me and said this was the only newspaper that wasn't communist. I looked at it and it was the most outrageous thing I'd ever seen! The guy was essentially crazy—a full-fledged fascist. I got along with him very well because I figured I had no reason to get into a political argument with him. As a matter of fact, I almost used his abbey, but when I found the abbey in East Anglia, it was such a great place I decided to use that. Then Dan and I went there and looked it over so we could duplicate the small portions of the abbey we would need in the studio. We just did a little bit of temporary construction around the abbey, putting in gravestones and things like that, but I only shot exteriors at the abbey. For all the interiors we went back to Shepperton studios and built all of the sets on the soundstage.

JD: Dan, how did you transition into becoming a director?

DH: After doing some initial work on *Tomb of Ligeia*, AIP asked me to direct *Die, Monster, Die* in England. After I did that movie, Roger asked me to direct some pictures he was producing for AIP. The first was a motorcycle picture with John Cassavetes, *The Devil's Angels* and after that Roger asked me to direct *Wild Racers* in Europe.

JD: I must say I love *The Wild Racers*.

DH: That movie began when Roger asked me to develop the script with Chuck Griffith. That meant I drove Chuck to Santa Barbara in my car and wouldn't let him out of the hotel room until he had a certain amount of pages done. Then we went to Palm Springs and he'd dry out there. We finally ended up in La Jolla writing for a day or so there. After a week, we came back with the finished script. Roger said, "Why don't we go to Europe and I'll direct the first unit and you can direct the second unit." That meant on Sundays I would photograph all the races. I thought that would be a good trip and I'd see all the formula race cars, but when I got to Europe Roger had already shot one of the races and he came back to me and said, "You know the script better than I do, why don't you direct the first unit, and I'll direct the second unit." I thought about it and at the time I wanted to do another film, *Paddy*, and Roger said, "I'll back you in that if you direct this one," so I agreed to direct *The Wild Racers*. So now I was going to direct first unit and Roger was going to direct second unit. Except Roger then said to me, "You know, you're here and you're going to be here the whole time, why don't you direct the first unit and the second unit and I'll go home." (Laughter)

RC: I went home but I came back.

DH: That's true, Roger did come back.

JD: The style of *Wild Racers* is rather unusual when you compare it to Roger's *The Young Racers*, which is a pretty straightforward picture. This one has all these fast cuts, short shots, and tinted pictures of race sequences that for all I know may have come from *The Young Racers*. Plus you had all this sort of Francis Lai, *A Man and a Woman* music.

DH: Well, we had a French composer, but I forget his name. But the editor was Dennis Jakob, who shot the water footage in *The Terror*. But we were sending all the footage back to Hollywood and we didn't see any rushes or anything, because we were just shooting and moving on to another city. I must say we didn't have one out-of-focus shot in principal photography.

RC: Wasn't Nestor Almendros the cameraman?

DH: Yes, Nestor shot the whole thing and Daniel Lacambre was the camera operator. But if I didn't think we had gotten a shot, I'd have Nestor shoot it over again and have them print both takes. But by the time we got to Paris we were totally exhausted, because it was a really grueling schedule and I would never even get to see a location. Talia Coppola was with us on the film, and she would be scouting locations for us, and I'd tell her, when you get to Rouen, or someplace like that, just go buy all the postcards you can and we'll use that to find our locations. That was how we did a lot of it.

RC: Talia Coppola was scouting locations playing the second lead and also doing the set dressings.

DH: Yes, and by the time we got to Paris, we had been shooting really long hours and Nestor said to me, "I can't do this anymore, I really need a break," so Daniel took over to give Nestor a break for a day. Nestor was Spanish, but he left Spain under Franco and went to live in Cuba, and his sister was the head of education for Castro, but he was not a communist. In fact, when the revolution got hot in Cuba, he left and went to Florida and taught at a girls' school there. Anyway, we made *Wild Racers* in 1968 and when we came into Paris it was during the May Day student uprisings, with everybody in the streets and throwing things at the screen and they had already shut down the Cannes film festival so Nestor said, "I've fled Spain, I've fled Cuba, and now we're right in the middle of an uprising in France!" We also had to shoot in Spain and Nestor was an exile from Franco's Spain, so he was a bit worried that they might remember him. We had these student drivers to take us around to our locations and we were driving down the streets in Madrid one day and we saw all these military cars and soldiers with automatic rifles, and I said, "What's going on?" They told me, "Franco's Palace is right over there and he's on his way back." So all these soldiers were on the street to protect him. But Nestor would really freak out if I started talking about the Franco government, because he thought that our drivers might have been put there to spy on him.

RC: Actually, the French had never seen anybody work the way we worked. We worked really hard. Thinking back on it now and looking at the movies I'm making today, people aren't working as hard as we did.

DH: Yes, that's true, but I will say this: when we were shooting on the beach for a scene, we filmed the whole thing and it took us three or four hours and I told Nestor we were ready to wrap. Nestor came up to me and said, "You can't wrap now. The light is just getting right." It was magic hour, his favorite time of day to shoot, as you can tell from his work in *Days of Heaven*. So he said to me, "Let's do the whole day over again." So in about two hours, we did everything over again. It was during the summer when it didn't get dark until very late. Well, everyone on the crew was very good about it and it was all up to them anyway, because everybody was working on a flat rate.

RC: On *The Wild Racers* I can tell you about one of the greatest examples of coordinated shooting I've ever been involved with. I really think this was one of the high points of all the shooting we did. When we were in Paris, we wanted a scene by the eternal flame of the Arc de Triomphe. Not only could we not get permission to shoot there, we didn't even have permission to be shooting in France! (Laughter) So we worked out a schedule where I was in one car, Nestor was in one car, Dan was in one car, Chuck Hannawalt was in one car, and the two actors, Fabian and Mimsy Farmer were in another car. The actors had already rehearsed the scene and we all drove around the Arc de Triomphe and then stopped our cars. We stopped traffic and everybody ran out to get the shot. Nestor put the camera down and Fabian and Mimsy knew exactly where to go. Dan got the shot and we all jumped back into our cars and took off!

DH: We also had a French production manager, Pierre Cottrell, who was a friend of Nestor's. They had worked together on several Eric Rohmer films. So every time we went to shoot someplace, Pierre would go and talk with whoever might ask us if we had permits. When we were in Nevers, we were shooting on the platform at a little train station and the stationmaster said, "Where's your permit?" Pierre says, "I left it in Paris at the hotel." So they sent someone to call Paris and Pierre says, "Everything is so screwed up in France, it will take them awhile to find out if we really have a permit or not." Meanwhile, I'm still shooting and Pierre is trying to stall the stationmaster. Finally, after a while, Pierre comes over to me and says, "I can't stall him much longer." I told him, "Try to give me another ten minutes." So I finished the shot and we are ready to leave, but Pierre stormed back up to the stationmaster and he started swearing at him in French. He said he would take it up with the authorities in Paris, because he had closed down our shooting! Then we all left. It was like that the whole time. We were one step ahead of the law.

JD: These are lessons that young kids today should know about.

RC: Actually, they should. But on a film like *Wild Racers*, the shooting is so easy compared to everything else you have to do. It's like you are doing all this stuff and incidentally, when you finally get it done, you are going to shoot a scene.

JD: It seems like a lot of hard work for a film that AIP ended up releasing as a second feature.

DH: Well, I don't think they wanted to release it at all! Another funny thing happened to us when we got to Madrid. We were in flamenco café and we had about seventy-five extras. So we had a guy who was catering the lunches and afterwards Joel Rapp, the assistant director went to pay him for seventy-five lunches, but the guy says, no it was eighty-five lunches. So they get into a big argument and finally Joel says, here is your money for seventy-five lunches, but the guy refused to take it, so Joel says, "Great, we just got seventy-five meals for nothing." So that night we're coming back to our hotel, Roger, Joel, Francis Doel, and myself and we see the catering guy with some plainclothes cops. They go up and ask for the producer of the film and Roger points to Joel and said, "There he is!" (Laughter)

RC: I don't think it was exactly like that. They didn't know who I was, but the catering guy had argued with Joel, so they went up to him. Anyway they took Joel away and he had to spend the night in jail. We bailed him out the next morning and said, "Joel, today's call is in half an hour; I hope you had a good night's sleep." (Laughter)

DH: What happened was Joel told them, "Okay, we'll pay you," but he kept saying, "This is absurd, this is absurd."

RC: That's what it was. I think the Spanish word for pig is *cerdoa*, so they thought Joel was calling them pigs. That's what really got them ticked off. So we had to bail Joel out, but he was good to shoot the next day!

LF: I was disappointed when you had to drop out of directing your episode of the *Masters of Horror* series.

RC: Yes, I was going to direct *Haeckel's Tale* from Clive Barker's story, but I was so busy I just didn't have the time to do it. They even postponed my segment for me, but then I got ill and one thing led to another and it just faded away. I would have liked to have been able to do it.

LF: Would you consider directing another episode?

RC: I'm not certain. Probably only be if it was something really special, like Joe's *Homecoming* episode was. Joe told me the story for *Homecoming* and then he sent me the first cut of it and I thought it was one of the best episodes of its kind I'd seen. It was so far above what is normally done, I thought he should have gotten some kind of award for it.

JD: So did we.

LF: All of your last films done for AIP had cuts made to them. Vincent Price told me he never knew how much authority you actually had as producer on the Poe films, because he said both Jim Nicholson and Sam Arkoff were very strong people to be working for. Did they ever do any cutting on the Poe films?

RC: No, not on the Poe films. I always put the Poe pictures in final cut. But later on what happened is I would finish a picture, put the picture in its final cut and then I'd find out after the fact that AIP had made cuts, which annoyed me a great deal. I was working a lot in Europe at the time, so after I finished a picture and put it in final cut, I might go to Europe. Then when I came back, I'd find out that changes had been made. This happened on both *The Wild Angels* and on *The Trip*, while *Gas-s-s* had incredible cuts made to it. Whole sections were taken out of *Gas-s-s*. "God" was taken out of the picture, and God was an important character in the movie. I think they were just offended by the fact that God was in the picture. I had him played by an actor with an outrageous New York Jewish accent and they were really startled by that. But cutting God really took the heart out of the picture. I think it was partially the fact that AIP had become a public company and Sam was Jewish and they didn't want to be accused of being anti-Semitic. But it wasn't anti-Semitism, because he was God! We all thought it was funny. But if they did object to God, they should have told me that early on, in the script stages. So a lot of the cuts AIP made to my later films were political cuts, very awkwardly made, whereas on the Poe films, there was no political statement, so there was nothing objectionable for them to cut.

LF: *Gas-s-s* turned out to be your last film for AIP, because after that you formed your own distribution company, New World Pictures.

RC: Yes, that was one of the reasons I started New World, because these cuts were beginning to happen with greater frequency, where it had not happened before. Now, I never had any objection to discussing the changes AIP wanted to make and if they thought something was wrong, I could make some modifications. But it was the idea that I would finish the film in good faith and then cutting was done to it afterwards. I'm not sure why that happened. I think it had to do with internal fears and problems at AIP. I was now dealing with contemporary subject matter and AIP had become a more conservative and almost frightened company. My own beliefs were liberal, if not radical, so their cuts were often done to change ideas or change things they felt might not be in good taste, and their taste was different from mine. So as my films in the sixties became more politically crystallized, more and more cutting was done on them.

LF: It's interesting that the Poe films still hold up quite well, unlike many other sixties movies set in contemporary times, such as *Gas-s-s*, which now tend to look rather dated. Are you surprised at how well the Poe films have stood the test of time?

RC: Yes, I am, and in fact, when I saw them again recently for the first time in many years, I was quite pleased. MGM had asked me to come in and do commentary tracks for their release on DVD, so I watched *The House of Usher* and *The Pit and the Pendulum* and I thought they stood up reasonably well, considering they were low-budget films. The special effects that we could afford at the time clearly do not measure up to today's standards, but allowing for that, I thought the stories, the acting, and the general level of production all held up very well. The strange thing was, as I was watching them they were a little bit different than I remembered. They ran the pictures for me and I was just looking at them, talking as I watched them. Then they cut together what I said in relationship to the scene I had talked about. But what surprised me the most was the plots developed a little bit differently than I had remembered them. So I started out on one tack, and then I thought, "Wait a minute, this picture is a little bit different than how I remembered it." While I was watching *Tomb of Ligeia*, for instance, I had completely forgotten that I burned the house down at the end. I thought I had stopped doing that. Also when I was shooting the Poe pictures, I was very aware that the scripts were dialogue heavy, so I was doing everything I could think of to try and make them as visual as possible. On all the Poe pictures I used quite a bit of dolly track. Then, after seeing them again, I was pleased that the pictures weren't quite as dialogue heavy as I had remembered.

LF: To end, do you have a favorite Poe picture? Sam Arkoff's favorite was *The Pit and the Pendulum*, Richard Matheson preferred *The Raven*, Floyd Crosby thought he did his best cinematography on *The Haunted Palace*, and Vincent Price liked *Tomb of Ligeia* best.

RC: I don't know. One day I would say one, the next day I'd say another. I liked *The Fall of the House of Usher* and *The Pit and the Pendulum* at the beginning and then later on I liked *The Masque of the Red Death* and *Tomb of Ligeia*. But I'm not certain, because it varies, so I wouldn't pick just one.

Corman: Godfather of the A's

Constantine Nasr / 2008

Previously unpublished interview. © 2008 by Constantine Nasr.

In November 2008, I visited the Brentwood offices of Concorde-New Horizon Pictures, the longtime production hub of Roger Corman. Nearly fifteen years had passed since I'd walked its halls and worked its floors as a development intern. The bustling nature of the office that I remembered was replaced by an unnatural silence of an enterprise in transition. However, Corman was still making pictures, and on the day I came calling, he had several meetings to attend; one film was in pre-production, another was in post. Business as usual. His presence remained just as powerful, and as purposeful, as my glorified memory. With a trademark smile that betrayed nothing but genuine courtesy, he gave me his full attention for the next ninety minutes. Seated beneath a framed poster of the Edinburgh Millenic Vision festival (perhaps to remind anyone who enters that his forty-year-old "vision" had in fact come true), the stoic Corman relaxed into our conversation, having little to prove yet much to teach. I found his every answer to be immediate, yet delivered with deliberate assurance. I discovered, as so many had before me, that Corman is not rehearsed. Where's the fun in that? No—Roger Corman enjoys the fact that he knows exactly what he wants to say.

Nasr: There's been a lot of discussion of the word "maverick" over the last few months. What would you say defines that expression, and do you believe you are still among the mavericks of Hollywood?
Corman: I'm not certain what the word "maverick" means. Obviously John McCain has made great use of it; whether he's a maverick or not, no one knows. I think a maverick is somebody who goes against the accepted rules, who's willing, if not eager, to do what he wants to do . . . as they say, to do his own thing. For me, it's to make the kind of films I want

to make, in the way I want to make them, without any particular regard for what mainstream Hollywood is doing.

Nasr: What was the last film you saw in the theater that you thought was a pretty good "bang for your buck" experience?

Corman: Weirdly enough . . . *Titanic*. I would assume you would have expected I'd pick a low-budget picture that looked big. But *Titanic*, when it was made, was the biggest-budgeted film ever made, which was done by Jim Cameron, who of course started with us. And I was talking with Jim about it. I've forgotten the names of the two companies. Paramount had it domestically, and Fox had it foreign or something like that. It was budgeted as a very big film and they were going over-budget. And both, let us say Fox and Paramount, just thought they had total losses, and they tried to get Jim to hold back. Jim said, "The only way that this film can break even is to spend *more* money to do exactly what I want." And this is an example of where the artist out-businessed the businessman. He said, "I will put up my own money to cover the overages, but I want a bigger share of the profits." And they agreed immediately, because all they wanted to do was to get back some reasonable portion of their investment. They assumed it would be a loser. The fact of the matter is that it was the biggest-budgeted film ever made, but Jim got the biggest bang for the buck. He really put it all on the screen. So, from the standpoint of what you get for the money, *Titanic* was a phenomenal film, and of course tremendously successful for the money.

Somebody else asked me in another interview, "What do you think of budgets like that?" I said, and I'll say this again, that for *Titanic*, I think the money was well spent. What bothers me—and I forget what the budget of it was, I think it was over $150 million—nobody had ever spent that before. I said, "What bothers me is not *Titanic* at $150 million. You look at it and you say, well, I can understand why. It is there on the screen. What bothers me is a $70–80 million film, and it's two stars walking around the room talking. And you say, "Where did the money go on that? I do not see the money on the screen."

Nasr: Do you feel the public's tastes have changed over the years since you've been making films, for better or for worse, and how has that affected what films are being made these days?

Corman: I think the public's taste has changed a little bit, and I think the motion picture business has turned slightly into a carnival business. We're seeing some actual well-made films, such as *Dark Knight* and *Iron Man* this year, both of which were giant, what they call tent-pole films.

They were very well made, they were good films. But they are now the biggest-budgeted, and the biggest successes, I would say, are exploitation films. They're the kind of films we formerly made. Whereas the more serious work, which on some level might be considered the more creative work, is being done on lower-budgeted films, very often independent films, and oftentimes don't even go into theaters, pictures made for television, primarily HBO and Showtime. So I think this has turned into an exploitation business.

Nasr: They call them genre films now.
Corman: Yes, as a matter of fact, I remember that at one time I made exploitation films. The major stars with bigger budgets—they couldn't call them exploitation films, so they decided to call them genre films. So now I'm making genre films. It's all the same.

Nasr: Who would you say has been the most influential person in your life?
Corman: Probably my father, who was an engineer and who taught me certain aspects of living and thinking. From a combination of logic and creativity, which is what an engineer does. From a filmmaking standpoint, I would say there are a number, and I would say they were either people I never met or only met slightly. I would say Eisenstein was extremely influential. At the same time Alfred Hitchcock, John Ford, Ingmar Bergman, Fellini. They were probably more influential than anybody who I'd actually worked *with*.

Nasr: Critics have said that your films speak to the obsessive fear of death that compels your main characters. Is this a theme you would acknowledge?
Corman: It probably is. There are various interpretations of my work. (laughs) There was a book called *The Millenic Vision* in England by two critics, and it was so intricate that I only read half of it. I didn't understand exactly what they were saying. On the other hand, there are some who have oversimplified what I've done. But I think anybody working in a creative fashion works partly out of their conscious mind and partially out of their unconscious mind. So I think you're aware of certain themes, certain things you want to do. But there are also unconscious drives within you that, as it were, come to the surface.

Nasr: I'd like to talk about *The Intruder*. On the surface, it seems to stand apart from the rest of your filmography but upon reflection, those same themes are carefully woven in. If *The Intruder* had been successful, would you have made films on other topics you felt strongly about?

Corman: If *The Intruder* had been successful, I would have probably continued in that vein. What happened was, I had been quite successful. I had never made a film that lost money. I'd made fifteen films or something like that before that, primarily for AIP and Allied Artists. It had got to the point where all I had to do was tell one of those companies an idea—I didn't have to have anything more than an idea—and they would back me because I never lost. *The Intruder* was a film totally different from what I'd been making. It had to do with racial integration in the American South, something I was personally very much concerned about. It was from a book by Charles Beaumont. I bought the book. I then had Chuck write the screenplay, and then took it to both Allied Artists and AIP. And to my great surprise, they turned it down. I'd never been turned down, on anything. And I'd made a certain amount of money, so I said, all right, I'll make it myself. My brother (Gene) and I produced it jointly and I directed it. And we had great difficulty in the South. We were run out of towns, we had a sheriff threatening us, we were threatened with murder. People threatened to kill us. And the picture opened to wonderful reviews. I still remember the opening line of the review of a New York newspaper, it was something like—"This film is a credit to the entire motion picture industry." It was the first film I ever made that lost money.

Now, eventually we got the money back, forty years later on a DVD release, in which Bill Shatner and I did a commentary, and it finally broke even . . . if you didn't count interest over the period of time.

But that made me rethink what I was doing. And I felt to a certain extent, it was my fault, in that I was too obvious in the theme, in the message. It was there on the surface. And the audience didn't want to come to see a film that was specifically a message film. What was a better way to do it, I felt, was to do an entertainment film. If there was a theme, a message, something that was interesting or important to me, it would be beneath the surface. It would be, as we say in method circles, sub-textual. So I changed my way of thinking, went back to the types of films I'd been making before, but now started to work themes and ideas beneath the surface of the film. I'd always done that a little bit, and now I began doing it more consciously. For instance, pictures like the science fiction picture *X: The Man with the X-Ray Eyes*. Also when I worked with the films about the counter-culture in the 1960s, *The Wild Angels* and *The Trip*. *The Wild Angels* was the first picture about the Hell's Angels, and it was actually the American entry at the Venice Film Festival. *The Trip* was about the drug culture and was the American entry at the Cannes Festival that year. Those pictures were incredibly successful. I think *The Wild Angels* at the time was the most profitable independent film ever made. And those two films, I was following my new technique, which was to say, "All right, these two films are about the Hell's Angels, or this film is about LSD, and I will deliver the entertainment that the public expects to see in these films, but sub-textually there will be certain themes in there that are important to me." And that way of making films worked. Had *The Intruder* succeeded, I probably would have done the same thing, but it would have been closer to *The Intruder* than to *The Wild Angels* and *The Trip*.

Nasr: Do you feel that *The Intruder* is still relevant today, especially in a time when many might feel we've gotten beyond many of the issues contained in the picture?
Corman: We have not gotten beyond the issues. I think we have partially solved the issues. But it's not complete. Some people say, with the election of Obama, we have transcended race. I don't believe we have. But race has become a diminished faction of American life. We have partially solved that problem. There is still much to be done.

Nasr: When was the first time you became fully aware of being in control, and maybe even enjoying making movies?
Corman: I would say it was probably halfway through the first film I ever directed, *Five Guns West*. It had a nine-day shooting schedule. At that time you worked six days a week in Hollywood, and on that film, I worked a week and a half on it. About the first half of the film, I was so nervous that I couldn't even eat lunch. I just laid down during the lunch period and tried to pull myself together for the afternoon's work. But about halfway through, I began to think that maybe I can do this. I was really wondering at the beginning if this was going to be a real mess. But after looking at the dailies, and they looked fairly decent, I began to think, "Well, this film is starting to come together." I think that was when I became comfortable.

Nasr: In this age of big, behemoth, blockbuster movies, do you feel that Hollywood has lost touch with not only its audience but with the key to great storytelling, regardless of budgets?

Corman: I don't think Hollywood has lost touch with the audience. In fact, the grosses of these giant special effects films indicate that they are continuing to resonate with the audience. I think however they have stepped away from the emphasis upon the narrative of the film, and now films are starting to be so emphasizing the special effects that some elements of the storytelling ability has been lost. I have great admiration for the special effects—I wish I'd have had that type of special effects work, particularly computer graphics, when I was directing films. But I think too many filmmakers and particularly the studios themselves are so insistent upon the wonderful work being done in special effects, that less work is being done on the screenplays.

Nasr: Can you name a few films that put to good use these tools that you never had at your disposal?

Corman: I think probably *The Dark Knight* and *Iron Man* and to a certain extent, the first American film of a Russian director who started with me, Timur Bekmambetov, *Wanted*, are examples of films that are special effects–driven but still maintain a story and a theme.

Nasr: Do you feel there will always be an audience for the low-budget, exploitation genre film?

Corman: There will always be an audience, I believe, for the exploitation genre film, but not necessarily the low-budget exploitation genre film. When *Jaws* first came out, Vincent Canby, the lead critic of the *New York Times*, wrote: "What is *Jaws* but a big-budget Roger Corman film." And I remember reading that and thinking that was very nice, but then I thought, he's right but he's missed one important point. *Jaws* is not only a bigger film . . . as a matter of fact, *Jaws* and the very first film I ever made, *Monster from the Ocean Floor,* have some similarities. There's no plagiarism or anything like that. They just had some similarities. And I thought, it's not only bigger, but it's better. And I thought that with *Jaws*, the major studios were starting to cut in to what I'd been doing. A little bit later, *Star Wars* came out. And when I saw *Star Wars*, I thought, my compatriots and I are in trouble. It was clear at this point that the major studios were starting to do what we did a number of years ago, but were doing them bigger, as Vince Canby said, and better, as I would add to his comment. And I've talked to Steven Spielberg and George Lucas, who made those films, and they said they had seen those films—not only my films and other people, Bill Castle and other people who were making films in the same genre when they were young—and they just decided to make bigger and better versions of it. And that has hurt us greatly.

Nasr: Was there a benefit to the genre when those filmmakers set out to expand its audience?
Corman: The benefits were to the studios that had the big budgets. There was no benefit whatsoever for us. (laughs)

Nasr: When you look at independent films today, what differentiates them from the independents of the past?
Corman: Most of the independents today are not truly independent. You can take two of the stronger independent companies, New Line and Miramax, who were quite successful, when they were truly independent. They were absorbed by the studios that recognized the flexibility and the innovative thinking that the independents had and decided to bring them into the fold. Both Miramax and New Line continue to be successful but gradually became less successful as they were part of major studios. And eventually the founders of both New Line and Miramax were forced out of their own companies.

Nasr: Would you say that they lost their identity as a result?
Corman: Yes, the independent identity and thinking gradually became diluted, for lack of a better word, by the thinking of the studios.

Nasr: You've tackled nearly every genre possible. Did you just rely on your instincts to help you move with the times, or were you simply recognizing and providing what your audiences craved?
Corman: When I was directing, I was much younger than I am today, and as a young filmmaker I was more attuned to what young people were thinking. And one of the advantages that I and my compatriots had was that we were closer to our audience in age and in interests. So we were able to tap into the culture that was around us. For instance, when I did *The Wild Angels,* the Hell's Angels were getting a great deal of publicity, and I just had the idea that somebody should make a movie about the Hell's Angels. There had been one biker film made before, a very good film by Kazan, *The Wild One* with Marlon Brando. But it was a different kind of a picture. It was a picture told from the story of a small town that the bikers come into. And that's the only picture on that subject that I am aware of. This was ten years or so later, when I made mine, when the Hell's Angels began to be an important part of American counter-

culture. And I admired *The Wild One*. I thought it was a very good film. I was aware of it, but I said, as good as it is, I don't want to make that film. I want to make a film from the standpoint of the Angels. I wanted to be part of the rebelliousness of these people. And I think that was the key decision that made *The Wild Angels* the success that it was.

Nasr: Do you believe today's Hollywood has taken full advantage of the possibilities of the youth market? Are there areas that have yet to be explored? Or is the market just fed what they are given and told to like it, such as with reality television?
Corman: I think Hollywood is doing a fairly good job at tapping the youth market. I'm not certain I could think of any area of the youth market that they haven't touched other than the possibility of probing a little deeper. Going beneath the surface and asking, "What do young people really think? How are they really living?" And I think that requires a young filmmaker to do that. I think we're tapping the surface or superficial qualities of what youth are doing.

Nasr: Do you believe in the auteur theory?
Corman: I believe partially in the auteur theory. I have always believed that filmmaking is a collaborative art, and that you have essentially three important people. You have the producer, the writer, and the director. You also have other people who clearly contribute: the director of photography, the editor, the actors themselves, the prop man, all the way down. Everybody is contributing to the film. But in general, it's the producer, the writer, and the director. And probably the director is the most important, so I would say I believe slightly in the auteur theory in putting the director forward. But I can tell you of any number of films where the most important person was the producer. And other films where the most important person was the writer.

Nasr: What does it mean to collaborate on a Roger Corman film?
Corman: Well, collaborating on a Roger Corman film today means this: Almost invariably the original idea for a film comes from me. I will have an idea. I may write down a three-, four-, five-page outline, or I may just have the idea. I will then bring a writer, and discuss the project with the writer, and then leave the actual writing to the writer. I'll give him my notes on the treatment, the first draft, the second draft, and so forth. But the writer does the writing. And so I'm collaborating in that I gave him the original idea and I'm discussing the way in which he's doing it.

I work the same way when the director comes in. And generally, not always, I will bring the director in, before the final draft is written, so that the writer, on the final draft, is working both with me, from my original idea to start the project, and the director, who's coming in and who will undoubtedly have ideas that will hopefully improve the film or change it in some way. And all three of us become collaborators on the final draft of the film.

Then during the filming, I leave the director 99 percent free to make the picture the way he wants to make it, having had a talk with the director before the shooting, in fact before the final draft, and specifically before the shooting, in which we discuss the themes of the film, how it's going to be made, and (because I finance the films with my own money) the budget and so forth. So, if the director and I are in agreement, and I don't start until we're in agreement, and very often I will take the director's viewpoint and say, "That's better than the idea I had." But the director and I are in agreement on the basic themes on how the film will be made. At that point I leave it totally to the director. I will very often only be on the set for the morning of the starting of the shooting day, to have coffee, talk to people, to generally just be a diplomat and nothing more. And on most of my films, I never come back. If I talk to the director, I make a point of never coming to the set. I will talk to him on the phone at lunch, or in the evening, because I find that if I come to the set, people start to look a little bit to me and I don't want them to do that. I want the director to be in charge.

Then, coming back in post-production, I tell the director, "Make your first cut, and then let me look with the editor." What they don't know is, when they say, "Okay, we're ready to show you our first cut," I say, "I'm just so busy, I don't have time to look at your first cut. Make your second cut, and let me see your second cut." Because I think, traditionally, the director has the first cut, and he shows it to the producer. I prefer to let the director and the editor make two cuts, really to refine their picture before I come in. I will then come in and look at the second cut with several members of my staff and give notes. And I work that way through the third, fourth, fifth cut, whatever.

Nasr: Do you believe that a film reflects a personal faith of a filmmaker, regardless of what they are attempting to put on screen, and if so, do you have any conscious personal beliefs that you can identify in your own work?

Corman: I do, but it varies. For instance, some of the science fiction or horror films we're making, there's not a great deal of personal faith in the film. There's more of simply the desire to work, not as an artist, but to work as a craftsman. To say, here is a special effects creature science fiction film, how do we as craftsmen make the best film possible involving this creature that we can?

Nasr: How about your Poe films, or *X: The Man with the X-Ray Eyes*? Do people read too much into these pictures?

Corman: There is, in those. In the Poe films, I was very much involved in Freudian theory and I was trying to work psychologically and on several depths involving, as much as one can, the unconscious mind. On *X*, I was talking about certain meanings of how we live. So I was investing more of my personal thoughts and feelings into those. What was significant on those, I was both the producer *and* the director, and in the case of *X*, the original idea and theme of the picture as well. As a producer, I'm still contributing that, but a little bit less.

Nasr: Are you surprised by the success of your "graduates"? This was your film school. You should have been charging.

Corman: I'm not surprised that so many of them have been successful. One or two have not, but actually it's an astonishing record, the percentage that has been successful. I chose them because I thought they were good and they were going to be successful. I could not have predicted how successful they were going to be. [But] they would have been successful had they never met me. Their own ability propelled them forward. All I did was be the first to recognize their ability, to give them a chance, and maybe to teach them a little bit. It's like, let's say, a coach of a successful college football team. He may be a great coach, drawing up the plays, figuring out what to do, teaching his players how to execute the plays. But he's probably recruited the best high school football players around. So he's working with the best talent he can have, and so the resulting winning football team is the combination of his choosing the best talent and then working with that talent.

Nasr: Your Poe films are situated almost too conveniently between the great horror tradition of the thirties and forties, and what would become the American horror resurgence in the seventies. It would almost seem as if you were the connection to America's Gothic horror tradition, between Browning and Whale to today's great filmmakers, many of whom you directly taught. Why do you think the horror film died after the war, and what did you do correctly to help bring it back?

Corman: I'm not certain I saved it. I think horror films have always been with us. I think not even in films, but just the concept of horror. For instance, what might be called the first novel in the English language is *Beowulf*, which is a creature-driven horror novel. I think this concept of the creature, the exterior monster that menaces us is part of our psyche. It's part of our unconscious. If we did not recognize that threat and react to it, the human race would've been destroyed. We were able to recognize that the saber tooth tiger or the mammoth or something was dangerous. The very fact that I—and obviously I'm not the first, so many people make their horror films at night. It's because, I believe, nighttime was dangerous when the human race was young. We stayed in the cave at night and we weren't going outside because we couldn't see the hidden danger. We went outside during the day. So I think all of these early experiences marked us.

Nasr: How influential was the success of Hammer Films and the Gothic resurgence that was taking place in England? Was the decision to go with Poe, one of your favorite writers, and later Lovecraft, simply a chance to make films based on an American heritage, or did Hammer help pave the way?

Corman: I never heard of Hammer when I started. These films, which are more or less classical horror films—which are what I did or at least think I did bring back, and I was obviously not the first, they had been made in the thirties—but that type of film had fallen out of favor. I had been making low-budget films, generally on ten-day schedules, in black and white, as double features. Both AIP and Allied Artists, two companies I was working with most, had a marketing tool or gimmick had the idea of putting together two $70,000–$80,000 black and white horror films, or black and white science fiction films or gangster films or teenage films, and sending them out as double features, two films for the price of one. And they'd been quite successful, very successful. But because I'd always had a percentage of the profits, I could see that they were starting to slide a little bit down, not much, but it was just easing slightly. And I took the fact that AIP wanted me to do two horror films, and I took the fact that while they were still successful, they were not as successful as they had been, and the fact that I was tired of doing it, and so I asked them to let me not make, say, two ten-day black and white horror films. Let me spend fifteen days—I never had a fifteen-day schedule—shoot in color, and double the budget. We actually more than doubled the budget, we went to about $200,000—and do one color film that will stand on its own. And they asked me what I wanted to do. I said I wanted to do Edgar

Allan Poe's "The Fall of the House of Usher," because I'd read the short story when I was in high school and always remembered it.

And it did not take a great deal of argument to convince them to do it. I think it was because AIP was a young, ambitious company, and they too wanted to, as it were, move up a little bit on the scale. So, the first of those films, *The Fall of the House of Usher*, was born of those two things. The fact that commercially what had been working before wasn't working quite as well, and the fact that I and, as I talked to them, AIP both wanted to move up.

I never started out to make a series of Poe films. I simply wanted to make *The Fall of the House of Usher*. It did very well. It was the biggest film that AIP ever had commercially, and it got quite good critical response, so they said, "Let's make another." And I just continued to make them. There were a number. I've forgotten but I think I've made five or six. They were all successful, and AIP wanted me to make more, and I said, "No, I'm starting to repeat myself. I'm beginning to use the same ideas." I simply wanted to go on and do something else. I'd always shot inside studios on the Poe films, for certain theories I had—I didn't want to show reality. Although on the last of them, I went against my own theories, and on *The Tomb of Ligeia*, I not only went outside, I went outside in the daytime—which was against all of my own theories because I was tired of my own theories by then.

And when they said they wanted me to do another one, I said I wanted to step away from this totally. I want to do a contemporary film, never going inside of a studio, shooting on natural locations, and I want to do a film about the Hell's Angels. And again, AIP completely agreed.

Nasr: Did you have a planned approach to every film you made?
Corman: Well, my thinking on the Poe films went through the others. And as I say to the young directors and writers working with me, you must have a theme or a theory or something that holds the picture together, that underpins the picture. It's good if your theory is correct, but it's still okay if your theory is wrong. At least something is holding the picture together. And my theory, for better or for worse, was that Poe in the mid-nineteenth century and Freud in the late nineteenth century, were working on similar things. They were working on the concept of the unconscious mind. I then built from that my own theory which is that the unconscious mind is not directly aware of the real world. The unconscious mind does not see. The eyes are connected to the conscious mind. It does not hear. It has no relationship. I have no idea whether this

theory is right or wrong, but it could well be right. It seemed logical to me at the time and still does. All the unconscious mind can do is filter through the conscious mind what the real world is, and interpret or misinterpret what is happening.

So therefore I said I wanted all of my pictures to be unreal. I do not ever want to go into the real world because the unconscious mind does not see the real world. I wanted everything to be shot inside the studio and therefore to be artificial. And, if I do go outside, I go outside only for brief periods because it's essential to the story, and I will go outside at night. And I remember I opened *Pit and the Pendulum* by the ocean, because, I think, we come from the ocean. And I thought there is something about the ocean that affects us. In *The Fall of the House of Usher*, the young man rides up to the house. There was a forest fire in the Hollywood Hills. We were not ready to shoot the picture, but all the trees were burned down. I simply got the cameraman, one grip, a horse and Mark Damon who played the lead; we went up, and for his ride to the house, he rode through this burned-out forest. I also had a special effects man, so I added a little ground fog to seep through. So it seems as if we were showing reality, but it was a filtered reality. The problem was that I just stayed with that theory for so long that on *The Tomb of Ligeia*, the last one, I said, "I'm throwing all my theories out. I'm going outside. I'm going outside in the daylight and I'm going to show the English countryside" simply because I got bored with my own theories. And that was my last Poe film. I then said I'd done enough.

Nasr: Why does Poe remain so influential?
Corman: I think Poe was one of the first to work with the concept of the unconscious. For that reason, he was writing stories that worked on two levels; one, as we as say in method acting, on the surface or textual level, which would be the narrative storyline and characters, but subtextually he was exploring universal concepts of fear, of horror, of fantasy and so forth. And that doubt-edged sword as it were is what has enabled him to stay significant.

Nasr: When you think back on Vincent Price, what memories spring to mind?
Corman: I remember one thing he said once to me. We had both been interviewed on the set by somebody, and there was some talk about art and so forth. And when the interviewer left, Vincent and I were talking, and he said he felt what we were craftsmen. That to say that we were try-

ing to create art was a pretentious and ultimately self-defeating way to work. That we should think of ourselves as skilled craftsmen, and if occasionally our craftsmanship could rise to the level of art, that would be wonderful, but that would simply be an outgrowth of working as skilled craftsmen.

Nasr: What does the title "producer" mean to you?

Corman: The producer has many functions. To me, this is why people don't understand what a producer does. It's very easy to understand what a writer does. He writes a script. You can understand what a director does. He's out there on the set saying "Put the camera here." The actors do this, you can understand what the cameraman or the editor does. You can't understand what the producer does. What the producer does is think. And therefore, you can be a producer lying in bed, unable to sleep. Or you can be a producer out at the beach. The producer, to me, comes up with the concept. He decides what picture to make and how to make it. That is the main job of the producer. It is what originates the motion picture. Now, it may be that it is not necessarily his idea. He may have read a novel, and he says, "I think I might want to make a picture from this novel." So the idea of making the picture may not be totally original with him. He may take something that exists in the world and say, "I want to make a picture about this." It may well be with the thousands of spec scripts that are written around, he looks at them and he picks one, and says, "Hey, I think I like this script." He makes a decision to make that script. Sometimes a director will come—and several directors have done this with me—they'll come to me with an idea. As the producer, I make the decision as to whether or not to make a picture from that idea. So his main job is to make that initial decision, and then to orchestrate the making of the film.

Nasr: I've been told that you don't know the meaning of the word "impossible." Is this true?

Corman: I have never found a challenge that was impossible. I found challenges that force me or inspire me, but generally force me to make the picture differently than I wanted to. Where something becomes impossible. An actor gets sick and suddenly you say, "What do I do?" A major studio will shut down and wait for the actor to get well. I can't shut down. I have to re-write the script and write the actor out of the picture, or even bring the actor in for a quick death scene before he goes to the hospital. In other words, whatever the challenge is, I've always found a way to solve it, and I have to admit, some of the solutions are made out of desperation, and not necessarily good solutions. But they were the best solutions I could do at the time. In other words, I've never started a film that I wasn't able to finish.

Nasr: Was there ever any one film that got away from you?

Corman: A couple that almost got away from me. But it's debatable as to whether they really got away from me or not because I was always found a way to at least finish the film. The film may have ended up quite differently than I had originally planned it, but we did finish.

Nasr: What about Robert E. Lee, a subject that captured your attention for so many years?

Corman: I've always been interested in the Civil War, and I thought Lee was one of the pivotal characters in the Civil War. He had actually been offered the leadership of the Union Army by Lincoln, and rejected it to fight for the South. I felt there was a theme there, as per the continuing question—ever since the Constitution was written, and while it was being written, between states' rights and federal rights. And I thought one of the major elements of the Civil War was that the South was fighting for the supremacy of the States' rights, and Lincoln and the North stood for the Union. I thought that that was an important part of the Civil War that hasn't been well-treated. And Lee believed in his state, in Virginia. I felt that was something that should be explored. Plus, of course, the action of the Civil War. I actually was going to do it for United Artists, and they approved the script, but they didn't want to give me a lot of money. I made a deal with a military academy in Virginia whose uniforms were the same as the Southern uniforms, for their exercises to restage several Civil War battles. I'd pay them a little bit of money and use them in the picture. But United Artists didn't believe I could do it, and that the military academy would do it, so the project was dropped. That was in the late sixties.

Nasr: Have you tried ever since to resurrect that project?

Corman: I've tried once or twice, but the Civil War has been treated so many times in the intervening years that it's just now a faded-away project.

Nasr: For a man so full of optimism, your films tend to have a rather pessimistic worldview. How do those views clash, if they do at all, on the screen?

Corman: I think as with all people, I'm not clearly one person. One part of me is optimistic, another is fairly pessimistic. For instance, the state of low-budget independent filmmaking at the moment. I'm quite pessimistic about where my compatriots and I stand and where we will stand in the immediate future. I have a little bit of optimism that the wheel turns, and that VOD, the Internet, and new methods of showing films will open up for us. So, it's that duality.

Nasr: You've had opportunities to work on major films with major stars for major studios, and you've turned them down to follow your own unique path. Would you do it all again? And will you ever return to directing?

Corman: I would probably have followed, more or less, the path I did follow. If I were to change anything, it might have been in 1970 when I stopped directing. I stopped directing only because I'd directed somewhere between fifty-five and sixty pictures in twelve or thirteen years, something like that, and I was just tired of directing. And I'd been offered the biggest budget and most important picture I'd ever had. John Updike, one of the best American novelists, had a very good novel, a bestseller called *Couples*. And I'd done a couple pictures for Allied Artists, and Allied Artists offered me the opportunity to do *Couples* on a much bigger budget. I turned it down, just because I felt . . . I just can't go out there and direct anything. I just planned to take the sabbatical, to take one year off, and then come back to directing. I never did because I started my own production and distribution company that was startlingly successful from the beginning, and I just stayed with it. The only thing I might regret: it didn't occur to me at the time but I might have said, "Yes, I will take this opportunity, but I want to rest six months before I make the film." I've sometimes second-guessed as to what would have happened had I directed that film, because it was a completely different picture than anything I'd ever done. But I made my decision and I have to abide by that.

Nasr: I'd like you to talk about your accomplishments with New World. Why did you champion these foreign filmmakers? Was becoming a distributor yet another crazy idea, or just another step in your evolution as a filmmaker?

Corman: It was something I did because I wanted to do it. It wasn't a charity. I didn't want to lose money. On the other hand, I didn't expect to make a great deal of money. I felt these films were not reaching the audiences they should and we had, at that time, really the most effective independent distribution company in the country, and I felt that we could distribute those films better than anybody else. And we did. We were quite successful over one period, I think it was five or six years. We won more Academy Awards for Best Foreign Films than all the majors combined. I'm very proud of that.

Nasr: Did you regret the loss of New World?
Corman: I didn't regret the sale. I regretted simply the mechanics of the way it worked out. I was giving up my distribution company to them, and in return, they were distributing my films for a low distribution fee. It seemed like a good idea in the contract, but in the working out, which had never occurred to me, they had very little incentive to work hard to distribute my films, because they were getting a very low distribution fee. And they were not doing a good job at distributing my films for that reason. They weren't making much money off of it. That was my only problem with them, and we were going to go to court, but we settled out of court. I had agreed not to go back into theatrical distribution, but after they didn't do a good job at distributing my films theatrically, they understood where I stood and I understood where they stood, and I think two years had gone by since we had made the original contract, they agreed to drop that provision and I went back into theatrical distribution.

Nasr: After you made *Frankenstein Unbound*, did that bug ever come back and bite you again?
Corman: *Frankenstein* was not a good experience for a variety of reasons, and I felt that the years had gone by. There would still be the possibility, there still is, that I might come back to direct one film, but at the moment, probably I will stay producing and distributing.

Nasr: Why didn't you take the offer to run a major studio when it was offered to you back in 1981?
Corman: I wasn't able to get complete authority. I had said that, in the days when the major studios were at their peak, in the thirties, forties, and early fifties, the heads of the studios really could make the decisions, and one of the problems was, at that time and still today, the heads of production at the studios really have to look to someplace else for ap-

proval. And they weren't ready to give me that kind of approval. And without that decision-making ability, I didn't think it was possible to run a major studio, at least the way I would do it efficiently.

Nasr: Do you feel today that many people in positions of power don't understand the process of making movies? Are their decisions really based on business or are there more challenges to balancing practical production concerns with business?

Corman: It's a combination. It's a fact that the heads of studio production today are former lawyers or agents or something like that. It's a different mentality, and again, even they do not have full authority in their own studios. So what I said in '80 or '81 is what I think is still happening today.

Nasr: How do you feel about the fact that all of these companies are owned by these profit-feeding mega-corporations? They are no longer companies led by creative innovators with business savvy but are smaller entities of giant conglomerates.

Corman: I think it is unfortunate for motion pictures that that has happened, but it's a natural growth pattern of capitalism. You can go all the way back to Adam Smith who predicted essentially that capital would be concentrated more and more in fewer and fewer hands. It's just the way capitalism works.

Nasr: What would you say to today's filmmakers trying to fight for their craft in this current economic climate, where YouTube and other avenues of distribution are open to virtually everyone, and the cost to tell stories is affordable to almost everyone?

Corman: I've always felt that the art of the moving image is the quintessential art of today. That includes motion pictures, television, YouTube, everything. It is the only art form that is new; all of the other art forms go back thousands of years. It is the modern art form, but it is a compromised art form, because it is a combination of art and business. And I think that anyone who works successfully in it has to be able to work with one knowledge of art, with one *thought* of art, and with one thought of business. If I had a choice between the two, I would favor the one who was more interested in art or craftsmanship. I think he would ultimately emerge as the best businessman as well.

Academy Award Acceptance Speech

Roger Corman / 2009

Speech delivered November 14, 2009. Printed by permission of the Academy of Motion Picture Arts and Sciences.

Needless to say I'm delighted to accept this Oscar personally, but I'd also like to accept it on behalf of my wife Julie, who's been my producing partner for many years, and also on behalf of those who've worked in the field in which I've spent most of my career, the independent filmmakers.

We all work in what I think is the only true modern art form. All other arts had their origins in antiquity and are therefore, to a certain extent, static. Motion pictures encompass movement, which is one of the key characteristics of our day, and for that reason they are modern. There's another reason as well. And the reason is that traditional art has been done, let us say, by composers, writers, poets, painters, who could create their art individually. Motion pictures require, the filmmaker requires a cast and a crew, and they must be paid. As a result our art is somewhat compromised. We're compromised between art and business and I think that represents something of the compromised world in which we live.

I think that to succeed in this world you have to take chances. Many of my friends and compatriots and people who've started with me are here tonight, and they've all succeeded. Some of them succeeded to an extraordinary degree. And I believe they've succeeded because they had the courage to take chances, to gamble. But they gambled because they knew the odds were with them; they knew they had the ability to create what they wanted to make. It's very easy for a major studio or somebody else to repeat their successes, to spend vast amounts of money on remakes, on special effects-driven tent-pole franchise films. But I believe the finest films being done today are done by the original, innovative filmmakers who have the courage to take a chance and to gamble. So I say to you: Keep gambling, keep taking chances. Thank you.

Key Resources

Articles

Alford, Henry. "The Merchant of Venice." *Vanity Fair*, April 1996, 136–38, 147–50.

Diehl, Digby. "Roger Corman: The Simonen of Cinema." *Show*, May 1970, 27–30, 86–87.

Dixon, Wheeler. "In Defense of Roger Corman." *Velvet Light Trap* 16 (Fall 1976): 11–14.

Krohn, Bill. "Interview with Roger Corman." *Cahiers Du Cinema*, January 1979, 29–33.

Levy, Alan. "Will Big Budgets Spoil Roger Corman?" *Status-Diplomat*, March 1967, 46–51, 78–79.

Strick, Philip. "From Ma Barker to Von Richthofen." *Sight and Sound*, August 1970.

Yates, Steven. "Invasion of the Mutant B-Movie Producers." *Kinoeye* 3, no. 1 (January 2003).

Books

Corman, Roger, with Jim Jerome. *How I Made a Hundred Movies in Hollywood and Never Lost a Dime*. New York: Random House, 1990.

Di Franco, J. Philip. *The Movie World of Roger Corman*. New York: Chelsea House, 1979.

Gray, Beverly. *Roger Corman: An Unauthorized Biography of the Godfather of Indie Filmmaking*. Los Angeles: Renaissance Books, 2000.

McGee, Mark Thomas. *Faster and Furiouser: The Revised and Fattened Fable of American International Pictures*. Jefferson: McFarland, 1996.

McGee, Mark Thomas. *Roger Corman: The Best of the Cheap Acts*. Jefferson: McFarland, 1988.

Morris, Gary. *Roger Corman*. Boston: Twain, 1985.

Naha, Ed. *The Films of Roger Corman: Brilliance on a Budget*. New York: Arco Publishing, 1982.

Will, David, and Paul Willemen. *Roger Corman: The Millenic Vision*. Edinburgh: Edinburgh Film Festival, 1970.

Documentaries

Roger Corman: Hollywood's Wild Angel (Christian Blackwood, 1979)
Corman's World: Exploits of a Hollywood Rebel (Alex Stapleton, 2011)

Audio Commentaries by Roger Corman

Crazy Mama, Roger Corman and Jonathan Demme
House of Usher, Roger Corman
The Pit and the Pendulum, Roger Corman
The Trip, Roger Corman
X: The Man with the X-Ray Eyes, Roger Corman

Index

CPSIA information can be obtained
at www.ICGtesting.com
Printed in the USA
BVHW040216200723
667423BV00001B/4

9 781617 031663